What Every Preacher
Should Know!

What Every Preacher Should Know!

(The Pastor's Success Handbook)

Simple Steps to Better Crowds, Bigger Offerings, More Results, Happy Church Relationships, Greater Revivals, Appealing Sermons, Solving Problems, and a More Effective Ministry!

By Hugh F. Pyle, D.D.

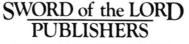

SWORD of the LORD
PUBLISHERS
P.O.BOX 1099, MURFREESBORO, TN 37133

Printed in the United States of America

Dedication

This volume is dedicated to the wife who has stood with me through the hectic, gruelling and exciting years of my ministry as pastor and evangelist.

My Queen, Esther, was to me the ideal pastor's wife—concerned, consecrated, conscientious, consistent, sharing the burden of pastor and people. She was ever aware of the needs of the members as well as their sorrows and triumphs, yet always the faithful and diligent mother of our own children. Our home was her domain.

At church she looked for visitors and made them welcome. She helped me with visitation, prayer and soul winning, always busy for the Lord but never wanting to be in the limelight.

Now as the wife of an evangelist she gladly endures the hardship of constant travel, the burden of being away from home and loved ones, and the responsibility of services night after night. Every week she must say goodbye to friends just made, move on again—sometimes hundreds of miles, and then start all over again with strangers the next week.

She is all that a prophet of God could ask for in a wife; loyal, loving, devoted and helpful in so many ways.

Esther, they named you well for surely you have "come to the kingdom for such a time as this," and much of whatever success I've known in the ministry is due to your devotion and faithfulness!

May a multitude of preacher boys who read this book find just such a help mate!

—Hugh F. Pyle.

Foreword

Dr. Hugh Pyle was ordained to the gospel ministry forty years ago. He has served over twenty-nine years in the pastorate and nine years in evangelism. He was pastor of several churches in the state of Florida, founding one church and leading in four church building programs.

For over fifteen years he was pastor of Central Baptist Church in Panama City, Florida. Under his leadership the church grew from one hundred to over sixteen hundred in membership. Dr. Pyle also served as president of the Panama City Christian Schools.

He holds a Doctor of Divinity degree from Tennessee Temple University, and has spoken in the largest Christian universities and colleges in America. He has also served as moderator of Southwide Baptist Fellowship.

The author of thirty books and several award-winning sermons, he is a charming and gifted writer. His sermons often appear in THE SWORD OF THE LORD. Dr. Pyle is a man of devotion and strong convictions.

This his latest book is a twenty-two-chapter manual written from a successful pastor's-successful evangelist's own experiences and point of view.

From the first chapter on how to get off to a good start through the last chapter filled with answers to questions that every preacher will need to know during his ministry, the book moves from one aspect of the ministry to another. Dr. Pyle covers in detail with helpful illustrations and pithy sayings most of the problems pastors face.

The section concerning facing and solving problems will help the pastor avoid problems. Fourteen common problems are dealt with at length.

Dr. Pyle is a great sermon builder, and the section on how to prepare and preach the sermon is a must for preachers.

In dealing with the evangelist-pastor relationship and how to plan a successful revival meeting, Dr. Pyle writes from both points of view and gives many helpful insights in the area of special meetings and visiting evangelists.

The book is practical, informative, and is written with common sense, sympathy and understanding.

I recommend the book to pastors everywhere. It will be a helpful addition to every pastor's library.

—Dr. Curtis Hutson.

1981

Preface

Pastor, have you wondered how to get more people to come hear you preach, how to get all the money your church needs, how to handle that ornery board member, how to reach visitors, how to steer your young people in the right direction? Here's how!

Have you longed for sparkling, well-attended Sunday night services, for a meaningful and effective music program, for workers who take their tasks seriously, for ushers who make people want to return to your church, for evangelistic meetings that succeed? Here's how!

Have you wondered how to get new, fresh sermons with appealing titles and good illustrations? Have you wondered what books would help you most to know how to build a great church and freshen up your sermons with pungent truths? Here's help!

Would you like to get the most out of your days, learning how to make time serve you? Have you had problems with staff workers or difficulty in replacing Sunday school workers (and others) who are not producing? Would it help to know how to care for visiting speakers and missionaries with a minimum of problem to the pastor?

Would you like to build a militant and strong church that is still cordial, warm and happy? One that will hate sin and crusade with you against the Devil, while at the same time winning the lost? Here's how!

Do you need a solution to the problem of getting tied up with counseling, committee meetings, difficult people, touchy situations that take you from your main tasks? What do you do with visitors who stay too long, people who want you to come see them too often and long delays that cut into your time at funerals, weddings and such? Here's help!

How can you have a Christian school without taking up your pastoral time? How co-relate the schedule of church and school and how to handle the personnel problems that crop up? How best advertise the church and school to make a real impression on your town or city?

How can you as a pastor have a happy home life while at the same time help to solve the difficulties that arise in your church and ministry? What do you do with your own perplexities?

After twenty-nine successful years in the pastorate and over nine years in the field of evangelism here are practical and pertinent observations you can use to build a work for God that will be dynamic, effective and pleasing to God. Try them, and may God bless you as you succeed!

—The Author.

Acknowledgement and Thanks

I am grateful for the men of God from whose material I have quoted in this book. Most are short quotes and too numerous to mention. Since I have referred to the men favorably I trust they will not mind being mentioned and quoted.

Thanks to Dr. W. E. Dowell for permission to quote a portion of his excellent article on The Philosophy of Music at Baptist Bible College. And many thanks to a number of pastors who have listed the books that have meant the most to them.

The following men have written specific paragraphs or pages for this book on particular subjects and I am very grateful to them for their permission to use the material: Thanks to

Dr. Gary Coleman   Dr. Bob Jones, III
Dr. E. J. Brinson   Rev. Bradley Price
Rev. Milton Ker   Rev. David F. Price
Dr. Frank Garlock   Rev. Norman Pyle
Dr. J. R. Faulkner   Rev. Howard Pyle
Rev. Gene Payne

May God bless each and all who have inspired much of this book and have thus helped make it possible!

—The Author.

Table of Contents

What Every Preacher Should Know!

(The Pastor's Success Handbook)

Jeremiah 42:4

Some time ago some young pastors and Bible school graduates asked me to write a book on *What Every Young Preacher Should Know*. For a couple of years now I have been observing, recalling and writing.

But I have become convinced that older preachers, too, need such practical and pertinent suggestions as well as *young* pastors and evangelists. So, after thirty-six years in the full-time ministry—here goes! How I wish I could have read this book thirty-seven years ago!

Pastor, have you ever wondered how to get more people to come hear you preach, how to get all the money from your people that the church needs, how to handle that ornery board member, how to have a music program in your church that will be effective and will truly glorify the Lord, how to reach those visitors, how to steer your young people in the right direction? Here's how.

Have you longed for sparkling, well-attended Sunday night services, for workers who really take their tasks seriously and fulfill them, for ushers who make people want to return to your church, for evangelistic meetings that succeed? Here's how!

Have you wished for success in getting new, fresh sermons with appealing titles, good outlines, pertinent illustrations and an effective conclusion? Would you like to have the titles of the books that will really help you build a great church and freshen up your preaching with pungent messages? Here's help!

Would you get the most out of your days with an organized plan of attack on the work at hand? Have you wondered how to inspire your Sunday school workers and others, how to replace staff members and lay workers without unnecessary heartache and stress, how to take care of visiting speakers, missionaries and others with a minimum of problem to the pastor? Here's how!

Would you like to build a militant and strong but happy and cordial church, a church that will love its pastor, hate sin, and crusade against the Devil, while at the same time winning the lost? Here's how!

Do you long for some solution to the problem of getting tied up with counseling, committee meetings, difficult people, touchy situations that take you from the main task of sermon preparation and soul winning? What do you do with visitors who stay too long, people who expect you to come see them more often than possible, long delays that cut into the pastor's time at funerals, and in preparation for weddings?

How do you co-relate the schedules of a Christian school and the church that sponsors it and keep the school from consuming too much of the pastor's time and handle the personnel problems that crop up?

How can a pastor roll with the punches, avoid heart attacks, pastor a strong church with all of its burdens without getting ulcers? Here's how!

Chapter One

The Starting Point
(On Your Mark, Get Set, Go!)

The race is seldom won by the runner who gets off to a bad start. How important for every pastor to begin right!

Here you have a clean slate. "Hats off to the past, coats off to the future," as Dan Crawford said. The new broom should sweep clean. Leap into the race with vigor, determine your priorities and fix your eyes on the proper goals.

"Everything rises or falls on leadership," Dr. Lee Roberson has often declared. You can lead people better than you can drive them. People will do what you *do* better than they will do what you say do.

Decide why you're here in this particular position. Remember who called you and who you're working for. Be sure your contract is with God. "If God be for us, who can be against us?" (Rom. 8:31). "What doest thou here?" God asked Elijah when he was cringing on the mountain in fear. It is a good idea to determine just what we're here for and what we intend to do.

Then, walk humbly with thy God. "By humility and the fear of the Lord are riches, and honour, and life" (Prov. 22:4).

The Devil can't do anything with a humble man, someone has wisely said.

Being humble and meek doesn't mean you're to be soft and spineless!

Write down some things you definitely want to accomplish in this work. Don't tell it all to the people at once. It is good to mention a few things that you are certain of and that will inspire and encourage your people. But to mention too many things may backfire on you. For one thing, many of those people may not be used to doing much of *anything*. They will feel you are taking too much on yourself and expecting too much of them. If you are young, they will possibly think of you as an upstart or a young "whippersnapper"!

Again, some of the deacons, elders or other mature members of the flock may think you're running ahead of them, and they may clip your wings and place you in a bad position at the start of your ministry.

Make your own list and then gradually share your dreams and aims with the people. As they gain confidence in you and learn to love you, they will be glad to follow you. You may determine (and I think you should) to visit (briefly) every home in your pastorate during the first few weeks of your ministry. Fine! But don't tell them you're going to and then not do it! Don't bite off more than you can chew!

If you plan to visit several hundred homes in a few weeks, you will probably not be able to push very many other projects at the same time. I would let the people know that you want to get acquainted with them and that you would enjoy long visits with them but that in order to get around to all of the flock, you will, of necessity, make those first visits short ones.

This will save you much time and it will relieve them also of feeling like you're going to take up their whole evening. Most people are busy and have many other things they want to do. The chapter on visitation will give you some good pointers on calling, but at the *beginning* of your ministry in a church, here are some good thoughts:

1. *Visit by areas*, taking several families within a few blocks of one another. This will save time and will be more practical than taking the church roll alphabetically. You may be able to start some evening before seven and visit four or five homes before 8:45 in this manner. Probably not too many people would appreciate your coming after 9:00 o'clock. Shut-ins, night workers and others you'll be able to visit in the afternoon, catching them before supper.

2. *Even though you may be in a hurry* to meet the people, and thus to get the chore of visiting every family quickly behind you,

it is important not to give the people the impression that you are in that big a hurry or that you're just anxious to scratch their name from your list.

3. *Be sure and include the children,* the teens, the grandparents or any other family member in your conversation on the get-acquainted visit. It would be well if the pastor's wife could accompany you on these initial visits. Then she will not be a stranger to them and she can help you remember the names of the children 'til you get to the car!

4. *Show interest in the people personally.* Don't be nosy, but it is a good idea to comment favorably on the lovely children, the beautiful painting on the wall, the new car in the drive, the beautifully kept lawn, etc. Talk more about them than about yourself. Let *them* talk a good bit during your visit and they will feel that *you* are a good conversationalist!

5. *Keep good records of your visits.* It may be that the church secretary will have already given you a card with the names and ages of the family members on it and if so, your work will be easier. Simply jot down the date of your visit and the pertinent things you need to remember about that family—the unsaved son, the grandmother in the rest home, the sister facing surgery, etc. You might even be able to make some of those notes while you are in their home *if* you can do it on a "let me make a note of that for my prayer list" basis. In that case, be sure you *do* make it a matter of prayer.

6. *Don't show favoritism,* but you might be wise to visit the families of the official board—if you have such—before you start the rounds of the families by areas. If certain families invite you for a meal, then, of course, you would temporarily break your routine of visiting by areas. It is good to accept those invitations for dinner and in such cases you would need to stay longer than your usual "get-acquainted" call. It may be that it will "get around" that some have so entertained you and others may take the hint and do likewise, but I would not mention it from the pulpit or "hint around" like a hungry hound. For one thing, as delightful as some of those family meals may be, it is a time-

consuming thing. In the country it may be necessary to eat with people often. In the city it will probably not become a problem.

7. *Should you call ahead* to let the people know you are coming to visit? There are pros and cons on this, of course. Most of the time I just made the visit. If we caught them home, fine. If we didn't, we went back another time. If we found them in the middle of a meal, a project, or hurrying to go somewhere, we would make it a very quick pop-call and promise to stay longer next time.

If you call ahead, it makes the visit seem so formal and official. The lady will probably feel she has to clean the house and fancy up the living room before the new minister comes. She may even feel she has to bake something, fix coffee, etc., and in that case you cannot make it a hurried call and hasten on to the next house. On the other hand, if you don't call ahead, then you run the risk of embarrassing them if they are in the middle of something they consider important, or if they are not properly dressed.

By the way, there will be some members who will never find it convenient for you to call and if you don't slip up on them you never *will* find them home! Play it by ear. You may find that the secretary or a good, friendly deacon and his wife will cue you in on the families who would definitely like you better if you called ahead for an appointment. I personally felt that, in most cases, it just made the call too official and took up too much time to call ahead and make it a "planned" visit.

8. *Be natural. Be kind.* Be genuinely interested in the people but don't be too familiar or talkative.

9. *Don't appear overly dogmatic about things* the people bring up with which you may disagree. You are new to them. There will be time to bring them around to your standards. Don't argue.

10. *Try to assume they will be in the services regularly.* If they happen to be people who have gotten out of the habit of coming to church, try to get a promise to "see you in church next Sunday"!

11. *Have a brief prayer* before you leave the home. Let the people realize that you walk with God.

At church you must be businesslike and organized and there will be time schedules to keep. Some people will stop you between Sunday school and church or at some other crucial time and want to tell you about the case of measles little Mary has or about the infected big toe their Uncle Charlie is suffering with out in Omaha. Try to take time for them. Listen to them and be sincerely interested. Promise to pray for little Mary or Uncle Charlie and then do it. (If you're like me you'd better write "Mary—measles" or "Unc. Charlie—toe" down somewhere.)

By the Sunday morning service I had several such cases inscribed on the margin of my bulletin. Add a few more announcements and the rest of the assorted prayer requests and your bulletin by Sunday night may look like a disaster area, but at least you've got it jotted down. One evangelist said I was the only pastor he knew who had a Sunday bulletin with Scofield notes! Perhaps a small notebook is better for such notes than the bulletin.

You can't run a church sitting in your office. Those are real live human beings you're working with—and their problems are very real to them.

You'll soon discover there are a few chronic cases, two or three hypochondriacs and a mental case or two, that you'll need help in handling or they'll consume all your time. One of the most distressing moments in a pastor's life is to see that sharp looking new couple going through the vestibule after church while you frantically try to figure out how to get dear old Sister Weep-a-Lot or Brother Problem-Plenty to stop talking to you long enough to meet the newcomers!

But be patient with even the feebleminded and the neurotic. Soon you'll find a trusted deacon, a loyal staff-member or even an overloaded wife who will "rescue" you in such cases. This is a good project for alert ushers, as we will discuss in the ushering chapter.

Don't be hurt (or surprised) if some of the people in your new parish do not take to you immediately. After all, if the former pastor was there for years, it will take time for some of them to transfer their allegiance and confidence to the new undershepherd. And you'll also find that some of them who just could "eat you up" when you're new on the field will act like they *had* consumed you when you've been around for a while.

Do your best to get along with people. There is no virtue in being hard to deal with. You may find that you have inherited a deacon or a Sunday school superintendent or an organist who would try the patience of Job and tax the wisdom of Solomon. But what would life be like without a challenge? God will help you to know how to cope with the problem-people if you walk in humility and keep your eyes on the Lord.

It is our sincere hope that this book will answer some of the questions that really plague young pastors. But stay sweet. Don't come on with a chip on your shoulders. I know the Bible is to be your main textbook but some preachers could well peruse Dale Carnegie's *How to Win Friends and Influence People*, too.

Problems will arise. In fact, they may abound. I remember Dr. J. R. Faulkner, then president of Tennessee Temple University, saying, "We have no problems, just challenges to adjust to the plan of God." The trial of your faith, though it be tried with fire, will one day be found unto praise and honor and glory (I Pet. 1:7).

Don't tell the people everything you know the first month you're there. They're going to need some spiritual food later on, too. I wouldn't use up all of my "sugar stick" sermons during the first few weeks or months just because they've been used well in other places. What goes over good down at Pine Bottom may not be what the saints at Society Hill need at all. Of course it is a blessing that you have some sermons with which you're already familiar. You may not have to study and prepare quite as hard during those strenuous weeks when you're trying to get acquainted and remember everybody's name, but I wouldn't preach a sermon just because it is familiar and you find it an easy one to remember. To depend upon past blessing may dump you in the middle of present failure.

"Learn to *love* your people—this is so important." I heard

Pastor Jim Brown from out in Batesville, Arkansas say that. How true. Even at the outset when the people are still new to you I'd begin to pray for God to give you a genuine love for His people. Learn to love them for Jesus' sake, and you'll soon find you love them for their own sakes, too.

Cultivate good habits from the beginning. Discipline yourself well. Get up early and get with the Lord at the beginning of the day. "He rose up early" was uttered concerning more than one of God's successful servants in the Bible. Get a fresh new start each morning. Every day will be different and every day should be glorious.

Several years ago I learned this poem. I hope I never forget it.

> I met God in the morning
> When my day was at its best,
> And His presence came like sunrise
> Like a glory in my breast.
>
> All day long the Presence lingered,
> All day long He stayed with me,
> And we sailed in perfect calmness
> O're a very troubled sea.
>
> Other ships were blown and battered,
> Other ships were sore distressed,
> But the winds that seemed to drive them
> Brought to us a peace and rest!
>
> Then I thought of other mornings,
> With a keen remorse of mind,
> When I, too, had loosed the moorings
> With the Presence left behind.
>
> So I think I know the secret,
> Learned from many a troubled way;
> You must seek Him in the morning
> If you want Him through the day.
>
> —Ralph Cushman

A pastor just won't have much time for the late show on the tube if he is going to meet God for a fresh rendezvous each morning before the family is up and the phone begins to ring. Dr. Oswald J. Smith said that he looked forward to the "morning watch" more than any other time of the day.

"Let your moderation be known unto all men" (Phil. 4:5). Be moderate in dining, driving, and dogmatism. Some pastors are guilty of overeating, overdriving and overreacting. A preacher should not have the reputation for being a glutton, a speed-demon or an incendiary.

Practice punctuality. Be *on time*, in other words. Services should start on time, appointments should be kept promptly, a hostess should never be kept in a frenzy wondering if "that preacher" will be late again for the meal he has been invited to enjoy. Nothing sours a lady member more than to have the dinner hot, the rolls ready to butter, and the family waiting nervously, only to have the pastor come puffing in late for the meal. The hostess will smile and pretend it doesn't bother her that the rolls are cold, the main dish overdone and the potatoes soggy from waiting, but don't forget it, pardner, it *does* bother her! Start in time to be *on* time!

It is good for a prospective pastor to let the church know what his main aims would be ahead of time, and let them know what he stands for. If they don't call you, well and good. You've saved yourself a lot of grief, anyway. Be honest with them ahead of time. This doesn't mean that you have to be rough with them or lambast them good so they'll know they're in for some stormy services if they call you. You can tread softly when you are new on the field and give them time to grow in grace and learn to have confidence in you. But don't be dishonest with them about what you believe and what you stand for. And, remember, there are, indeed, "many ways to skin a cat," and if you can't accomplish what you feel God wants done one way you can sometimes do it another way. Don't be discouraged if all does not go to suit you as you begin your pastorate.

Be an example to the flock. "The husbandman that laboureth must be first partaker of the fruit." If you don't have your priorities straight neither will they. If you are lazy you can expect your people to be. If you are selfish they will be selfish, too. If you don't win souls, your people are not likely to.

Die to yourself from the very beginning. The pastor should

never be pouty, haughty or puffed up with pride. Discipline yourself. This is so important.

But for Jesus' sake, hitch your wagon to a star, aim high, and believe that God is going to use you there to bless and help His people. Read carefully the chapters of the rest of this book. Study other good books by men who have done a good job for God. Visit great soul-winning churches to observe how they do it. At least observe them by reading their periodicals, church bulletins and everything else you can lay your hands on that will help you with ideas. And as you settle down to a routine in the pastorate make the most of your time, which is what our next chapter is about.

Chapter Two

Squeezing the Most Out of a Day

"The time is short," Paul wrote, and every diligent pastor wants to make the most of it. Most of us are hamstrung with delays, interruptions, and problems that seem to rob us of the precious time we need to accomplish our goals. How can we tame time and squeeze out of a day all that God has for us?

First, make up your mind that you're going to master time by first mastering yourself: "Through idleness of the hands the house droppeth through," wrote Solomon (Eccles. 10:18). By nature most of us are lazy. Even the most conscientious person has a lazy streak. "It is high time to awake out of sleep" (Rom. 13:11).

So master *yourself*—then your *day.* "As thy days, so shall thy strength be." The management of time is so important for a successful man in any vocation and especially is this true in the ministry. Make up a daily schedule. Even if it does get riddled with interruptions on some days it will help to know what you intend to do. Plan your day.

Get organized and do your best to keep organized. File things so you'll know where they are. If you have a secretary give her time to keep things properly filed for you. In the case of sermon material, illustrations, etc., you'll probably have to have a filing system of your own. I have spent hours of precious time looking for an illustration, a clipping or a letter that I should have had properly filed.

Get up early! If you make a habit of rolling out immediately when the alarm sounds you can save precious minutes. What is there to be gained by groaning, yawning and rolling over for a few more winks? Some of those winks may merge into another hour of wasted time. If your family is still asleep you can lay your clothes out the night before and have them right ready to slip quietly into the next morning. Ease on out into the study, or to the place of prayer before the noise of the family and the telephone sounds. Some cold water in the face ought to wake you up. If the early morning is the time for your exercise period (jogging, etc.) then, of course, you'll be wide awake when you get back from that. You might find it advisable to read a bit of the Bible before you pray, lest you get sleepy on your knees in the early morning.

"No Bible, no breakfast" was a good resolution of a noted Chinese Christian.

"He rose up early" was the rule of many a successful person in the Bible. David, "Early will I seek thee" (Ps. 63:1). Moses, "Satisfy us early with thy mercy" (Ps. 90:14). Solomon, "Let us get up early to the vineyards" (Song of Sol. 7:12), "Abraham gat up early in the morning to the place where he stood before the Lord" (Gen. 19:27); "Jacob rose up early in the morning" (Gen. 28:18); "Joshua rose early in the morning" (Josh. 3:1); "Gideon . . .rose up early" (Judg. 7:1) to attack the Midianites; and our Lord Himself "rising up a great while before day. . .went out, and departed into a solitary place, and there prayed" (Mark 1:35).

In one pastorate I had my study off a porch away from the main body of the house. In another my study was a large upper room over our garage. In my last and longest pastorate we made my study out of a utility room away from the house out by the carport. It will be a great help to any preacher if he has his study away from the house. Too many, I fear, try to study in their church office. One successful pastor I know had his study in the back of the church, behind the choir loft and baptistry, and almost a block away from the church office. The secretary could thus intercept most of the interruptions before they got to the pastor.

If a pastor tries to study in his home it will be impossible not to hear the sounds of the wife and children as the household activities go on. The doorbell will ring and (if only unconsciously) the preacher will wonder if it is for him and if he will have to get up from his work. The little children in the house will want to know why they cannot go in and see Daddy if he is at home, but if he has gone "out" to his study they will soon realize that "Daddy has gone to work."

If a pastor tries to work in or too close to his house it will be easy for his wife to call on him for little errands ("Honey, could you run to the store and get me some soap powder?"); or for the solution to trivial problems ("Dear, could you help me with these curtain rods?"); or baby-sitting jobs ("Sweetheart, the baby is asleep, I think, and I need to run over to Mary's; would you mind listening out for him?") Of course, as soon as she gets out of sight the Devil will see to it that the baby will wake up crying and thirty minutes or more may be lost from the study.

Don't let yourself become a nursemaid or errand boy. If mowing the grass and cutting the weeds are your sole means of exercise, well and good, but if you jog, swim or play tennis for exercise then probably it will pay you to hire a boy to cut your grass. Too many such activities will kill valuable time.

You're the boss when you're a preacher. There is no time clock to punch, no manager to report to, no prescribed number of hours to "put in." For this reason the preacher must be honest with himself and with God and discipline himself as to the proper use of his hours. Since we are "on our own" it would be mighty easy to get into a habit of "goofing off" with the morning paper, talking to the "boys" down at the corner garage, picking up grocery items for the little woman or swapping tales with neighboring pastors. The busy pastor will be too conscientious to become so occupied.

Shall I spend my time *studying* or *visiting*? Well, BOTH, of course! But time must be set aside for each. In the earlier days of my last pastorate I made from 50 to 70 calls a week. This is one main reason why our church grew from 100 members to 1600 during the pastorate! As the church grew larger there were many more hospital visits, church and school difficulties, funerals and weddings, parishioners with problems they wanted help with and so I had to reduce the calls to perhaps 25 to 40 visits per week, as other staff members could (by then) be given some of the visitation load.

But don't ever let yourself become a slave to the office chair and expect others to do all the outside work. Have some definite visitation hours for soul winning. Other calls will have to be taken up with backslidden and discouraged Christians or with prospective members. Then, of course, there is the never-ending burden of the hospitals and other sick calls.

And no pastor can afford to neglect his shut-ins. These dear people will be the ones most likely to spend much time in prayer for you. They are lonely and need encouragement. They need the pastor because many of them cannot get out to the services if they are truly "shut-ins." While other staff members or your "shut-in" committee can assist with this, periodically, there is no substitute for the pastor's going personally from time to time. It will strengthen you and encourage your own heart to have been in the presence of those who suffer and are confined. It is a good idea to have cassette tapes made of the Sunday services which can be taken by and played for them in the week that follows. Perhaps the church can afford to buy the tape player for the shut-ins who do not have their own.

By the way, those shut-ins will love the pastor who visits them and sometimes the very property the church needs will be donated by that shut-in you may not have known even *had* any property! Well-cared-for shut-ins sometimes leave substantial amounts to the work of the Lord and the church in their wills. No church can afford to shun or ignore the sick and the shut-ins.

I usually tried to do soul-winning visitation a couple of nights a week, such as Tuesday and Thursday, and again on Saturday afternoon, though we, of course, kept our eyes open for souls at all times.

Committees can be selected to take care of many things the pastor would normally have to do. I know some preachers and churches boast of having "no officers except the pastor and deacons," but I have found some committees greatly helpful. There is nothing in the Bible that says it is wrong to have committees. While many committees "take down minutes and waste hours," there is no reason why this has to be true.

"Separately they do nothing while together they determine that nothing can be done," some wit has said about committees (I've had a few like that!). But if these groups are very carefully chosen, with a good responsible chairman (or chairwoman), and if officially approved by the church to make the importance of their task all the more impressive, there is no reason why these committees cannot be a great help to the pastor.

For instance, there is no earthly reason why a pastor (or even a pastor's wife) has to take care of selecting the flowers for the communion table, arranging the meal schedule for the visiting evangelist, or seeing to it that the nursery has adequate toys or crib sheets! If committees are chosen carefully and then allowed a certain amount from the church budget to get the things they need to function, the pastor should never have to touch many of the things with which some pastors are burdened down. Here is a list of committees that might well be considered:

GROUNDS COMMITTEE. (Flower planting, weeding, shrub trimming, etc.)

NURSERY COMMITTEE. (Making sure the nursery has adequate help, proper furnishings, clean facilities, etc.)

HOSPITALITY COMMITTEE. (With a wise and discerning lady heading this one up the visiting missionaries will always have a place to stay, the evangelist will have a good meal with the pastor in some clean home each evening, visiting guests from other churches will be properly recognized, etc.)

SHUT-IN COMMITTEE. Some of the healthy and active senior citizens may be the ones to head this one up. They can visit the shut-ins more often than the pastor does and can inform him of special problems, serious illnesses, hospitalized members, etc. The Shut-in Committee also can see to it that shut-ins hear tape recordings of the pastor's messages last Sunday, that they are remembered on their birthdays, and that they are taken care of generously and happily at holiday times like Christmas, Thanksgiving, Mother's Day, etc. They can also arrange for such shut-ins to get a way to church on Sundays when the weather is nice enough for them to get out to services.

FLOWER COMMITTEE. Sees to it that the flowers in the church are fresh each Sunday and that indoor plants and arrangements are kept cleaned and attractive.

YOUTH FELLOWSHIP COMMITTEE can be a big help in slating special events for the young people, especially if the church does not have a youth director. Parents can be organized for refreshments during "After Glow" or other times for youth to get together. Don't make the poor pastor's wife have to do it all. Whoever the youth leader or youth director will be, a good committee working with him will be of great help.

A MUSIC COMMITTEE would need to work very closely with (and under) the pastor unless he has a full-time music director who thus would head up such a committee. Variety in choir presentations, great care in selecting singers for solos, duets, trios, etc., elimination of the wrong kind of music, scheduling of numbers for funerals or special events—all of these things are to be considered. A music committee could also see to it that songbooks are kept clean and in good repair, choir music is properly filed, records kept of music previously used, etc. In the church where there is a full-time minister of music, of course, much of this would be under his direct supervision. He, in turn, would be responsible to the pastor.

A FINANCE COMMITTEE can work with the pastor, particularly when it comes time to draw up a proposed budget for the new church year. This committee also can be aware of undue spending, emergencies, financial problems that arise, etc. These men should certainly include some deacons, and in some cases it might be wise for all of them to be deacons. The treasurer, too, should be a member of this committee.

A VISITATION COMMITTEE could be of great value in some situations. If the church has a full-time visitation minister then such workers could work under him and he, in turn, would be responsible to the pastor. Never let the congregation get the idea, though, that all of the visitation and calling is to be done by this committee. They would spearhead it, inspire it, set the example, and could help find prospects, meet newcomers to the city, keep visitation files fresh and active, etc.

Pastor, learn to delegate! Sometimes I know it will seem like you have to end up doing it yourself, anyway. There will be times when staff members will slip up and forget something or when committee chairmen will go out of town without informing you. Still it will be wise to trust your workers and delegate responsibility. You'll have to be aware of what's going on, of course, and sometimes you'll have to change chairmen on some committees, or call in a worker to have a briefing of what needs to be done, but with all of the problems you may incur you'll still find it easier to have someone helping you with the work. Then, too, of course your workers and members need some tasks to perform for the Lord.

If you have a paid youth director then a youth committee may not be necessary, and if you do have one it will perhaps be best for the committee to be chosen and directed by that youth director. Likewise if you have a paid choir director or music leader then the music committee can report to him and he, in turn, can be responsible to you.

Some of these problems will be discussed under separate chapter headings.

Every pastor will have to arrange his own schedule, but sometimes I've been asked to suggest a good time arrangement for the day. Perhaps this one I frequently used will be helpful.

6:00 A.M. (or earlier), into the study or prayer closet for Bible reading and prayer. Perhaps 10 minutes for jogging, bicycling or exercise too, in the early morning hours. Jot down brief outline of tasks to be accomplished today and pray over them.

7:10-7:30—Shower, shave, dress.

7:30-8:10—Breakfast and family Bible reading.

8:10-8:30—Off to radio broadcast, pick up mail, etc.

9:15 to 10:00—Go by church office, open mail, dictate brief letters.

10:00 till 12:30—Study time, followed by lunch with your wife.

1:15 to 3:00—Study time, answer mail, etc.

3:00 to 5:30—Visitation, including hospital calls, go by church office for tasks that may have accumulated there.

5:30 to 7:00—Dinner with family, time for children, etc.

7:30 to 8:45—Visitation or board meetings or prayer meeting depending on which night of the week it is.

9:00 to 11:00—Time spent with wife and/or family.

On Wednesdays more time would be spent in study on evening message and less time for visiting and miscellaneous items. On Saturdays I spent 6 or 8 hours in the study from early morning until perhaps mid-afternoon before venturing out for calling. Then again in the study Saturday night, Sunday morning early, and Sunday afternoon. Mondays were considered a "day off." Sometimes I got it by leaving town. Other Mondays we would take off after the early broadcast and necessary hospital calls. Monday night and possibly Friday night would be family nights with wife and/or children.

Emergencies and disasters will, of course, alter the schedule. You might just as well adjust without groaning!

And what about counseling? I personally believe many pastors have ruined their preaching and soul-winning ministries by too much counseling. You can use psychology (mostly good common sense!) but God didn't call you to be a psychologist or a psychiatrist—He called you to preach! Keep the pulpit hot and your own heart saturated with the Bible and you can answer the questions most people have in a very few minutes. If they are willing to take the Bible formula and obey God you have accomplished something. But if they are not willing to do this you will only stifle your own ministry by spending long hours "counseling" with them!

But what about those who *insist* on talking to you and keep demanding counseling time? First, I would give them God's Word and let them know that this Book (the Bible) has the answer to their every problem. Encourage them to attend every service, Sunday morning, Sunday evening, Wednesday evening, Sunday school, Bible classes, in addition to their own personal Bible study at home.

Second, pray with them and pray for them. Try to teach them to pray for themselves and stand on their own two feet.

Have an abundant supply of good tracts and booklets on hand to help those who need counseling. Dr. Brandt or Dr. Narramore may well help them with their books and save you many hours. However, the books I've found most helpful are smaller tracts; or pamphlets by Dr. Rice, Dr. DeHaan and such men. At the close of this chapter I'll list some literature you should have on hand in a nice rack or on a long counter for such counseling needs.

Give them the radio time of good broadcasts that will help them.

Get them to order (or supply them with) *Our Daily Bread,* a good devotional booklet.

Try to appoint a spiritual and strong Christian to help you encourage them.

Be sure your Sunday school or some other active group gets to this person and gets him or her busy doing something worthwhile, preferably something for others. Many people find that their own troubles vanish when they get busy doing something for someone else.

If your problem-persons really are mental cases then, of course, you may need to recommend a Christian psychiatrist if one is near at hand. If not, at least insist that they get a thorough check-up by a competent physician. Many of our mental or imagined spiritual ailments are really a result of some physical malfunction.

If their problem is spiritual and they will not accept the counsel of the Word God, and will not come consistently to hear the Bible preached, then you have lost nothing by letting them drift on to another church.

A young pastor should be especially careful and on guard if the person who wants counseling is a member of the opposite sex. A good practice is to set a time limit—say 20 or 30 minutes that you can talk with her. (If she is needing salvation and willing to listen you may need a bit more time than this). It is not a bad idea to do such counseling when your secretary or someone else is nearby—preferably in the very next office. In some instances if you as a pastor feel that the lady is lonely, emotional and/or starved for affection it may be best for you to have your wife along for the counseling session.

If a person keeps talking and lingering how does the pastor get him (or her) to go? In other words, how does he terminate the visit?

When I've said all that I know to say and felt the visit was over

I would shove my chair back and shut the Bible or notebook to which we had been referring and suggest that we have prayer. Even if you have already prayed about the problem at hand you can always have a "benediction." Whether you kneel or stand for the prayer will be determined by the pastor and the circumstances. If you feel he is going to talk on incessantly and that it will be hard to wrap it up, I'd say, "Well, let's have prayer before you go." Then bow your head and thank God for the privilege of the conference and pray God's blessing on him as he goes his way. Even the thickest person should by then get the idea that you had other things to do and that it was time for him to be gone. If he *still* persists in hanging on after that I would just say, "You're going to have to pardon me now as I have others waiting to see me," or "I'm going to have to get on to the hospital," or "I mustn't keep you any longer," and open the door for him.

In some cases, where you know the person is long-winded and overburdened, it may be well to have your secretary (or your wife, or someone else) to interrupt you after twenty minutes or so to let you know that this or that appointment is waiting for you. There are people in every community who will stay on forever if you let them!

Time marches on. You will never get "caught up" if you're an honest servant of God. There will always be many other things you can do. Franklin said, "Do not squander time, for that is the stuff life is made of." Time *is* short, so 'redeem the time'!

"Are there not twelve hours in the day?" the Saviour asked. Perhaps by this He is teaching us that we ought to be busy and accomplish all that we can in the twelve hours meant for working. Then with seven hours or so spent sleeping one will still have five hours each day left for recreation, eating and family pleasure.

Plan your twelve hours well. Sometimes it may pay you to take inventory and see how the last (working) day was spent. Perhaps today you may improve on the use of those twelve tremendous, golden hours!

By the way, time will be wasted if we have not prayed. If we are attempting to do the job *our* way instead of God's way the day will be a failure. In Mark 4 the storm ceased when they prayed.

> **O what peace we often forfeit,**
> **O what needless pain we bear,**
> **All because we do not carry**
> **Everything to God in prayer.**

"The effectual fervent prayer of a righteous man availeth much."—Jas. 5:16.

Use the extra minutes of the day well and you may find you have gained an extra hour of study and valuable accomplishment. Keep a good book in your car. Some Bible verses typed out on cards and left on the dashboard or over the sun visor will remind you to memorize while you drive or wait for a traffic light. Have good tracts or small booklets in your coat pocket to read when waiting for someone or standing in line at the tag office. You could read several chapters in a book while a tire is being changed or a small repair job is being done.

Read the paper at night when you are too tired to concentrate on anything important. Have a book by your easy chair while your wife is putting the final touches on the evening meal. Use idle moments to work for you in mastering something for the Master.

Many pastors keep a cassette recorder in the car. Thus you can listen to good sermons or Bible lessons while riding and while waiting for the light to change.

Yes, time marches on. Use it well. Too soon it will merge into eternity.

List of helpful tracts and booklets to have available in lobby or on the pastor's shelf for help in dealing with certain problems people will have:

SALVATION BOOKLETS:

"What Must I Do to Be Saved?" by Dr. John R. Rice, Box 1099, Murfreesboro, Tennessee 37130

Operation, the Only Hope by Dr. Hugh Pyle, Box 1508, Panama City, Florida 32401

Salvation booklets of Oliver Green, Box 2024, Greenville, South Carolina 29602

Books from Chick Publications, Box 662, Chino, California 91710
Tract, *God's Simple Plan of Salvation,* Lifegate, Box 1771, Martinsville, Indiana 46151
Tracts from American Tract Society, Box 402008, Garland, Texas 75040

BOOKS ON ASSURANCE AND SUCCESS IN CHRISTIAN LIFE:

Safety, Certainty and Enjoyment from Back to the Bible, Box 82808, Lincoln, Nebraska 68501
The Truth About the Christian Life by Dr. Hugh Pyle, Box 1508, Panama City, Florida 32401

BOOKS FOR HOME AND FAMILY PROBLEMS:

Taming of the Toddler
Taming of the Teenager
Taming of the TV
How to Live Happily Ever After
Keeping the Honey in the Honeymoon all by Dr. Hugh Pyle, Box 1508, Panama City, Florida 32401

BOOKS ON CULTS AND ISMS:

Truth About Tongues by Dr. Hugh Pyle, Box 1508, Panama City, Florida 32401
Mr. Confusion order from Back to the Bible, Box 82808, Lincoln, Nebraska 68501

Mormonism, Latter-Day Confusion order from Back to the Bible, address above.
T.M., Is It Only Meditation? order from Back to the Bible
Jehovah's Witnesses order from Back to the Bible
Sunday or Sabbath? by Dr. John R. Rice, Box 1099, Murfreesboro, Tennessee 37130

BOOKS ON GENERAL CHRISTIAN LIFE AND GROWTH:

Our Daily Bread, Radio Bible Class, Box 22, Grand Rapids, Michigan 49555
Booklets by Dr. M. R. DeHaan, Box 22, Grand Rapids, Michigan 49555
Booklets by Dr. John R. Rice, Box 1099, Murfreesboro, Tennessee 37130

BOOKS ON PERSONAL PROBLEMS:

Nervous Christians (Little)
Why Do Christians Suffer? (Epp)
Master Secrets of Prayer (Thompson)
How to Know the Will of God (Weiss) all from Back to the Bible
Truth About the Homosexuals (10¢) Dr. Hugh Pyle

BOOKS ON CREATION AND EVOLUTION:
How Did It All Begin? (Whitcomb) Back to the Bible
Why I Accept the Genesis Record (Hand) Back to the Bible
Problems of Evolution (Stewart Custer) Bob Jones University Press

BOOKLETS ON SMOKING AND DRINKING:
How to Quit Smoking Without Pills, Pain or Panic (Hugh Pyle)
Liquid Devil—The Bible and the Bottle (Hugh Pyle)

BOOKLETS ON ROCK MUSIC:
What's Wrong With Rock and Roll? Bob Larson, Box 26438, Denver, Colorado 80226
The Rock Blast—The Big Beat by Frank Garlock, P. O. Box 6524, Greenville, South Carolina 29614.

Chapter Three

Brethren, We Have Met
to Worship

Why not have services to which people will want to come back? Your meetings for worship and service can be so pleasant, proper and profitable that people will look forward to coming again and again.

This chapter is not to deal so much with the order of service as with practical things we have observed along the way. Some suggestions will be so commonplace as to appear trite indeed. But many pastors are so close to their own work that they cannot see it, like the man who couldn't find the forest for the trees. These are common-sense suggestions. I have visited in a great number of churches and have also talked to many people who either came to a church or left one for these reasons. So please don't take these simple observations lightly. They could make a big difference in your church.

1. The First Appearance Is Important!

Your church may not be fancy, expensive, majestic or ornate, but it can surely be neat, clean, freshly painted and orderly. When worshipers walk up to your doors let them see a parking lot with lines neatly drawn, sidewalks swept and clean, grass trimmed, leaves raked and shrubbery properly kept. As they walk up onto your porch or into your lobby let them be impressed with the fresh, clean, ready-for-company look. Many pastors are so busy with the spiritual problems of their churches that they never seem to notice what visitors notice immediately. If the church is fortunate enough to have a good grounds man and a good custodian, then much of your problem is solved. Even so, unless they are rare workers indeed, you'll either have to keep in behind them and remind them of just what you want the church and grounds to look like or else have a committee (preferably one good, concientious man) to be responsible for these hired workers. Most custodians resent having several "bosses." Whoever is responsible for outlining the duties of the grounds man and custodian must be a perfectionist, but an even-tempered one. Don't appoint a man whose own house and yard are not neat and clean.

A good thought to keep in mind: It is generally best not to hire a custodian from your own membership. But whatever you do, don't hire one whose own yard and house look like a disaster area!

Let your church be known as a beauty spot, if possible. At least, don't let people go away remembering the messy lobby, the stale bulletins in the songbook racks, the unmowed grass and the littered parking lot. Some people who are used to spotless houses, well-kept lawns, bright, cheerful shopping centers, im-maculate banks and clean restaurants are going to be "turned off" by a messy, littered, cluttered church building.

If you happen to have a small church and must depend on volunteer or part-time janitorial help, then keep stressing the importance of the service rendered by those who keep the church clean, fresh and bright. Remind them that 'cleanliness is next to godliness.' It may not be in the Bible but it is true, nevertheless! And stay on it! Determine to keep up a good first appearance.

If the church is too poor to hire a custodian and too small to find volunteers who will do it right, you might try hiring your own teenage children to do it *if* they're well-disciplined and old enough to do a first-class job. Someone has suggested that there are three ways to get something done: do it yourself, hire some-one, or forbid your kids to do it! If the kids do it you'll have to be the supervisor and make sure they do a "finished" job. I would use them only if you have to, and only temporarily.

2. Make Sure the People Hear You!

I'm certain that in most churches the services would be more effective if the volume was turned up! In fact, surprisingly enough, there are many churches where they have no sound system at all! The pastor assumes because he can hear himself that everyone else can. Not many people have a built-in sound system like Dr. Ian Paisley. Maybe Billy Sunday could preach to thousands with a sounding board, and John Wesley could preach in the churchyard from his father's tombstone, but most of us do not have the lung power of those great old war-horses. I imagine that if they lived today and had to combat cushioned pews, carpeted floors, overhead jets and humming air conditioners they would use a sound system too.

As I have waited to be introduced in Sunday school assemblies, church services or youth rallies around the country I have reached this conclusion: 50% of all preachers and from 75% to 90% of Sunday school superintendents and other laymen are not being properly heard. In fact, many of them in making announcements or introductions would have fared just as well if they hadn't said anything at all!

So, turn up the sound! Visit the big, flourishing soul-winning churches in this country and you will note that they have a good, adequate sound system and that they have the volume turned high. It is impossible to sleep under the announcements or the preaching of Dr. Lee Roberson. You can't miss a word when Dr. Jack Hyles thunders at you. Choose any other dynamic and successful pastor and you'll find the same thing is true.

I have sometimes started a crusade and felt that I was not being heard in a loud and effective manner. Nothing much was happening. Then when I prevailed upon the pastor or the sound engineer to give me some volume the whole spirit of the meeting changed and results were soon forthcoming.

Maybe the liberal and liturgical fellows can get away with a mild-mannered and soft-spoken service but those of us who want to shake Hell's foundations and snatch souls as brands from the burning are going to have to come through loud and clear!

Years ago I heard Evangelist Hyman Appelman say something like this: Some men asked why he shouted and cried when he preached. He pointed to a huge concrete ledge hanging over the sidewalk on a building across the street. Dr. Appelman said, "If I saw you standing over there under that massive ledge and it began to crack and crumble and was about to fall on your head, would you want me to cup my hands to my mouth and whisper (very softly), 'O Sir, that ledge is about to fall and crush you to death. Perhaps it would be best for you to move out from under it'?" The man replied, "Go on and shout! And I'll come to *hear* you!"

Speak up! Even when you use a P. A. system. Some speakers mumble, mutter, lower their voices without getting closer to the microphone, and consequently are not heard. All people will appreciate you for it if you speak up, especially those who are hard of hearing—and many people are.

A good sound system is a "must." We've had trouble getting a good one and getting it to work right in every church I ever pastored. Acoustics are very tricky. In my last and longest pastorate we had an expensive and an adequate sound system, but still, it took a while to get it adjusted just right. Even now the proper volume for the choir or for one preacher may not be the proper volume for another preacher or for the Sunday school superintendent. You need to get a good sound engineer to "ride the gain" on it all the time. Don't be afraid to let him know that you think it needs turning up (or down). The technician back in the sound box may not be getting the same analysis that you are. You're the pastor—ask for what you know you need to make the service right.

If the people cannot hear you they are not going to be impressed even if you have a wonderful outline and a terrific closing illustration. A noted evangelist taught me in the first years of my preaching ministry that evangelistic preaching is not going to be effective if it is not *loud.* He was right!

Now I don't mean screaming and screeching at the people. Don't try to substitute perspiration for inspiration (or for an adequate sound system). I don't mean to rant and rave. But if you have an adequate sound system, and someone managing it who knows what he is doing, you can speak in a conversational tone, save your voice from exhaustion, and still reach the ears of the people (and their hearts) very effectively.

You need a sound system for a number of reasons: To overcome crying babies who may cut loose in the service; planes that may fly over; or trucks or motorcycles that go roaring by. If you have fans or an air conditioner running you have still another problem. Then, when your crowd increases and the building fills up, that much more sound is going to be absorbed by the people and the clothing they are wearing. Most churches being built today also have carpeted floors and many have cushioned pews. Without a good sound system you can just be ruined, in such cases. Again, the pastor may want to lower his voice for effect in a message sometimes. You can do it if you have a good P. A. system and get close to the "mike" as you speak more softly. But you won't be heard at all if you lower your voice without that sound system.

And don't forget, if you already have a good sound system, *turn up the volume* and see what happens! That old sinner who has been withstanding your sermons for years may wake up and come to Christ next Sunday! The Sunday school superintendent may finally get through to his adult assembly. And the next time you have testimonies the people may hear and get a blessing. And remember, small churches as well as big ones need a good P. A. system.

3. Do Your People Freeze or Fry?

Some churches have it so hot in winter that you can hardly breathe. And in summertime while the men are comfortable in their long-sleeve jackets the ladies may be shivering in their lightweight dresses.

So what do you do? Spurgeon said that good oxygen was most important, next to good preaching. Be sure you have a good circulation system for the heat in winter that will bring in some fresh air. Those backsliders who seem to be in a stupor may just be asleep because it is so warm in there! If your heat is not a central, circulating system then you need to train your ushers to have windows cracked or doors opened at proper intervals to allow the air to cool off or freshen up as the need arises.

In the summer most churches have the air conditioners set at too cold a spot on the thermostat. If people are shivering they are not likely to be convicted about how terrible it would be to go to Hell. Anything warm would be welcome at the moment when their bare arms are turning blue! Many of our ladies learned to bring along a sweater or a stole or cape even in summertime so they would be comfortable on the inside of the church. We have lost older people with arthritis because the temperature was too cold for them. Try to find a happy medium. You'll never please everybody, but many churches really do go to extremes with the cooling system.

4. Start on Time!

Most churches do not. Many churches begin the service from one minute to ten minutes after the set time for starting. Nothing so irritates people as to hurry like mad to get the children ready, weave through traffic, hunt that parking place at the church, struggle through the crowd in the vestibule, and then when they finally sink into their pew on time, have to sit there for several minutes waiting for the pastor, the choir and the music director to finally get things together for the opening hymn. The truth of the matter is that this order of service and preparation should have been made long before 11:00 on Sunday morning. Pastor, if your church has a bad habit of starting late it may take you a while to educate them properly but it will be well worth while!

Our organist would be playing for the congregation several minutes before the services began. Thus, if the pianist needed to be back in the choir room until the last minute the service could still easily begin smoothly. The music director or song leader, be he paid staff member or volunteer helper, must learn that God's work is the most important in the world and should be done right! This includes starting *on time*.

If your church is extremely small and you have no organist, then probably there is another piano player in the church who would be glad to play up until time for the choir and the regular pianist to march in. I know that last-minute rehearsal is important to most choir directors. But he can graciously and firmly lead his choir members to realize the importance of getting right on back to the choir room to rehearse and be ready to walk out into the auditorium a minute before the service is to begin. Start without them one or two Sundays (if need be) and they'll soon get the message! "The pastor wants us to start on time."

Another good reason for starting on time is so the pastor will not have some of his precious preaching time stolen at the other end of the service. I usually had a 25-to-30-minute sermon planned for Sunday morning. If the service started late, then I was (if unconsciously) tense over the fact that I was either going to have to preach overtime or whack off some of that message somewhere along the line.

People who may be prospects for your church are going to have confidence in you and your church if you are well-organized and get under way properly and on time. And they are more likely to come back Sunday night if they like the way things went on Sunday morning.

If you, as a pastor, see the service getting away from you, it would be well to cut down on some announcements, read a shorter portion of Scripture before you preach, and do your own praying before the sermon so you can keep it short. Don't do desolation to the sermon. But remember, if you go very far overtime at the end of the message you've pretty well lost the people, anyway. I frequently have conducted my *invitation* after twelve noon but if possible I always try to have the message finished and the people's head bowed for prayer by the time the clock reaches twelve. If not, they're going to be thinking about the roast in the oven at home or the growing line at the cafeteria just when you want them to be thinking about what they ought to do with your sermon.

"If you don't strike oil in thirty minutes you might as well stop boring," someone has wisely said. Now, on Sunday *night* you may get away with preaching a slightly longer sermon. But even then, in this day of calculated timing, with our ulcerated and tranquilized society, I imagine you are going to be more effective if you do not get the reputation for being long-winded.

Another reason for watching the clock on Sunday morning in many of our fundamental churches is that many soul-winning churches now have a bus ministry. Those hundreds of bus children have parents. Many of them were assured by the bus workers on Saturday that their kids would be back at a decent hour on Sunday. Try to keep faith with them.

By the way, see to it that the Sunday school superintendent starts his opening assembly on time, too. This is one way to keep the whole schedule from getting out of line and making everybody late all the way through the morning.

Let your music man know how many specials you have time for. If he has the people sing all 16 verses of some hymns let him know that we'd better make it 2 or 3 verses of those hymns. These things will be worked out in the pastor's office, of course, and not on the platform.

Sometimes a young preacher hears about a successful pastor who preaches long sermons, spends a great amount of time on promotion, and carries the invitation through the tribulation and on into the millennium. Be it known unto you that, if he does all of this and still succeeds in keeping the crowds coming back for more punishment, he is the exception and not the rule. The crowds are coming back *in spite of* his long-windedness, not *because* of it!

5. The Announcements

If you have a bus superintendent or a Sunday school leader who makes announcements during the worship service make sure that he jots down what he is going to announce so he does not ramble and waste time. And keep your own announcements brief and to the point.

A very good suggestion: Don't say, "Now it is time for announcements." Or, "I have several announcements to make." If you do, that is the time most people catch up on their sleep, read the bulletin, adjust their ties, whisper to the kids, or write notes. If the announcement is not important don't make it. (It's best to have most of them in the bulletin, anyway!) But if the announcement is worth making and there's no way of getting out of it, try this:

"Here's something very important I want to share with you!" Or,

"Before we sing anymore I must tell you *this.*" Or,

"Please note the very important statement in the bulletin about. . . ." Or,

"Here's something tremendous I've been waiting to tell you."

Now if it's not "tremendous" you could probably just have a reference to it in the bulletin and not announce it at all.

Sometimes the ladies of the church or some class will just insist that you make an announcement for them. In that case, you can say, "Oh, yes, the Sunshine Class wanted me to say that their monthly meeting will be. . ." and hurry on to something of general interest to everybody. But try to get the Sunshine Class to learn that if they do not want an eclipse, they should put that in the bulletin from now on.

Promotion of certain growth projects in the church is sometimes necessary from the pulpit. Indeed, if you, as a pastor, want that project to succeed it must be heartily stressed by you. But in such cases don't call it an "announcement." Just *present it* enthusiastically and positively. If it involves the whole church, of course, you can spend a bit more time on it than if it is just a project for the choir, the Sunday school or the youth department.

Another touchy matter will be the requests for prayer for the sick that will come to you. Some people (who usually never come to the prayer meeting on Wednesday night) will expect you to go to great lengths to secure the heartfelt intercession of the entire flock for Patricia Pain-a-lot's pancreas or Gus Groan's gout flare-up. Some preachers feel it their heartfelt duty to give a complete organ recital of the hospitalized members during the announcement time. Then they wonder why the crowd diminishes! In fact, I have sometimes heard such intimate details of a female patient's condition discussed from the pulpit that I wonder how the member's of the afflicted one's family kept from sliding under the pews!

A good idea is to train your people to realize that the prayer time for the sick and afflicted is on Wednesday night. (Even there I would have a prepared prayer list and not let the time get away from you.) Then, if there is some emergency or some very critical illness that arises you can mention it earnestly and briefly and flash an instant prayer during the Sunday service. God hears short prayers as well as long ones.

Of course, if there has been a tragic accident Saturday night involving one or more of your members, or some of your people have lost their home in a fire, or some other calamity has occurred, then you should mention such and urge the people to pray earnestly for the suffering ones.

Also on Sunday *nights* you can mention in prayer the seriously ill or those who are hospitalized. This pleases the loved ones of the sick person and also keeps the need for intercession upon the minds of your flock.

6. Variety Is Still the Spice of Life

The story is told of a man who was declared to be dead. The undertaker prepared the body for burial. An ornate funeral service was soon in progress at the church. The flowers were all in place. The mourners were present. The organ was playing. The pallbearers were ready for action. Suddenly the "corpse" began to sit up in the coffin, deciding that he was not dead yet, after all. The preacher looked aghast and cried, "Don't do that! You're disturbing the program."

Now in some churches the program is so stiff and such routine has been established that one can set his watch by the yawns in the choir. Don't be afraid to "disturb the program" and change things around a bit now and then. Your services should have a measure of dignity but not be so formal that they are stiff and dead. And don't get in such a rut that everybody always knows exactly what is happening next. (Who was it that said that a rut is a grave with the ends kicked out?)

The service does not have to always start with the doxology, which is for many churches just a musical carpet to come in on. Surprise the people sometimes and let the service begin with a rousing choir number or a verse of "Sound the Battle Cry"!

Instead of praying after the first song, wait until after the second now and then. Startle them by making your announcements when they least expect them. (If you do that, and don't even mention the word "announcement" they may get the shot without feeling any pain at all!)

Don't always say the same thing when you pray ("Lord, bless all those the world over for whom it is our solemn duty to pray"). Plan ahead and even make notes about the things you want to remember to stress in public prayer. I do not think you should read a "canned" prayer but if it is all right to have notes for your sermon why not have a few notes for your prayer? Pray for our nation (Heaven knows we need it!). Let the people know you are informed by praying for things of national and monumental interest. A President should not be elected without pastors of Bible-preaching churches ever mentioning the matter in public prayer. If entire towns are wiped out in a tornado it behooves the people of God to remember the suffering survivors in holy prayer. If a city is being threatened with a nuclear explosion or a devastating crisis is putting thousands of people out of work, these are timely subjects for public prayer. These burdens are on the minds of people. They will be blessed and relieved to know that their pastor knows and cares.

Do pray for those in authority, as the Bible commands.

Be aware of the great issues of the day, and urge your people to pray. Be a crusader! I know some preachers get off the main track and get "carried away" on projects, be they ever so noble, but others just never get their people to write their congressmen about things that could be changed for the better in this nation. If there is a fight on about abortion, pornography or television profanity your people ought to know where you stand and where you expect them to stand.

An X-rated movie house ought not be able to operate in your community without feeling the stinging assault of God's people. By constant protest we saw the X-rated ones removed and the only "Adult" book store closed in our town. I was on the radio every day as well as influencing people from the pulpit and otherwise. God's people have been sitting around long enough letting the perverts and porn-peddlers get away with murder and mayhem.

You will, of course, want to mention some matters in good taste and very carefully, since children are present. Also I would be careful about advertising the Devil's business any more than is necessary. I don't think I ever mentioned the pornographic *Playboy* magazine by name when I was a pastor as I did not want the curiosity of our teenage boys aroused any more than already was the case. I wonder how many weak Christians have gone to see a certain movie because some pastor had inadvertently called attention to it in a sermon? Thousands of extra copies of the very filthy *Hustler* magazine sold during the trial of Larry Flynt as a great amount of publicity was given publicly to the lurid publication.

However, in my messages I would lambast the *Playboy* philosophy in connection with a broadside against the new morality of the day. The adults knew what I was driving at.

7. Welcome the Visitors

However I would be very careful about calling visitors by name and having them stand. A few might like such attention, but many of the people you want to reach do not want to be made conspicuous or put on the spot. Some like to slip in and "case" the church before they get too well known and feel "pressured" by the pastor or the congregation. Especially is this true of unsaved people. They feel awkward and are embarrassed enough already without the pastor making them stand and give their names. You can demand their rank, name and serial number but you probably won't find them back in your congregation very soon.

If you pass out visitors' cards why not ask them to give them to you at the door, (or to one of your assistants or ushers) as they leave? That way you get to know them personally, and they just might put an offering in the plate instead of that visitor's card when the offering is received. They will be less likely to be embarrassed to give you their card and meet the pastor this way than to have to be "shown off" and introduced to the entire twelve tribes of Israel at the morning service.

In my chapter on "Bigger Offerings" I will go into this in some detail but let me say in passing that the choir, the pastors, and those on the platform should set the example in public giving; the plates should be passed down every aisle; plenty of ushers should be used; and the offering plates should be used for the *offering of God,* not as a catch-all for visitors' cards, voting ballots, reservations to the youth banquet and prayer requests for the ailing. No wonder some churches have a financial deficit! By the time you eliminate all of the above, plus the buttons and bus tokens in the plate, where is there any room left for tithes and offerings?

8. Pastor, Be Optimistic and Positive

If you are not enthusiastic how can you expect your people to be? Our preaching (if we preach the Word) must include a good many negatives as we urge our people to live godly, separated lives. But there are so many other things we can be happy and positive about. Though things look black on the world scene that may mean the coming of the Lord is all the more a soon possibility! Sometimes it seems only a few Christians are concerned but remember the seven thousand who have not bowed the knee to Baal. We are ambassadors for Christ. God is on our side. The promises of God are still yea and amen. Heaven is a sure thing for the child of God. The Lord answers prayer. The Bible is our sure foundation. Jesus Christ is the same yesterday, today and forever. God is still on the throne. Remember these things when you are prone to get dull and pessimistic.

Lester Roloff has asked, "How can we expect to help our ulcerated congregations if we are all torn up ourselves?"

Look at the churches that are growing and fruitful. The pastor, in each case, will be a man of optimism, faith and enthusiasm!

Be cheerful. "A merry heart doeth good like a medicine."

It will pay you to occasionally read a self-help book by some outstanding motivator in the business world. Or listen to the tapes of men like Clement Stone, Zig Ziglar, or "Tremendous" Jones.

Let us use good sense if we would lead people. Keep yourself in the love of God and saturate yourself so with the promises of the Bible that when you stand before the people they will be convinced you know what you're talking about and that you walk in faith and triumph with God.

9. Above All, Preach the Word

Keep your ministry Bible-centered! "Throw the *Book* at them." Keep abreast of the times, but the people don't come on Sunday to hear current events or to "face the nation" and "meet the press." They are hungry sheep and they come to be fed.

Surely they need fleecing and flogging at times. But be sure you feed them, too. They won't stand for the former without the latter. Stay much in the Word yourself so you'll have something fresh and wonderful from God for them when they come to church. Don't give them warmed-over religious hash.

"Be instant in season, out of season." Let them learn that the interpretation of life's perplexities and calamities will be found at the church as our pastor unfolds the Book.

One of the sweetest things I ever heard at the door after church on Sunday in an earlier pastorate was the voice of a sweet, saintly old lady saying, with feeling, "the *sheep* have been *fed*"! Memorize Scripture. Nothing will so bless your preaching. Be a man of the Book. They need not, "Thus thinketh the mind of man," but "Thus saith the Word of God"! In this you can be absolutely positive.

A Few Closing Thoughts

Have a good light over the pulpit shining down on the man of God. Many pastors preach partly in the shadows. One hopes they do not love darkness rather than light because their deeds are evil. Be sure the light illuminates the pastor's face. They need to see the expressions of a fervent, dynamic man as well as hear what he has to say. Then, too, the preaching of the Word is the main event. Yet in some churches the brighter light is on the choir or the congregation rather than on the man of God. Also the pastor will probably see his Bible and his notes better if he has a good light.

Have a bright, cheerful, well-lighted auditorium. Some churches remind you of a monastery or a tomb. "Let there be light!" If your building is dark and gloomy cut some windows, install some chandeliers, paint the inside white—anything to brighten up the place. We're talking about going to Heaven where all is clean and bright, and where the Lord Himself is the light. Let us not "dwell in darkness" down here.

Incidentally, in some churches the pulpit light is not turned on, even though they have one. A pastor has to watch it. That custodian or technician may have gotten into a bad habit of failing to turn your switch! In the entertainment world the technician would be fired if he didn't turn the spotlight on the main performer. How much more important is this Spirit-filled man with the burning message of God!

Don't have too many preliminaries in the service. Get on into the proclaiming of what God has to say.

Let the service not be too formal—yet not a three-ring circus, either.

Don't be too chummy or flippant with God or with the people. This is a high position of great honor—to be God's representative. Don't cheapen it with claptrap or horseplay.

Yet, keep your sense of humor. Don't tell jokes for the sake of having a joke. But sometimes a humorous tidbit in the message, if it falls naturally into place, will be of great assistance in driving home a point you wish to make. And don't be afraid to laugh at yourself. If you make a mistake, be the first to admit it. Don't let the natural laughter of others get you rattled or embarrassed. They might even learn that you are human, after all.

Don't use the pulpit to lambast some old goat. The innocent sheep will get blasted too. Satan sometimes gets us to assume that because one family is "in a huff" that the whole crowd is against us. Most of them won't even know anything about it if you ignore it and go ahead and keep sweet.

Be genuinely interested in people. Love them and pray for a passion for souls. Be sincere and honest. Keep your faith up. After the benediction they might decide to come back on Sunday night too.

Chapter Four

Making Sunday Night
Services Sparkle!

Any *good* preacher will have people to preach to on Sunday *morning*. But what about Sunday *night*? How do you get them to come back? Is it possible to compete with television, ball games, family rides, reunions and just plain indifference? Yes, it is! But don't wait until Sunday night to start competing! On the radio every day I was pushing for Sunday night. If I had an interesting topic the town knew about it before Sunday night. If I could think of a catchy or enticing title for the message, I advertised it in blockbuster letters in the church mail-out, the bulletin, and of course, in the daily papers, as well as on radio.

The choir would have some of its most beautiful and rousing numbers all ready for Sunday night. The quartet or trio would sing on Sunday night. If we had a good brass duet or cello or string number available we'd have them do their best for Sunday night!

We did everything possible to make the Sunday morning crowd feel they were really *missing it* if they were not in church on Sunday night.

In other words, *build all week toward Sunday night!* Sunday morning, then, will pretty well carry itself. People with any religion at all will come on Sunday morning. But in times like these you've got to have something out of the ordinary to get a good crowd and keep them coming consistently on Sunday nights. And you've got to *work* at it. Here's how!

1. Train Your Sunday Morning People to Be Sales People for Sunday Night

All of them will not do it, of course. But the good Christians in the Sunday morning crowd can be taught to be friendly and to be genuinely helpful in getting people for Sunday night.

You'll have to stress this *friendliness* constantly. People forget. The best of Christians get taken up with their little "tempests in teapots."

It's natural after church to want to rush over and speak to those personal friends or our own loved ones who may be in the congregation. So the matter of being friendly to others, and especially to strangers, has to be drilled into them all the time until it becomes as natural as breathing.

In our travels through the years, my wife and I have slipped into services of many churches and often we are completely unknown to the pastor or people. On many occasions we have gone in and out with scarcely a nod or a smile and seldom a handshake. And this is in our good, warm, evangelistic churches, some of whom bill themselves as "The friendliest church in town!"

It is ludicrous, if not pathetic, to go to the church that advertises, "The end of your search for a friendly church," and have people pay absolutely no attention at all to you when you worship there. But it happens all the time!

Again, it depends upon leadership. If the pastor and deacons and other leaders do not set the example and constantly gear others toward this, the friendly church just will not evolve automatically.

How do you go about curing this malady?

Get your Sunday morning "friendliness crew" out of your Wednesday night crowd. On Wednesday night you can informally and earnestly explain to your people what "we *must* do" if we're going to reach people and keep them coming. Also, the recruiting of such representatives can be done through Sunday school classes and among the people who come to visitation. They are usually your soul winners, the people who really care about others.

Then the pastor as he preaches on soul winning can constantly stress that this is vital if we would reach people. Remind them that the lost people who do venture into our services (and many of the saved ones) are people with problems, burdens, heartaches and some of them are lonely and searching for friends, wishing for someone to care that they exist. Then, you can appoint certain of your personable folk to be hosts and/or hostesses on set Sundays to watch out for people and get acquainted with the new people and prospects. Teach them that on the days they are the official church greeters that neither flood nor storm nor wintry blast can deter them from mingling with those newcomers and other nonmembers and making them feel at home. Be sure they pass the names along to others—to the pastor, the Sunday school superintendent in whose department they would be, even to the teacher in whose class they probably would be. If they are Christians and you find out they can sing, let the choir director know about it. If they are young people, be sure and "sic" the youth director or youth leaders on them. Don't let them get away unloved and unwanted!

2. Make Much of Music on Sunday Night

Be sure your music director or choir leader keeps his choir pepped up and excited about the Sunday night services. No exceptions! This is the big one! If you have a real good choir you might want them to open with a number and then sing another or two before the song service is over. If your choir is small or mediocre then it may be best to use them for the congregational singing but only use them once for a "special." Don't bore the people with second- or third-rate "specials."

If you have a male quartet or a ladies' trio or a good singing young people's group, this is the time to let them "rise and shine." But don't compromise your convictions and let them use cheap, worldly music just to "please the youth." Use good music. See the chapter, "Whatever Happened to God's Music?"

USE GOSPEL CHORUSES. From two to four good choruses during the Sunday night service will do wonders to loosen up or liven up the song service. Caution: Don't sing the same ones over and over again. "Heavenly Sunshine" or the first verse of "Amazing Grace" will lose some lustre (and some meaning) if sung every Sunday night from New Year's to Labor Day! Use a chorus or two that will appeal to the children, then one that teens love, then a more serious chorus for the older folk. Keep a variety of choruses before the people. And learn a new one now and then. Once in a while you can have "request night" for choruses the people love. Sing some old ones and some new ones. Don't get in a rut. At the end of the chapter we will suggest some good choruses that will sparkle.

When switching from chorus to chorus don't make it a stiff thing. Try to avoid long pauses. Instead of announcing, "It is now time for us to sing some choruses," and then proceeding methodically down the list, try saying happily, "It is *chorus time* now! And we'll start with 'Some Golden Daybreak.' Notice the sequence in theme as we sing this medley of choruses tonight!" Chorus time is frequently spoiled by a long pause between numbers while the pianist looks for the next one in the songbook. Have them planned ahead and the pages already clipped and ready for action. Of course, if you are fortunate enough to have a musician who can play them all by ear or by memory and modulate out of one into another, that is all the better.

Young people love choruses and so do the children. But adults, too, will loosen up and warm up to good-spirited choruses.

USE INSTRUMENTAL NUMBERS on Sunday night. In addition to the piano and organ if you have a few students who play in the band at school it is likely that some of them are capable of playing along with the hymns on Sunday night in a little "orchestra" of their own. If you have a trained orchestra man, of course, then he may be able to actually produce a good church orchestra that will add greatly to your "drawing card" for the services.

If several of your people play instruments then vary the special music. Again, don't get in a rut. Good violin music is beautiful but very few people want to hear the same person playing the same kind of special every Sunday. Next Sunday let it be a trombone special or the brass trio or something else.

If your trumpet virtuoso performs for the musical service be sure he doesn't stand so that every loud blast goes right into the microphone to be amplified fifty times for the ears of the listeners. Sometimes older people complain about instrumental music hurting their ears. A good sound man will turn the volume down (or off) if the trumpet or other instruments are to be played right into the "mike."

USE EVANGELISTIC MUSIC and spirited songs on Sunday night. A vesper service may sometimes have its place, but to play soft, dreamy music on Sunday night will not have the people very wide awake or receptive by the time the sermon begins. "Holy, Holy, Holy" or "The Stranger of Galilee" hardly prepares folk for a message on " 'Prepare to Meet Thy God.' "

Of course, if the pastor is planning to preach to Christians at the Sunday night service the songs can be adapted accordingly but they still should not all be long, slow, dismal songs. "Count Your Blessings" or "To God Be the Glory" will go good just ahead of that sermon on "The Trials of Life," or "What to Do With Life's Burdens." If the Sunday night sermon is on prayer, why not keep "Sweet Hour of Prayer" for Wednesday night and try "I Believe the Answer's on the Way" or "Tell It to Jesus" for Sunday night? Of course, such prayer songs as "What a Friend We Have in Jesus" and "Did You Think to Pray?" can be sung with a moving spirit and a stepped-up tempo at times. Far too many song leaders *drag* songs that could be easily sung with a bit more life and feeling.

Be sure your music director or the pastor or someone in charge carefully "screens" the special numbers, and never throw the special music "open" to just anyone who cares to sing. You may please those amateur would-be concert soloists in your crowd, but you sure won't excite your Sunday night visitors about coming back regularly. Now, it would be better if the decision about who is to sing the special did not have to be made by the pastor. At least, don't let it be *known* that he is the one who decides! Of course, he can always make a "request" that the trio or the quartet sing just before he preaches.

Another word of caution, don't let the song service get away from you. Don't allow the song leader to schedule so many "specials" that the people are exhausted before the message begins. Be sure the song service is so well planned that the service does not drag.

3. Use the Element of Surprise

You can preach on the great themes of the Scripture, and do so in a reverent way, and still keep the people guessing about just what that topic in the bulletin means. You may or may not want to always let the people know just what new series the pastor starts this Sunday night. But be sure that enough is said about it that they would surely not want to *miss* the first one in the series.

"Our mystery soloist will sing tonight," or, "We'll have a guest musician you'll greatly enjoy tonight—don't miss her," keeps the element of surprise. If you plan to start a new attendance contest on Sunday night don't let them in on the details Sunday morning. Save it as a surprise for Sunday night.

If awards are to be given for something special, let them be made on Sunday night. People will come to see who wins.

Have a good testimony or two sometimes on Sunday night. In some cases you may keep it a secret as to who the guest "testifiers" will be. If it is one of your own people you can say on Sunday morning or in the mail-out to members, "One of our very own men will be heard from this pulpit Sunday night! He will give a brief testimony about an exciting rescue (or a "thrilling conversion," or a "wonderful answer to prayer")!

Baptize on Sunday night at the close of the service. Make much of it. Be sure the relatives and friends of the ones to be baptized are notified. You thus will have a larger crowd to preach to and some of them will probably be unsaved folk. Your people may be surprised to see who some of the visitors are who came to see their friends baptized.

4. Keep Things Moving

Don't let the Sunday night service (or any other one) drag along at a poor, dying rate. From the opening song or chorus to the closing "Amen" keep things moving and interesting.

Be sure the choir is in place and ready to go on the stroke of seven (or whatever time you begin the service). Musicians should have their cue cards well in advance of the opening moment of the service. Ushers should be alerted if the pastor wants anything passed out or taken up that is out of the ordinary. Let no delays take place.

Fortunate the pastor who has some radio and television experience. If you do not have, it would be good to observe some good pastors whose services are telecast and whose success is evident. Watch how they do it. Then pretend you're on the air even if you are not. I don't mean that we should be precise and "professional." I *do* mean we should be synchronized, smooth, alert and well-organized so that the service moves along beautifully and in such interesting fashion that no one would dare sleep through a minute of it.

If a deacon has that opening prayer, be sure it is one who will pray out clearly and distinctly and is not afraid of the "mike." If yours is a very small church he may stay at his seat to pray, but be sure he stands and speaks out very clearly. Though he talks to God for us he will not edify or encourage the saints if they do not hear him. If he is to come to the platform let him know ahead of time so that he can be making his way up there and already at the pulpit when the pastor says, "Let us pray." The pastor may say, "Brother Jones is coming to lead us to the throne of grace. Let us remember especially to pray for. . . . Now let us bow as Brother Jones leads us." By that time Jones is on the spot and ready to pray.

Be sure song numbers are chosen in advance. Don't let long pauses put a damper on your service. Make certain the ushers know where the visitors' cards are ahead of time. Don't have the hands of the visitors in the air while some usher runs out into the vestibule to try to find the cards, as I have frequently seen them do.

If the trio is going to sing, be sure the song director motions to them to be making their way to the platform on the closing verse of the preceding song so that they immediately step into place to sing.

Don't allow your singers to give a speech before they sing.

Some singers, both male and female, think this is their chance to "preach."

Be sure that your song leader does not consume time by talking about every verse of every song, or by pumping the people with anecdotes all along the way to try to keep them singing. Encourage him to use songs the people can sing. "Wonderful Grace of Jesus" is a good number for a trained choir but most congregations choke to death on it! To be sure, once in a while a good music man will refer to the "wonderful truth" contained in this next verse, or will sometimes call attention to "the words in this oft-neglected third verse." But such comments and commentaries should be few and far between.

If "The Old Rugged Cross" is to be sung, I would sing 2 or 3 verses instead of 5 or 6. Then let the next hymn be a fast moving one. Stay out of the rut.

By the time the choir or the quartet takes their seats, the pastor should already be making his next introduction or the song leader should be starting the next song. If there was as much "dead space" on television productions as in the average church service the sponsors would lose millions of dollars in advertising time. Keep things moving.

At invitation time, be sure the musicians are near their instruments and do not have to travel from "the backside of the desert" to get on the bench for this important song. When the pastor starts his invitation the whole staff—personal workers, choir, musicians, ushers, all—should be most alert. Never have a musical introduction for the invitation hymn. Strike while the iron is hot. When the preacher says, "Now we will sing," the chord should be sounded and the invitation hymn begun at once. Don't give the sinner out there a second or a minute of silence or delay to change his mind about coming forward.

5. Have Plenty of Light and Sound

Be sure the lights are all on and bright, especially over the pulpit and choir. But don't let it be too subdued in the congregation either. People do not doze very well under bright lights.

As was said in an earlier chapter, make sure the sound system is on and that it is turned up plenty loud. This is the most important message in the world. Don't muffle it. If young people are to sing, children are to recite or a testimony is to be given, the sound technician will probably need to raise the volume or the effectiveness may be lost. Then, of course, the sound will be adjusted again when the preacher (most of *us* are loud mouths) or the choir comes back on for the next thing to be done.

Make sure the choir comes out loud and clear on the invitation song. Some people never hear the words of an invitation appeal, the words are sung so softly.

6. Be Optimistic and Encouraging

People have left churches and moved away from good pastors because the discouraging word and the minor note were sounded so frequently from the pulpit. Read some good motivational material now and then. Be optimistic and cheerful. "A merry heart doeth good like a medicine." Many of these people chose you tonight over their favorite comic or some exciting story on TV. You are not to be an entertainer or a dunce but at least you can be happy and cheerful. It is contagious. Use good psychology with your people. Some Christian leaders are so down in the dumps themselves that their followers can hardly be expected to be otherwise.

Instead of emphasizing how many are absent tonight, rejoice over "all of you who came." Never fuss at those who came for the sins of those who didn't come. Remind them that "a crowd draws a crowd" and that by being faithful in their places, as they are, others will be encouraged to come, too.

Keep your chin up during the service even if you feel like falling on your face when it is all over.

7. Plan a Series of Messages or Follow Through on Some Exciting Themes From Time to Time

While the series should not be too long, I find that a frequent series of messages will do much to generate interest.

"The Book of Revelation Speaks," "Thrilling Themes of the Second Coming," "Successful Giants of the Old Testament,"

"Men Whose Prayers Were Answered," "How to Have a Successful Marriage and a Happy Home"—these and many others could be the subject for a fascinating series of messages.

"What the Bible Teaches About. . ." is another way to go about it, dealing with worldliness, abortion, lust and pornography, capital punishment, marriage, compromise, music, the Holy Spirit, Hell, etc., etc.

Try to get the people committed to attend the first message in the series and then enlist them for the rest in the series. We'll always pick up a few regulars for Sunday night who were not regulars before.

When Biship Pike died in the desert, when Marilyn Monroe, the sex goddess, died from an overdose, when the Silver Bridge fell in the Ohio river, when the lights all went out in New York City, our people knew there would probably be an exciting message on the subject in the light of the Bible soon. And so on Sunday nights we had such sermons as:

> The Case of the Wandering Bishop
> What Killed Marilyn Monroe?
> The Fatal Fall of the Silver Bridge
> The Night New York Disappeared
> The Death of the Rock King
> The Invasion of the Beatles
> The Space Walk
> My Trip to Outer Space
> Was Betsy [a hurricane] an Act of God? etc., etc.

A brief story for the little ones sometimes during the song service, a special presentation by the teens, a "pocket sermon" for the kids (speaking briefly on some object a child takes from the pastor's coat pocket), a contest to see which boys and girls can bring the most visitors, an occasional (or perhaps a regular) refreshment time for the youth afterwards—all of these things help to keep some "sparkle" in the Sunday night service and also keeps the interest of the younger generation we're always fuming about.

8. Variety Is the Spice, Here, Too!

Perhaps a series of "pulpit editorials" on current events in the light of the Bible, brought by the pastor and well-planned, can be intriguing. They would be from 3 to 5 minutes and would be read during the song service or just before the sermon.

A pew-packing contest among the adults when the pastor is preaching a series of sermons to the unsaved would be good.

Some unusual contest with couples or individuals competing to get people to church will help in regular services (if not done too often) as well as during revivals or for Sunday school contests.

A presentation from our Christian school or some other good Christian school in the area once in a while is good and makes for variety.

Carefully chosen and well-named topics for a sermon will help gather interest even if the subject matter is that with which they are quite familiar.

A fellowship time afterwards, either at the church social hall or in the homes of the people, will sometimes help. Adults as well as young people need some times to get together just for fun, food and fellowship.

9. A Few Things to Remember:

Start on time—always, and end at a decent hour, too.

Pick a starting time that will help you reach the most people. It is easier to start early in a city environment, perhaps, than in a farm community where many have to do the "milking" before they can come to church.

Get your ushers excited about this important service. Make sure they are there early to greet people and that they really serve as ushers, before, during and after the services. (More in the chapter on "Ushers.")

Make sure your deacons are geared-up for the Sunday night service. They need to be with you in making this a great "church night" or "soul-winning effort" or whatever you are striving for currently in your Sunday night services. The deacons and their wives should always be a welcoming committee to mingle among the people and make sure weak Christians are encouraged and visitors come back.

Youth meetings or other training services before the main Sunday night hour will often feed crowds and interest on into your evening service.

But I wouldn't let the early study or training hour degenerate into a dry, dull, lifeless meeting where your main workers feel obligated to attend when they could be out witnessing and bringing people into the night service. Decide which is most important to what you are trying to do.

Play up the Sunday night service in every way possible. Advertise widely. Announce it on the radio in exciting terms. Get television spots if you can afford to do so. Use the church page in your daily paper.

Don't let the service drag. Keep it alive. Keep announcements brief and to the point. Don't call on men to pray who will pray all around the world and put people to sleep. Don't have too many preliminaries. Have plenty of spirited music and singing, but not too much. Don't keep the people overtime too often if you want to keep them coming.

Have a good, clean and well-staffed nursery in which parents can have confidence. Many will come so they won't have to wrestle with the baby for an hour or so.

Watch the kids! Don't let children or teens talk, giggle and otherwise disturb your service. The very people they are disturbing may be the ones you're trying to reach for Christ. Keep at least one or two staff members on the platform to "eyeball" them while you preach. Make sure the ushers are alert to "trouble spots" in the congregation. Don't hesitate to let parents learn that children are big enough to sit by themselves or with other children in church *only* if they're old enough to be still and listen reverently. Try to train a host of your youth to sit near the front. This encourages others to do so, too. It is better for parents or ushers to handle the discipline problem than for the preacher to have to call down offending children from the pulpit.

(In the case of teens, make friends with them, love them, let them know you want them there and are genuinely interested in them. If they *like* you and know that you like *them,* you will not have as much discipline problem with them.)

Stress your Wednesday night service to this Sunday night

crowd. Let them know about the absorbing Bible studies and the important prayer time while you have them there with you. You may soon have as many on Wednesday night as you do on Sunday night!

10. Good Choruses for Sunday Night Services:

My Lord Knows the Way Through the Wilderness
Come and Dine
Christ Is All I Need
Some Golden Daybreak
It Is Summertime in My Heart
All Because of Calvary
Safe Am I
He Owns the Cattle on a Thousand Hills
We'll Never Say Goodbye in Glory
Sing as You Ride
Constantly Abiding
Surely Goodness and Mercy
The Windows of Heaven Are Open
I Will Sing of the Mercies of the Lord
Behold He Comes
Happiness Is
My Sins Are Gone
I Am the Resurrection
If You Want Joy
Every Day With Jesus
Everybody Ought to Know
Altogether Lovely
He Careth for You
Lead Me to Some Soul Today
Jesus Is the Sweetest Name I Know

There are many, many more. Don't get in a rut!

Chapter Five

How to Get Bigger and Better Offerings

"Money answereth all things."— Eccles. 10:19.

Most churches could take in far more money than they do! Many pastors lament the fact that certain needed projects have to "go begging" because the money is just not there. In great numbers of churches the budget is overdrawn, checks bounce, bills are unpaid and the work of the Lord suffers because of a lack of money.

Yet many churches do not even nearly take in all the money they *could* be receiving. Why? There are many reasons:

1. Some pastors are timid about preaching on money. They have listened to some backslider or tightwad complain about the "church always asking for money" and they feel intimidated.

2. They read about the economy being in bad shape and prices going up so they feel sorry for the people and are reluctant to urge them to give.

3. They do not use many easy and God-given opportunities to give people a chance to give.

4. They do not really challenge the people to give.

5. The pastor himself is not happy and optimistic and excited about giving.

6. He may not set the right example himself. Or he does not lead his staff members and the choir and others in leadership to set the proper example.

7. He is apologetic when he preaches on tithing.

8. The offering is not taken with confidence and enthusiasm.

9. Crude and slipshod ways are used in taking the offering. The ushers are not properly trained.

10. The wrong kind of music frequently accompanies the "lifting" of the offering.

11. Other things are going on while the offering is being taken.

12. It is not made clear to the people what the offering is for.

13. The offering plate is used as a "catch-all" for things other than the offering.

14. Proper care of the money is not taken when it is received.

15. The people have no confidence that the money is being handled in a businesslike manner.

16. The people are not taught that this offering time is a grand act of worship when all of us can participate in doing something for God who has done so much for us.

Pastor, would you really like to see your people cheerful and happy about the offering? Would you enjoy seeing a good increase in contributions? Would you like to have all the money your church needs for its projects? Well, your needs and the needs of your church can be met. Let's begin with the last reason (number 16) for not getting good offerings and work our way back to reason number one. I have been a pastor for 29 of my 39 years in the ministry. The other 10 years I have observed other churches—hundreds of them. Here's how to get bigger and better offerings:

1. Worship Is an Act of Bringing Something to God

In Genesis 22 when Abraham said, "I and the lad will go yonder and worship," he was ready and willing to *give* the dearest and the best that he had to God. The sacrifice on Mount Moriah was an "offering" to God. So the *first time* "worship" is mentioned in the Bible it was an *offering*. And some people think you can have a worship service without an offering being taken!

Train your people to realize that this is a high and holy part of our worship and service to God. Here every individual can share in this wonderful act of worship—the bringing of tithes and offerings to the Lord. It is possible, of course, to give to God other things besides money (time, energy, service, talent), but money is that which is mentioned far more often than anything else. In fact, giving is mentioned more than any other thing in the New Testament except faith. A book by Dr. Earle V. Pierce on *The Supreme Beatitude* ("it is more blessed to give than to receive") will help you immeasurably in getting material for your people on this aspect of worshiping God by giving.

2. Be Sure the Money Is Handled and Used in an Honest and Businesslike Manner

Only then can business people and hard-working would-be contributors have confidence that their giving is being done in the right way.

A financial statement of all monies spent should be readily available to the people at least once a month. Let them know in this manner that their offerings are being used for the pastor's salary, for church expenses, for missions, and for the various projects of the church. The church financial secretary (if you have one) can be responsible for working this up each month, working closely with the treasurer, the finance committee, and, of course, approved by the pastor. In churches that are quite small you can probably use some good volunteer among the lay people who is familiar with figures, has good common sense and is thoroughly in accord with what you are doing, to draw up the financial spending sheet for your people each month. This can be done by listing every check, or by a very accurate and complete resume of the input and the output of the church monies.

Wild spending by the pastor or deacons or by some committee will soon cause contributors to lose confidence in the way the church is doing business. God's business is the greatest in the world. We should not be careless and deceitful in the way things are handled.

People lose confidence if they feel that the pastor or chairman of the deacons or treasurer or any one person (or group) has unlimited access to the church funds and is purchasing or running up bills indiscriminately.

No pastor in his right mind ought to want to have the monies of the church at his disposal. As a pastor I would never sign a check, count the offering, take the offering home with me, or anything that would ever give anyone in the church (or out) a chance to say that I wanted control of the finances. There are enough shysters and charlatans around to keep that old story circulating. Let *them* get the bad reputation for money madness, if they must, and let the shysters get locked up for running off with church funds, but let those of us who would win souls and pastor a flourishing church have sense enough to stay out of trouble. Don't get sticky fingers.

If business people in the town are circulating the news that your church isn't paying its bills then people who might otherwise give to your church will be reluctant to do so.

If you say "use the envelope in the pews" then be sure there are plenty of fresh envelopes in the pews. In order to do so your custodian or someone on the finance committee will probably need to check it out before every service. Children scribble on the back of envelopes, teens write notes on them, even adults sometimes use them to doodle faces on, especially during announcements!

Many times I've heard pastors say, "Use the envelope in the pew," when there wasn't an envelope in sight. To be sure he told "Brother Casual" to put out the envelopes way back last fall. But they have long since disappeared and "Brother Casual" was just too casual about it to replenish the stock!

Be sensible, honest, and businesslike if you want people to trust your church to distribute their tithes and offerings properly.

3. Take *Care* of the Money You Take *Up*

Almost every week I read about some thief breaking into a church and stealing the Sunday night offering or some other offering. Usually the cash had been put in a file drawer or in some office desk. Why? Often, because some church official was too lazy to run by the night depository at the bank.

Don't keep the money at the church unless you have a

foolproof safe. Let at least two men put it in the safe and be sure it is properly locked. Or if you are taking the money to the bank, be sure at least two men go together to deposit it. Across this country men are leaving churches in disgrace because someone suspected them of taking some of the church's money. Most of the time it was not theft—it was just poor management and thoughtlessness. Suppose the one man taking the money gets robbed on the way to the bank? There will always be some suspicious souls in the church who will look askance at him because they want to believe the worst and will very likely assume he "just made up the tale" about the robbery. How can the man ever clear himself if he was the only one with the money?

For this reason never, but NEVER, let the money be gathered up by just one man (or woman) and carried off to a back room or to the treasurer's home to be counted later. Even if that man or woman is as honest as the Angel Gabriel, there may be someone who someday will say, "Well, I know I put $50 in that Sunday, and there is no $50 on record here." How can the treasurer or counter ever prove that he was innocent of "the great transgression"? I have been in churches all over America where just one person comes up and takes the money and carries it off. It is not fair to the one man, nor is it good business. Suppose that tried and trusted treasurer does get in a bad financial bind sometime and the Devil whispers, "Some of that cash they'll never miss. You can always pay it back later"? Stranger things than this have happened. Many people succumb to temptation in a moment of weakness who would never have fallen if the "easy way out" had not been there to tempt them.

Another reason for using several men (at least two) instead of one is that sometimes that one man (treasurer or whatever) may fall out with the preacher or he may not like the evangelist. He may think he is doing God a big favor if he juggles things around a bit to be sure the money goes into this account instead of for the cause it was given. When a church worker gets backslidden he (or she) will do strange things indeed.

If you become pastor of a church where this one-man finance committee is already in operation, don't assume he is crooked.

He probably is not. He's probably doing it because no one ever thought of the risk involved. He may be the most honest man in the church so everyone just assumes he is the right one to always handle the money. Don't get yourself in hot water by jumping on him about it or by bringing it to the church as a matter for discussion. The poor honest fellow will probably then assume that someone is suspicious of him.

The best thing to do is ask some questions and find out what certain practices are *before* you ever take the church. Then no one can think that you just have it in for the treasurer. If the man is honest, he will be happy to have someone else work with him when he sees the risk involved. Perhaps you could just let your finance committee read this chapter on "How to Get Bigger and Better Offerings" and he'll be begging for someone to help him count the money!

If you send around to Sunday school departments to pick up envelopes of money on Sunday mornings be sure that at least two people go to pick them up. Make sure that two or more secretaries count the money in the Sunday school office. We are told to avoid the very appearance of evil.

4. Use the Offering Plates for the Offering Only

Let people hand you their *visitors' cards* at the *door*. If you have one hundred visitors in your Sunday service you may get one hundred visitors' cards if you have passed them out. But you would get from $100 to $200 or more instead of visitors' cards if you have them hand you their cards at the door. In the case of a large auditorium you will need associate pastors and good ushers to help you meet the visitors and gather their cards at the door. People will generally put *something* in the plate when it goes by. If they have not been instructed to put in a visitor's card they will usually put in some money. It's as simple as that! When I learned that lesson our offerings picked up.

Also, I could meet many of the visitors personally and remember their name because I was looking at them when I saw their name on the card at the door. In the pulpit when welcoming the visitors I would simply say,

"We are so happy to have you visitors and would so much enjoy meeting you personally. So would you please fill out the visitor's card, *hold it* for me and give it to me as you leave so I may have the privilege of shaking your hand? If I have your card when I shake your hand I may remember you next time."

Then at the end of the service, just before the benediction, you can again remind the visitors to be sure and let you have their cards at the door. Some will still drop the card in the plate, but not nearly so many. The offerings will pick up and the plates will not be cluttered with cards. When people see greenbacks in the plate they will be inspired to give too. Imagine what they think when all they see in the plate is a stack of visitors' cards!

There may be times when you will want to pass the plates for ballots or to receive petitions, or to give out invitations or some such, but if so, be sure and do it *separately* from the offering. Don't confuse the people. They're confused enough, already.

Some churches actually have blank envelopes in the plate and ask people to take one out for the offering as the plate goes by. But how on earth could anyone take out an envelope, put money in, address it, and get it back in the plate, all in the second that the plate goes by him? Then, too, most people would not be caught *dead* taking something *out* of the plate as it is passed.

5. Always Make It Clear for What the People Are Giving

Now if it is on Sunday morning most people assume that the offering is for the needs of the church. But even then, it is good to say, "We now have the wonderful privilege of giving back to God some of what He has entrusted to our care. The offering today, of course, will be for the work of the church here, for our new building, and for missionaries around the world," etc., etc.

If the offering on Sunday night is for missions, or is a special offering to the building fund or for the Christian school, then be sure and make this plain to the people. People get confused easily and they will give better if they know exactly what they are giving for, if it is a worthy project. The same would be true on Wednesdays, or during special meetings.

If you want extra money put in for your gospel broadcast or for some Christian school venture, then I would have envelopes for these special projects and call their attention to the fact that the envelopes are there for them to use.

Announce any special offerings well *ahead* of the actual offering so the people will have plenty of time to fill out their envelopes, get the money in, and get their name on it.

6. When the Offering Is Taken, Don't Have Other Things Going on Too!

Dr. Bill Rice had a wonderful message on the taking of the offering. One thing I have always remembered was how he stressed that no vocal specials, choir numbers or announcements should be going on while the offering was being taken. If this really is an act of devotion and is an offering to God, then we should be thinking about God and our gifts to Him while the monies are being received. I don't think you should "kiss it goodbye" but this *is* the only money you disburse that you'll ever see again, so part with it tenderly and thoughtfully. "Lay up for yourselves treasures in heaven," Jesus taught in Matthew 6.

If an exciting choir special or some important announcements are happening at the same time, some people are going to be distracted from giving in the offering. And what about the choir? They should be worshiping God with their gifts, too. An appropriate offertory on the organ or piano is probably best during the offering.

About the worst thing I've ever witnessed during the offering is to have the song leader ask everyone to grab a songbook and stand and sing hymn number so-and-so while the offering is being taken! Can you imagine how anybody could possibly get into their pockets or purses and *give* when they are standing there holding a songbook in one hand while passing the plate with the other hand? Unless you preach to three-handed people, I surely wouldn't try that one. Yet it has been done more than once.

Needless to say, it won't take long to count the offering that night!

7. Use Appropriate, Cheerful Music on Organ or Piano During the Offering

Many organists play heavy classical music or dead "funeral" music during the offering. Perhaps they feel that this will be a good sedative to make the extraction less painful.

Appropriate for some long-faced worshipers might be, "When we asunder part it gives us inward pain," as they are relieved of their offerings, but other songs would be more inspiring.

Don't use "Precious Memories," "Beautiful Isle of Somewhere" or "Into the Woods My Master Went, Clean Forspent" as an offertory. And while some songs may seem too vague or too slow for a good offertory you may not want to use "Master, the Tempest Is Raging" or "The Fight Is On" either. While the former may make the worshiper drowsy or have a negative reaction on him, the extremely fast songs may unconsciously cause him to hurry and pass the plate before he has had time to give as he ought.

There are many beautiful hymns that, tastefully and cheerfully played, make wonderful offertory songs. Some of these are:

> How Great Thou Art
> He Is Able
> Joybells
> At the Cross
> And Can It Be That I Should Gain?
> Trust and Obey
> Make Me a Channel of Blessing
> It Pays to Serve Jesus
> God Will Take Care of You
> Give of Your Best to the Master
> Will There Be Any Stars in My Crown?

All of these hymns are positive, cheerful, challenging, and will make good offertory specials. They remind the giver that God is great and can easily provide a good return on our investment.

8. Train Your Ushers to Take the Offering Properly

I'm sure this sounds trite but you might be amazed at the way some churches allow the men to take the offering.

In many cases only two men take it when four or six are needed. There should be *at least one usher* on *either* side of *each section* of pews. But how often we've seen the plate go down the aisle and the worshiper on the far end has to juggle the plate over his shoulder and try to find someone behind him to take the plate and pass it back. In some instances this is a child or a feeble adult. More often than you think the plate is dropped on the floor in such cases.

Even worse, in some country or small-town churches two men will go down the center aisle. One will stick the offering plate out in the direction of the east side. The other will stick his plate out in the direction of the west side. If someone wants to give an offering he must wave his envelope or his hand to flag the usher down. If the church is lucky the plate will get over to the worshiper and back. In some cases I've seen the worshiper have to get up and walk half way through his section in order to make his offering, or stretch out over others like an Indian rubber man!

Now, let's face it. A lot of people are just not going to go to all that trouble to make an offering. It is embarrassing to have to get up and make a show of his giving in the first place. In the second place he may not feel too much like his offering is needed very badly if the ushers are not willing to get the plate to him so he can give easily and without confusion and display. Again, some people may not want to give anyway, but most people *will* give something if the plate is actually passed to them and they have to handle it and pass it on to someone else. If the plate is passed to them they know they are expected to give; it is the proper thing to do, and they feel a bit awkward about *not* giving in such cases.

Untrained ushers sometimes are careless and miss whole rows of people. Others have been known to double-up and pass the plate down the same row twice! Of course, this is accidental, but it shows the importance of using trained, careful ushers.

Some churches use teenagers or even junior boys to take the offering, especially on Sunday night. This does not give the offering its needed dignity and importance.

Use clean, neat, sharp-looking men for ushers. The usher should be dressed in a neat suit with a coat and tie, of course. (In some resort town churches in the heat of summer it may be that everyone comes to church in casual sport clothes. In that case the ushers might get by with a neat, clean dress shirt and tie, without a jacket.) The well-dressed usher adds dignity and authority to his position by being properly attired.

If teens are to be used they should be sharp-looking, mature teenagers with a good haircut, and should be young men who are anxious to serve and will gladly receive the proper training and instruction from the head usher. Even then, it might be best to let them "practice" on the Wednesday night crowd until they mature and are grown into manhood.

Use only ushers who have a clean reputation and a good Christian testimony. If a man is engaged in questionable practices during the week or does not have the best reputation in his business I certainly would not have him taking the offering in my church!

If you just "gather up the men" for the offering on the spur of the moment (as some head ushers do) you will have a duke's mixture of Heaven only knows what. Hence, the importance of properly training your ushers. A separate chapter will be given to this important work.

Is it even necessary to suggest that the men walk down the aisles in unison, pace themselves so that they do not outrun the other ushers, watch carefully to be sure that a small child does not drop the whole thing, assist where there is an afflicted person, and be sure the money is carefully taken care of after the offering is received?

It is good for the money to be put back on the communion table unless it is to be immediately taken to the safe by the men.

And how should the money best be counted? Some banks allow the secretaries or other trained workers to count it in the bank on Monday. Generally it is best for the finance committee or deacons to count the money at the church immediately after the service and the entire amount taken by a team of at least two men immediately to the safe deposit vault of the bank.

I would not allow the men to get into the habit of taking the money to a room and counting it during the service. The men need the blessing of the hymns, the special music and the sermon. They interrupt when they make their grand entrance during the sermon. And it is a poor testimony to others when some men are allowed to treat the message and/or song service as if it were not as important as the money.

9. Take the Offering With Enthusiasm and Optimism

Be joyful about the offering yourself, Pastor. Appear confident that the money needed for the church (or missions or the building or whatever) is going to be supplied by the Lord through His people. God loves a cheerful giver, yea, even a "hilarious" giver. So it behooves the preacher to be happy and thrilled that we have come to this part of the service. Use such verses as Malachi 3:10, Luke 6:38, II Corinthians 9:6-8 and Philippians 4:19 to encourage their giving.

10. Do Not Apologize for Preaching on Tithing

This is as much a part of the Bible message, Christian living and missionary opportunity as any other part of the Bible. The Word of God has much to say about it. We would be robbing our people if we did not teach them to tithe. They can never outgive God. So preach it!

It is true that, under grace, we should not stop at the tithe. But the tithe is a good starting place. "You can do more than tithe *after* you have tithed but you can not do more than tithe until you have tithed" is a good way of putting it. I always reminded our people that they could get along far better on 9/10ths with God than on 10/10ths without God, and that God would *prove* that to them as they became faithful tithers.

Don't hesitate to let them know they are robbing God if they do not at least bring the tithe to God (Mal. 3:8,9). Sprinkle your tithing sermons with good illustrations not only from the Bible but from Christian life itself. There are some good little humorous thoughts and illustrations along the way that will make your tithing sermons better received and will make the nontither laugh at himself for having been a stingy, tightfisted tightwad. Don't fail to have envelopes handy for your people. Be sure each member gets his box of tithing envelopes at the beginning of each year. Keep records of tithing.

Preach a full message on tithing at least once a year, probably twice a year. Scatter tithing truths in other messages during the year. Have an occasional study on the subject of stewardship. Use pithy sentences on tithing in your bulletin and church paper. Get some good tracts on the subject and be sure all of your people get them from time to time.

And before you preach a tithing sermon, remind yourself that this is one of the best things you could ever do for your people. Thus, you never have anything to apologize for in asking them to become faithful tithers.

11. Set the Right Example Publicly and Be Sure Other Leaders Do

Attend a church like Highland Park Baptist Church in Chattanooga and you will see the pastors, staff members and choir members all putting in an offering when the plate is passed. This sets a very good example to others and inspires them to give.

I know that some churches lead the people to put their envelopes in the Sunday school. But it seems to me that this leaves the church offering plate rather bare and is a poor example to the visitors and others who just attend the worship service. Are they sitting there thinking, "The members of this church must not have much confidence in their church. None of them seem to be putting anything in!"?

I would put in a dollar or so in the Sunday school offering when I was a pastor and save my tithe envelope for the morning service. Then I would try to have something to put in at night, also.

12. Be Excited About Giving

Your own happiness and optimism about tithing will prove contagious. Always take a positive attitude. Test God frequently. Keep your own heart hot about giving.

When there is a special offering or a building bond to buy, be among the first to happily have a part. Let your people know that you wouldn't miss the joy of giving for the world!

Be sure that your own wife and children share your enthusiasm. People notice the pastor's family. If they know that you and your family give sacrificially they will want to do so, too. Be generous (Prov. 13:7)!

13. Challenge the People to Give

People will respond to a real challenge. Have a stewardship banquet once in a while and bring in a speaker who will thrill your people with the message on giving. Keep interesting items before your people about churches that are really doing great things for God because the people worked together and gave happily. Use Ezra and the book of Nehemiah to inspire them, as well as the words of Jesus and Paul.

Have a tithing campaign or a stewardship contest sometimes. Some churches do so, with the inspiration of a stewardship crusade and tithing banquet at the beginning of each year.

If you have a good report to give about a great offering last Sunday don't give it until *after* the offering is taken today! To get up and boast about or rejoice in big offerings already received may automatically give some people the impression that they do not need to be so generous this Sunday!

Think big. Keep challenging projects before the people without overloading them, of course. In a Volkswagen factory was a sign, "Think Big and You're Fired!" That may be true in a Volks factory, but the preacher who wants his people to get involved and give in a challenging way must, indeed, think big!

14. Use Every Opportunity for People to Give

Take an offering on Wednesday nights, for example. For years we never did this in my pastorates. The men said, "Preacher, the people who are going to give will give on Sundays, anyway." But I finally said, "Well, let's try it and see." We did. Immediately we began to take in $50 and $60 on Wednesday nights. Soon it was $100 and $200 per Wednesday. Now when I look at the church paper from my former pastorate I see that the Wednesday night offerings are regularly $300 and $400 per week, sometimes more than that! What pastor would not like to increase his offering $300 or $400 per week so easily?

Some people will make out a check or fill an envelope for Sunday. Then they get sick or they are called out of town. Not many will bring their envelope by the church as they leave town but many will put it in on the following Wednesday. But by the next Sunday they may have spent it.

Be sure to pass the plates to the choir. Believe it or not, in some churches they never take an offering in the choir. In some instances the choir is singing at the time and they never give unless they track down an usher after church and say, "Hey, how about seeing that my money gets in the counting room?" Now really, if the bringing of an offering is an act of worship then choir members should so worship, too.

Take an offering on special occasions. Most people expect an offering at the service where you show a film, have a guest speaker or present a missionary challenge. Why not take an offering and give the people a chance to share in the need? Keep them in the habit of giving.

During revivals or Bible Conference meetings I would take an offering each night. More will be said about this in my chapter on revivals and the revival offering, but let me assure you that people are not going to give too much. Some people will be there one night who may not get back again. Others may have money tonight but may be broke the next time they attend the meetings. Visitors may have come especially to hear your evangelist or guest speaker. Why not let them share in the blessing by giving?

Use deep offering plates! Some of the little shallow plates made for churches would discourage nearly anyone from giving. To see a few bills floating around on the top of plates not as deep as a soup bowl would make me afraid that if I gave an offering it would blow off long before the usher ever got it to home plate. It would probably pay you to buy some new collection plates if yours are the thin, stingy, shallow kind.

Observe the big revival crusades or the mammoth religious extravaganzas on television and you will see that they use huge buckets or deep containers from the fast food chicken outfits to receive their offerings. This inspires people to give and it keeps any of it from blowing away in the wind. It is an act of faith, "Open thy mouth *wide*, and I will fill it," God says in Psalm 81:10.

USE ENVELOPES, NOT CARDS, FOR SUNDAY SCHOOL PUPILS AND VISITORS. It is not possible to put an offering in a *card*. If you have envelopes it will be, even if subconsciously, realized that an offering should be included. People may put the information or registration card in the plate without an offering but they're not likely to put an *envelope* in the plate without an offering! Think about it. Also when you pray before the offering don't say, "Bless each nickle and dime given." It would be better psychology to say, "Bless the generous offerings of thy people. We thank Thee that these dollars are going to win souls and reach people with the Gospel." Some of those visitors will be reaching for their billfolds right after the prayer.

15. "When in Debt, Tithe!"

. . .was the name of one of the first articles I read after I surrendered my life to the Lord. Things *are* tight for many people now. The economy *is* in bad shape. Prices *are* going up. But this is all the more reason why people should not *drop God* or neglect their church. God will take care of those who, like Elijah at the Brook Cherith (I Kings 17), will put their trust in Him. If we tithe we actually back God into a corner (I speak reverently). It gives us a chance to really "prove God" just as He exhorts us to do in Malachi 3.

Take a positive attitude about things. If you feel sorry for the people don't let them know that you do. They buy the other things they need. Why shouldn't they contribute to the greatest cause in the world and the only thing that will LAST FOREVER? (See Matthew 6:19-33). In many cases if you don't inspire them to give it to the Lord they are going to waste it on something they will never see again after this life.

16. Never Be Intimidated by Selfish People

The fellow who gripes about the pastor "always preaching on money" probably isn't giving much, if any, himself. If he was tithing and giving generously he wouldn't mind the pastor mentioning it. In fact, he'd be giving a testimony about it, himself.

Don't let one or two stingy tightwads make you rob the people of the blessing God wants to give them by teaching them generosity.

Use good psychology. We are inviting them to a feast, not to a funeral. Lead them to "be unselfish and see what happens"!

You know they can never outgive God. Challenge them to try it! *God's Loving Money Rule for Your Financial Prosperity* was the name of an excellent tract that I used to use in my tithing message. Yes, "whatsoever he doeth shall prosper" was never any more true than it is in this matter of giving. You are showing them how to prosper. Who should mind that?

Before the offering either pray a joyful, expectant prayer yourself or call on some dedicated, enthusiastic man who will, by his prayer, inspire people to want to get in on this great chance to prosper.

God doesn't need our money so much as we need His blessing. So never be timid about the matter of the offering.

Chapter Six
Make a Joyful Noise!

ADVERTISE! Everyone in your county should know where your church is, what it stands for and what's going on there!

Try not to let a day go by that your church is not mentioned in the daily papers. Certainly never let a *week* go by without the community knowing that something is happening at your place!

Most preachers never use one fourth of the opportunities available to them. Many never use *one tenth* of the options for making their church known to the community. "Make a joyful noise," the Bible tells us. Let the whole countryside know that you're there.

"It was *noised* that he was in the house" (Mark 2:1). Mostly word of mouth, to be sure. But how do you get people talking about your church? There surely must be some way besides the pastor running off with the organist or the treasurer absconding with the funds!

Yet the only time some churches are mentioned in the press is a small notice on the church page meekly inviting the public to "special meetings." One possible exception—a wreck happens in front of the building or an occasional funeral is conducted in the sanctuary.

Now surely we can do better than that! Why is it that some churches are growing constantly and that people flock to the services? Others, meanwhile, drag along at a poor dying rate and hardly anyone in town knows the church is there.

A church I once pastored caught on fire and burned to the ground. A whiskey-drinking sinner later told me that he had been to my church once. "I was there the day the church burned. . .watched it burn right down to the slab," he assured me. Now that was some consolation. But that sinner taught me a lesson. Set our churches on fire and the people will come around to see what the smoke is all about. Vance Havner has suggested, however, that the only fire in many a church is down in the kitchen where a defeated little handful drink hot chocolate and read the minutes of the last meeting.

Now how can you be sure that everyone remembers your church and knows that it is there? Better still, how can we best attract them and make them want to visit us?

Some of the preceding chapters have told us how to keep them coming back once they come, but how do we attract them in the first place?

1. A Strategic Location Is a Big Help

If you are starting a new work or if your present membership plans to move its location be sure and hold out for a good location in a prominent place. When we had only a handful of people in the church I last pastored in Panama City, Florida, we stuck our necks out and bought a 35-acre airport (hangar and all) right in the heart of town on a prominent thoroughfare. The town had grown up around that private airport. Needless to say, we were soon known to everyone in our county. Anyone driving into town and asking where the Central Baptist Church was located immediately found someone who knew. "Oh, yes, that's the church meeting in the airplane hangar by the shopping center on West 11th Street." Or, "Sure, that's the church that has the big Christian school at 11th and Balboa."

Every church, of course, cannot obtain such a prominent piece of property but every church that can would profit by doing so. At least get the most prominent piece of property you can get. You say, "Why, we could never afford 35 acres at today's prices." You know what we did? Instead of trying to erect a pretty new building at once we bought the property we felt God wanted us to have and moved our little shot-gun building (it looked like a sawed-off army barracks) right over next to the hangar. We made a deal with the airport manager. He could keep his planes around our church for a while if we could use his property and part of his hangar for our church while he was re-locating at the municipal airport. It was rough and we had problems. (Ever tried to air condition an airplane hangar?) But we made it, the airport is ours and all paid for, and we had a piece of property that was the envy of every church in town and almost every businessman in the county. A good location with an attractive sign out front is built-in advertising everytime someone drives by.

If people see that you have a nice piece of property and you keep it looking nice while you're having "growing pains" and paying for it, they know you mean business and that you'll soon have a good building there.

Our hangar was not attractive. But at least it was big and it stood out! We always had something going on there. The Christian school started adjacent to it. We were on the radio daily mentioning our plans for the future. After a few years we were erecting the big new auditorium and the hangar came down. The wait was worth it. Get a prominent location if at all possible.

2. Keep Your Grounds and the Outside of the Building Attractive

This was stressed in Chapter Three and is so important. If you cannot afford to hire a landscaper and grounds man there probably are people in your membership who would feel honored to be turned loose on such a project. If not, you can appoint a committee of energetic folk to sound out the local nursery and landscaping places, scan the magazines on gardens and shrubbery and set out to make your place a property to be proud of. God's work deserves the best.

3. Put an Attractive Sign Out Front

If you are on that prominent thoroughfare or boulevard you will need a large sign that will stand out and cannot be missed by the passersby. If your church sits back on a quiet residential street where traffic moves slower and the same residents come by every day your sign can be smaller and less expensive.

But get a professional sign man to do your sign. Unless you are blessed by having a topnotch sign man in your church it will be important to hire an expert. And there are all kinds of sign men.

Look around. Examine the yellow pages. Look at some signs they have made. Wait until you find someone who can really do what you want done.

Meantime, you can possibly rent a portable (and lighted) sign to draw attention to your church until the sign man has created his masterpiece for you. Some special "sign" offerings or a few good men in your church to "sponsor" the sign might well pay for it. Or you might turn the teens loose on raising the money for it. But don't let that willing *house painter* do your sign. He may be able to slap paint on the side of a structure but sign painting is something else.

I've seen some crude and grotesque church signs indeed, and it didn't take a Ph.D. to ascertain that they had been turned out by an amateur.

4. Use Your Newspapers

This is most important!

While advertising rates are high in the big city newspaper I would get some kind of ad in there at least once a week. Also, there are suburban papers and even free community supplements that go into thousands of homes in and around the large cities.

In a medium-sized city the advertising rates will not be so high. The options are greater. You can perhaps get a larger ad here and it will be easier to get free news stories.

In smaller cities you have a great opportunity to reach your community each week. In a city between 25,000 and 75,000 in population it will not be so difficult to get acquainted with the advertising department workers and the city editor and church editor, too. Usually they are interested in stories of local churches.

In the small towns and villages you've got it made. They are anxious to get news of any kind and the advertising rates will be cheap, too. An alert pastor can keep his church constantly before the people in such places. If your church is a country church the nearby towns will be glad to publicize your work in their local small-town newspaper.

5. Learn the Difference Between Ads and News Stories

I have been surprised to see how many pastors would speak of putting in an "ad" when they really meant a free news story. Visit your local newspaper, look around, ask questions, get acquainted with people. Let them know that you are anxious to advertise with them and that you want to do your very best to help them and yourself, too.

Study the ads in your paper—church ads and otherwise. Notice that each good ad is there to really tell the people something. An effective ad will include not only what, but who, why, where and how much.

You may be able to find out from other pastors in the area or from some trusted Christian friend whether or not there is an advertising man on the local ad staff who is a Christian and will be sympathetic to your church. I frequently had such a person who was very helpful to me on the papers in towns where I pastored. I took time to meet them and get acquainted with them. I let them know that I wanted to spend some *money* with them. That always helps!

An ad is an 'ad-vertisement'—a paid advertisement. A pastor shows his ignorance if he walks into a newspaper office and says he wants "to run a free ad" for his church. There isn't any such animal! What he means, of course, is that he wants a story on the church page, or some news item describing an event in his church.

Dress up when you go to meet the editors. Don't go in looking like a slob *or* a playboy. Don't start out by asking how cheap it is, whether you can get it free, or how big the *discount* is to churches. There *may be* a discount to churches. Some newspapers do have such a thing. But a better way to phrase it would be, "What is the rate for advertising our big church events in your paper on such and such a day?" If they don't mention a church discount—usually they will—you could then ask, "Is there a special rate for churches or religious organizations?" In some cases there may also be a special rate for an ad run several times in a row or for an advertiser who runs an ad every week, etc.

Let them know you are interested in *advertising* first. Then you can go into the newsroom. Unless it is a *big* city newspaper you can probably meet the city editor without too much trouble. If so you can say, "I've been anxious to meet you. We've enjoyed and appreciated your paper. I'm Pastor (or Dr.) So-and-So, and have moved to the city from _____ to become pastor of the _____ Church here. I've just made arrangements to advertise in your paper and wanted to meet you while I'm here." In the course of the conversation ask about who you will be talking to when you have some news for them. Don't call it "free" stories. All the news stories are free. The editor will probably take you and introduce you to the church editor. You may or may not want to give all of your stories to the church editor. If he (or she) is friendly to your church and seems interested in you and anxious to help, then you may have found your newspaper contact. But sometimes the church editor is just someone hired to whittle down every church story and try to cram as little of it as possible into the church page next Saturday. They may not have any real interest in your church and especially if they find out yours is a fundamental, Bible-believing church.

In such cases I would keep asking around among your members and friends to see if there is an interested and compatible Christian in the news room who might help you. If such a person cannot be found then do your best to make a real friend out of the church editor. It's not as hard as you might imagine.

Get your story to them *early* in the week, not right on the deadline.

TYPE OUT your news story. *Double-space* it on *one* side of the paper only, and let at least the first page be on church letterhead. Don't make them have to guess whose church the story is from. Stories written out single-spaced, or (even worse) with pen and ink, are frowned upon if not completely rejected by the editor. When I've taken my stories in for publication I've seen some atrocious pages sprawled out on the church editor's desk. No wonder they dislike some pastors and churches!

Leave at least an inch margin at top and bottom of the page and on either side. Make it neat. Spell correctly. Don't wander around and say a lot of unnecessary things or repeat yourself. That just means more work for the editor crossing out what you've said.

Here is a sample of the kind of story many an editor has to deal with:

> The Maranatha Fundamental Bible Church announces special meetings with Evangelist Bartholomew Blowhard at the sanctuary of the church, meeting at 1779 Hard-to-Find Avenue. Special music is being planned. Sunday school is at 9:45 and the Sunday services will be at 11:00 a.m. and 7:00 p.m. The pastor wishes to take this opportunity to invite the public to attend the meetings. The revival will run through Friday night. Rev. Blowhard is a nationally known evangelist. Everybody is welcome.

What's wrong with the story? Several things. Since the evangelist or the revival is the main thing you want to emphasize I would build up a heading saying so, and start the story that way. It is obvious that the meetings would be held in the sanctuary of the church if you never said so. Since Hard-to-Find Avenue is hard to find, I would give directions about where the church is located. The public should be told who will furnish the special music. The time of the services should be mentioned in conjunction with the date of the campaign. The editor will strike out the part about the "pastor wishes to invite the public" as that does not really say anything. Just stating that Blowhard is "nationally known" doesn't tell the people much. There isn't much news in the story. Here is a better way to write it up:

CHURCH CRUSADE TO FEATURE
OKLAHOMA MINISTER

A noted Oklahoma evangelist, Dr. Bartholomew Blowhard, comes to our city tonight for a revival crusade beginning Sunday in the Maranatha Bible Church. Blowhard, whose preaching has taken him into 35 of the 50 states, is the author of 10 books and is a popular speaker on the campuses of American colleges and universities.

The pastor, Rev. J. Edgar Hooper, states that Dr. Blowhard will speak for six days, through Friday, June 10th, with services at 7:30 each evening. Sunday services will be at 11:00 and 7:00.

Special music will be furnished by the Maranatha Revival Choir under the direction of "Spring" Birdsong, and the Maranatha Quartet. A popular youth choir from nearby Singdale will also be featured with a special program of music during the campaign.

Dr. Blowhard has an appeal to all ages with a puppet performance for the children and a teenage soul-winning class for the high schoolers while he is here.

A nursery will be maintained for babies and tots at all services.

Plenty of off-street parking is assured.

Maranatha Bible Church is located at 1779 Hard-to-Find Avenue, two blocks west of Comfort Causeway, near the corner of Jinx and Sphinks. The public is invited.

Now the editor may not run all of the above but he is likely to, and even if he "bleeds it" a bit, it will still have far more meat on the bones than the first story that didn't really say anything.

They may tell you that you do not need to put a *heading* on the story since they write their own headlines but if you head it up yourself they just *might* use your idea and at *least* they get the *main thrust* of what you are trying to say in your news story.

Many stories brought to newspapers are rejected or cut to smitherines because the story is not really *news*. How can you have a fresh news story for the paper week after week?

Well, any week I could make a "newsy" story of my sermon topics for the next Sunday. But you cannot get away with that every week. One week it may be the revival, another week a special program the choir is doing, the next the dedication of your sign out front, and the following a trip your teens are taking. Then you can build up that vacation Bible school you've planned for months; the next Saturday it may be the big commencement extravaganza to close out the Bible school. One week it may be the Christian school project, the next the new buses you are sending out as you enlarge your bus outreach. This week it may be the start of a new series, "PASTOR TO BEGIN NEW SERIES ON THRILLING BIBLE THEMES," or "MAKING THE OLD TESTAMENT COME ALIVE," PASTOR PROMISES. Next time it may be the special home classes your ladies are beginning. The new building addition, of course, should be played up with pictures of the building committee standing by the pastor along with the architect, the builder, etc. And on and on we could go.

Special days, bus contests, Bible conferences, missionaries who are to speak, new arrivals on the staff, new departments formed, socials enjoyed, seminars conducted, trips made, special guests—all of these are newsy.

Announcing that the pastor will speak on *prayer* the following Sunday is not considered very news worthy. But if the topic is "HOW TO GET THINGS FROM GOD," explaining that the pastor will show how to actually "touch the Invisible," that is considered newsy.

Saying that you will bring a prophetic message will not raise the eyebrow of the church editor, but announcing that the Sunday night topic will be "ISRAEL AND THE MIDEAST CRISIS IN THE LIGHT OF THE BIBLE" will be catchy and far more likely to take his fancy.

While the Bible doctrine of the Holy Spirit may not sound very fascinating to the average reader, "A BIBLICAL ANALYSIS OF THE MODERN CHARISMATIC MOVEMENT" may kick up quite a bit of interest!

Once I would get a Sunday night series on Great Bible Heroes under way and had said about all I could about that in a news story, I would keep that one rolling under its own power and stewing in its own juice while I concentrated my ads for a few Sundays on the topics of the Sunday morning messages. Then when I got my Sunday *morning* crowd there I could sell them on coming for the Sunday night series.

Instead of announcing that you will speak on "The Blood," why not name it "Heaven's Blood Bank"? Rather than announce a message on tithing why not call it "A Sure-Fire Way to Financial Success"? Billy Sunday, when wanting to preach on "Be Sure Your Sin Will Find You Out," dubbed it, "God's Faithful Detective." Mine was "The Boomerang"! Instead of "The

Doctrine of the New Birth," how about "People Who Are Born Twice"?

If a pastor plans to speak today on abortion, homosexuality, capital punishment, the race problem or the Equal Rights Amendment, these topics will be considered *news!*

In writing up paid ads for the advertising department you can be a bit more demanding and at least make requests for space preference. Many times they will put your ad in the most out-of-the-way spot they can find and if you can make friends with the ad man and get him to try to place it in a conspicuous place it will be to your advantage. Ask for page 3 or 5 if possible. They sure won't run it on page 1 and page 3 is better than page 2. Page 5 is good because in most papers it will be ahead of the big grocery or furniture ads and possibly across from the editorial page. If you are going to have a news *story* on the church page then I would either run my *paid* ad in another issue of the paper or insist they not have it on the church page. Pages 3, 5, or 7 are better than 2, 4, or 6 because when a man opens his paper he will see these pages first and if he is hurriedly thumbing through the paper he will catch your ad quicker.

The back page is good if you can get it. Try to stay out of the sports section with your ad unless you are featuring Joe Boyd, converted All-American football star, or someone the sports fans will be interested in.

The financial pages are not good and I would steer clear of the amusement and theater section. The TV page would get attention but they very probably will not run it there. And don't run it in competition with TV ads or other entertaining items unless you have a big ad, well written, with at least one good picture in it.

Always have a picture in your ad! The pastor's picture is good as you want to keep your church and your name before the people of your city or community. When the evangelist is coming be sure and run his picture in the ad no matter what he looks like! A picture is worth a thousand words, they say. The picture draws attention to the ad. Put a black border or a striped border around your ad to draw attention to it. You will have to request this of

your ad man if you want it. A picture of your church will sometimes be good if you have an attractive building. Sometimes I
would run a picture of a huge crowd outside our building. If you
can get a good shot of your auditorium *filled* on the inside this
will go good in some future ad.

If you can only run very small ads study the ads that appear
once a month in the back section of THE SWORD OF THE
LORD and fix yourself up one like that.

6. Get on the Radio With Your Church Message

Some preachers are "naturals" for radio and others are not. If
you enjoy radio work, feel at home in front of a "mike," and have
the ingenuity to work up first-class broadcasts, then I would try
to get on the air every day with a topnotch morning broadcast.
Anywhere from 8:00 to 9:00 is a good time to be on the air. Earlier
is not too bad. The noon hour is fair. At night you've got a lot of
competition from TV.

If you do not feel that you have the time, money or inclination
for a daily broadcast then you could make 5 tapes a week of 5
minutes each. Be sure you have a professional help you do it just
right. Broadcast them in the early morning hours, 7 to 9:00 a.m.,
one each morning preferably at the same time each day. These 5-
minute programs will likely cost nearly as much as the 15-minute
ones would but will probably do just as much good.

I would not buy 30 minutes or an hour and put your choir and
other singers on the air unless you have a fabulous singing group.
The recorded productions of the professionals will outshine you
unless you have a topnotch musical man and really fine singers.

The next best thing would be spot announcements on the
radio. If you can get some of these on a Christian radio station
and some of them on a good FM station it would be good. While
you might want to get on worldly country music or rock stations
(if you could) to preach the Gospel to the heathen you're not likely to draw from that crowd to your church with spot announcements.

Don't spend precious preaching-and-inviting time by praying
on the radio. With the possible exception of a few shut-ins, peo-

ple are not going to be drawn to your church because they hear you *praying* on the radio. Do your praying before you go on the air. Someone who has been on the radio in a city for many years like Dr. Lee Roberson or Dr. Bruce Cummons and has won the hearts of thousands can use a "prayer-time" effectively for the shut-ins, the troubled or the afflicted, but for the rest of us I would do public praying sparingly and "enter into my closet" for that vital practice.

Begin your broadcast with a pithy statement, a timely quote or an exciting invitation to stand by for what's coming on, and then go right into a first-class musical number unless you are the rare preacher who can capture the attention of people with your voice and message and start shooting them down with the gospel gun the minute the broadcast begins.

Make use of radio and TV "bulletin boards" for public announcements. They welcome such. But again, type them out, double-spaced, and be brief and to the point. Take the announcements in person or find out exactly to whom to mail them. Be on time with your announcements.

When you are on the radio make much of the topics of your messages for the next Sunday. Keep people aware that something highly interesting is going on over at your church. Whet their appetites.

On the radio don't let yourself develop a ministerial "whang" or a professional put-on sound. Be natural. Speak in a conversational tone. You can put urgency and enthusiasm into your voice without screaming, puffing and hollering at the people. No one likes to be screamed at on the radio.

Use Meloids or some good throat disc before you go on the air to get rid of hoarseness or early morning hang-ups in your throat. Some of us who have sinus problems will do well to irrigate our sinuses before broadcasting. Don't go on the air sniffing, snorting and clearing your throat.

Either conclude your program with a strong appeal to receive Christ or a warm invitation to your church. One other option would be "a thought to remember" as you leave the air.

Of course, promote your "special days" at the church while

you are on the air (briefly) but don't spend all your preaching time doing so. Don't beg for money on the air!

7. Use Billboards on the Highways Coming Into Your Town

Be sure a professional helps you with this so it will look good and say what it ought to say. If you cannot afford these, there probably is a businessman in your church (or in your radio audience) who will share a sign with you or perhaps sponsor one.

8. Use Lights to Focus on Your Church at Night

When you have an attractive lawn and building a spotlight or two on the building will help. A lighted cross on the steeple will help people find you from all directions. Dr. Dino Pedrone at Chambersburg, Pennsylvania, has a lighted cross on the top of the peak of his big auditorium, and his church on the hill (The Open Door Church) can be seen at night from all over the city. Some churches may be able to afford a huge spotlight sweeping the sky at night and thus draw attention to the church from all over.

9. Have Small Arrows and Signs at Intersections Near Your Church

All roads should lead to your church. Let people know exactly how to find you. If your church is on a back street or out of the limelight, then I would run a map of how to find you in an ad now and then. Some churches find it helpful also to have a small map printed on the back of tracts they give out so everyone can readily locate them.

10. Print an Attractive Card on Slick Stock and Salt the Town Down With It

Use the name of the church, picture of it (if attractive), picture of pastor, music director, youth man, school principal, etc., along with a cheery and enthusiastic resume of the wonderful things that go on at your church. Make it a fourfold one if you have several ministers on your staff. Be sure you give the time of all services, complete address, map if needed, etc. Be sure all of your people have a quantity of these at all times to give out—on visitation, in the mail, at stores, in the shopping malls, in their places of business, everywhere. Let the whole town know you're there and the church is doing things for God.

11. Promote Special Days and Other Events That Will Draw People

Don't go along at a humdrum rate. Keep something going on. For good ideas on special days and promotion, see books by Dr. Lee Roberson at Highland Park Baptist Church, 1819 Union Avenue, Chattanooga, Tennessee 37404, and by Dr. Jack Hyles, First Baptist Church, 523 Sibley Street, Hammond, Indiana 46320, and others. You will not be able to use all of their ideas but you will get some good help and many of these things will work if you work at it.

Everytime you have a big "special day" you'll keep a few people who will become regulars, and you will also remind the people in the town once more that you are still around and can't be forgotten.

12. Use Buses, Keep Them Painted, Have Your Church's Name on Them

A bus ministry will be rewarding. Souls will be won, families will be reached, children will be kept out of trouble, Christians will have a good opportunity to serve, people will know you love them, and your church will grow. Much has been said and written about busing and the bus ministry. Get the bus books of Dr. Wally Beebe and others who have succeeded. See ads in THE SWORD OF THE LORD and look at books on the subject in reliable Christian bookstores for further help on the bus ministry.

As people constantly see your attractive buses rolling through town they are made aware, once more, that you are there to help them and that you're doing things for God.

13. There Is No Substitute for Bible Preaching and Soul Winning

No matter how attractive your building or how much you advertise and promote you've got to have something there for the people when they come. Win souls and you'll find others doing it, too. A prominent midwestern pastor was asked how he happened to have such good crowds on Sunday and he replied, "Well, I preach the Gospel on Sunday and I have five hundred members who are out there preaching it all week!" Fire up your people. Keep the platform hot. Stress soul winning. Preach the Word. Feed the sheep and they'll come back for more.

14. A Few Closing Thoughts:

As you become successful and your church grows, other churches will want to get on the bandwagon and use your ideas to compete with you. Don't be surprised, and don't let it get you down.

In Panama City when I first began running ads I was almost the only pastor who did (except when other churches were having revivals) but soon others began to have weekly ads, too. Now the church page is loaded with cults, Catholics, Campbellites, charismatics—you name it. Even the liberals are advertising quite a bit now. So you just have to make yours a little better and a little bigger (if possible) and try to stay out in front. If it gets too bad, try to stay off the church page with your ads.

We began using buses and soon the denominational die-hards and the wildfire heretics were running buses, too. It just turns out that way. Preachers all over America have had to put up with this "competition."

Be sure the sound, lights, heat and air conditioning are as near perfect as possible when the people do get to your church.

Use floats in parades, fire trucks in vacation Bible school convoys, and any other proper and legitimate way of drawing attention to your church when you are doing something worthwhile.

Get a reputation as a church where people find the Lord. Some of those folks in town and in your radio audience are going to remember you someday when they have trouble or sorrow and they will call for you.

If you have a Christian school keep the proper balance between advertising your church and your school and let one complement the other.

Use Direct Mail to send out a church paper and other materials that may eventually draw others in your direction.

Consider running an ad in THE SWORD OF THE LORD on the church page they have once a month. This will draw outsiders who may move to your area and when people are on vacation they will know where to go to church.

Keep stressing to your people the importance of boosting your church, inviting others and passing out the church cards wherever they go in your city or community. Never for a day let the people forget that you are there!

Chapter Seven

Whatever Happened to God's Music?

Next to the preaching of the Word itself, the *music* of your church may be the matter of most importance.

The evangelistic fervor of a church or the effectiveness of a sermon may be chilled or killed by dead, solemn, ritualistic music. On the other hand, many churches have let the bars down and accepted the music standards of the world, the liberals and the charismatics. In such places you could sometimes close your eyes and you wouldn't know whether you were in a nightclub, a barroom or a "holy roller" camp meeting. It is no wonder that many of the older saints, sick at heart, just stay home from church and read their Bibles and long for the old days when a church service looked and sounded like one!

Generally where the music is shallow and worldly, the church will be the same.

Several years back when I was a pastor, I knew that some churches were compromising in the matter of music and heard that even some (liberal) churches were having social dancing for their young people. But I never would have dreamed that *rock* music would ever be brought into *any* church—much less into those of our churches that preach the Bible and believe in trying to honor God.

The choir need not be the "war department" in your church. The *pastor* is the key! If he leads his people to be a spiritual, God-fearing, Bible-loving congregation, they will automatically appreciate and insist on having the right kind of music. The preacher who believes what the Bible teaches about separation and leads his people to live spiritual lives will not have any big battle over the kind of songs the church sings or over the guest musicians who are invited to the platform in that church.

Great care must be exercised to make certain that you get the right kind of choir director or music leader for your church—one who will agree with your position on worldliness, consecration and separation. I have not heard the music from *all* Christian colleges and Bible schools, of course, but I've heard a great many of the products of some schools. When I was a pastor we secured our music men from Tennessee Temple University or Bob Jones University, so we never had any problem with the wrong kind of music in our church. From my observation as an evangelist, the music men who have had their training at Tennessee Temple, Bob Jones University, Maranatha Baptist Bible College, Massillon Bible College, Piedmont and Pensacola Christian College will likely not give the pastor heartaches and ulcers in the music ministry of the church. I'm sure there are also some other schools that are holding the line on the right kind of music, but these are the ones I've had the most experience with, and whose music ministries I can endorse.

Philosophy of Music

Sensing the trend toward compromise in music, the Baptist Bible College of Springfield, Missouri, recently stated its Philosophy of Music in an outstanding message by Dr. W. E. Dowell, the school president. Not only had the trend been observed by school leaders, but the trustees of BBC have determined that the college be protected from this liberal trend and that the representative music of Baptist Bible College should be traditional music. Among other things, the excellent *Baptist Tribune* article states,

> The throbbing drum beat or the loud bass guitar is not acceptable at BBC. Great hymns and spiritual songs are preferable in all our singing groups.
> "Background music," when used with special groups, should be at least somewhat subdued—not the loud, throbbing kind you often hear. This is also applicable to the use of a soundtrack. I have heard some good singers who sang songs beautifully, but the songs were ruined by their soundtrack. Any lyric that refers

to God as "somebody up there" or "the man upstairs" is not acceptable.

If the accompaniment of a song dominates the melody or lyrics, it is not fitting. Rock music of any kind is not to be performed or listened to at Baptist Bible College. Good gospel music should have sincerity and devotion. Frivolous trash and meaningless musical sounds, rhythms and drums attract the flesh, but they cannot assist in worship and in devotions. Church music should be moderate in its pretentions, because it is not the physical passions, but the pure feelings of the heart that are here to be touched. IF THERE IS ANY DOUBT THAT A MUSICAL NUMBER IS ACCEPTABLE, IT SHOULD BE TREATED BY THE RULE OF MODERATION AND THEREFORE AVOIDED. [Capitals mine, HFP.] A throbbing beat is a sign of rock music. This is not just a regular pulse of the meter, it is a pulsating beat. I have heard the same beat in the heart of Africa. This effect has infiltrated a slow pop-style of gospel music. The musical sounds were designed to excite the emotions and the physical stem. The change of words to religious text does not alter the effect of the music. The use of this style is an attempt to compromise with the world.

Now I have not quoted all of Dr. Dowell's message for the sake of brevity, but this philosophy of music at BBC would be a good one for a church, also.

Bible Standards

Here are some verses to think about as we consider music in the church:

The songs should glorify God (I Cor. 10:31).

The message should be scriptural (Eph. 5:19).

They should be in the name of the Lord Jesus Christ, giving thanks to God (Col. 3:17).

As new creatures in Christ all things should have become *new* (II Cor. 5:17).

We are not to be "conformed to this world," but "transformed" (Rom. 12:2).

We should sing with the Spirit and with the understanding also (I Cor. 14:15).

In Leviticus 10:10, God tells us to "put a difference between holy and unholy, and between clean and unclean."

We are to "learn *not* the way of the *heathen.*"

We are not to "turn. . .again to the weak and beggarly elements" of the world (Gal. 4:9).

"When the burnt-offering began, the song of the Lord began also" (II Chron. 29:27), which indicates along with Romans 12:1 that every believer is to present himself a sacrifice to the Lord.

They should be the "psalms and hymns and spiritual songs" of Colossians 3:16, not the raucous, clashing clatter of an obscene world.

In describing the sins of the priests, Ezekiel said, "They have put no difference between the holy and profane" (Ezek. 22:26).

We are not to "love. . .the world, neither the things that are in the world" (I John 2:15).

"Holiness becometh thine house, O Lord, for ever" (Ps. 93:5).

Pastor Colis Thorn of Calvary Baptist Church, Fort Walton Beach, Florida, in commenting on how to know the music is "right," suggests:

1. It should glorify God.
2. It should prepare the congregation for the message.
3. It should prepare the preacher to preach better.

Forrest L. Keener writes, "There is a need in our day for returning to Bible principles in our music. It needs to be scripturally sound in doctrinal content as well as worshipful in its presentation." Then, in commenting on a hippie singing religious songs with a rock beat and hillbilly whang, he states, "This destructive flame is fed by the pitiful fact that many churches today are infinitely more interested in 'relating' to youth, the public, the world, than they are in glorifying God in the church. . .let us insist that our singing be worship, not performance."

In the *Baptist Tribune,* Dale Peterson asks, "Do we really have to give teens '*their* kind of music'?" He continues,

> We as fundamental Baptists, believe in separation in dress, abstaining from alcohol, tobacco, dances, and hard rock, but when it comes to "church music" feathers can get ruffled

quickly. Many youth workers say you have to be like (lost) teenagers to reach them. They say you have to wear mod clothes, be hip, and jive. I say "hogwash!" Young people are looking for men and women to lead them. The Southern Michigan Youth Fellowship has not followed modern trends in music and by God's grace will not! We still sing the old songs and sing them heartily in the "old way."

When I was a Florida pastor, I watched church after church around us adopt the worldly dress, habits and music of the world to "try to reach the youth." Yet our church with its preaching against sin and worldliness, and holding the line on good, traditional music, had more young people than any church in our part of Florida, and we also had the largest Christian school.

Do We Have to Be Relevant?

Pastor Richard Kidd of Shrewsbury, Pennsylvania, in his church paper, writes about those who insist, "We've got to be relevant," or "We've got to be contemporary if we are going to communicate the gospel to our young people," and he reminds us that this contemporary "relevance" had taken us farther and farther away from all standards of decency and morality and the God of our fathers. He then quotes G. Campbell Morgan who said, "I am often told that the church needs to catch the spirit of the age if it is to succeed. I reply that the church succeeds only in proportion as she *corrects* the spirit of the age!"

An Ohio pastor used to sing in a Nashville (sound) quartet. "I know these people. That's why we *don't* have them in our church." Again he said, "We don't have charismatic *preachers* preach for us—why have their *music?*" He reminded me of one popular writer of modern (and mod) gospel music who claims his music is just as "inspired" as the Bible is! The pastor also stated, "If the 700 Club or PTL Club pushes the sound, I don't want it."

Vance Havner in his book, *Song at Twilight*, laments:

The distemper has invaded the churches in what goes for gospel music. It would be bad enough if jazz had remained in the nightclubs amidst the darkness of heathenism transplanted from the African to the asphalt jungle. But when the church borrows both the language and the livery of Sodom, it is time to hang our heads in shame.

A. W. Tozer in *Born After Midnight* writes,

The influence of the erotic spirit is felt almost everywhere in evangelical circles. Much of the singing in certain types of meetings has in it more of romance than it has of the Holy Ghost. Both words and music are designed to arouse the libidinous.

In *Why Our Churches Do Not Win Souls*, Dr. John R. Rice states:

Where are the songs of the great revivals? It is sadly true that now few songs are written with a gospel appeal to the unsaved, or to the unchurched, or cold Christians. Once multitudes were moved with "Tell Mother I'll Be There". . . .What new song do you know like "Ye Must Be Born Again," "For You I Am Praying" or "The Great Judgment Morning"?. . . .Where are the songs on soul winning like "Must I Go and Empty Handed?" and "Will There Be Any Stars in My Crown?"

In the chapter on "Church Music Usually Does Not Tend to Soul Winning," Dr. Rice continues,

Where there are no great revivals and no great evangelistic preaching, then song writers do not write evangelistic songs. And the music of our churches does not emphasize soul winning and usually does not fit into a soul-winning program.

Dr. Rice quotes Dr. Jack Hyles in saying, "If you want Billy Sunday results, you must have Homer Rodeheaver music. If you want Moody and Torrey revivals, you must have Sankey and Alexander music!" How true!

Singer Mike Coyle writes:

Much of our contemporary "religious music" is written to consider personal experience or to use general truth in such a way that would make even a modernist comfortable. Most lack dignity, honor, and are not directed towards God, but are horizontally oriented.

Reece Randle states,

Music can literally make or break a service. If the music does not reinforce good doctrine, it is not good music. If the music speaks to the foot and not the heart, it is the wrong kind. If the music works on the emotions alone and does not speak to the mind it is not right. Many churches reek of charismatic, shallow, worldly music that has been penned, popularized and pushed by those of another camp. Brethren, why must this be so? Why must we feed the flesh in the name of trying to save the soul? Why do we pat our feet and say "amen" to fleshly songs that have no more spiritual content than a nursery rhyme?

He then speaks of the bad music, bad lyrics and bad associations of much modern "religious" music, and in summing it up wrote,

If the song has been taken from or modeled after the rock or folk culture it will prompt the wrong thoughts and emotions from those converted from that culture. . . . Even if the song is basically good, but is performed in a manner akin to that of the T.V. or stage entertainer, then it is dangerous. Examine the association. Does that wild, raucous sound you've been hearing really prepare hearts for your message? Does the shallow, sentimental lyrical content really edify the saints? Does the sound that is so much like the world's music really reach the lost?

My Testimony

I was saved as a young boy during the "jazz age" of the world. But I would have been amazed if the Southern Baptist church I attended had brought jazz music into the church. I'll tell you what I remember; I remember "Brighten the Corner Where You Are." I remember "He Keeps Me Singing," "Beulah Land," "Loyalty to Christ," and "Will You Be Enlisted as a Volunteer?" I remember "Power in the Blood" and "Standing on the Promises." And that's what I expected when I went to church.

I surrendered my life to Christ for His service during the "swing age." But I think I would have been repelled—even shocked—as a teenager, if my church had brought in a swing band or had used theatrical "stars" to "reach the young people" in my day. If they had done so, I would never have surrendered. Swing music I could have found without going to church to get it. I wanted something better.

The Cop-Out

Bill Harvey, gospel singer, has written about the church's cop-out compromise with the new sound in music:

> The cop-out is the songwriters we thought we could count on for scriptural, spiritual and musical accuracy and consistency turning to the new "art form" (rock music) for the vehicle to convey their lyrics. . .words that would no doubt bless if the voo-doo rhythm didn't confuse them. The cop-out is the professional quartets putting gospel cliches to the rock beat and refusing to sing without a guarantee. . . . It is unfortunate that even some fundamental schools and churches are using soft-rock and choreography with their singing groups to prove they are "up-beat" and "with it" and to attract the crowds!

Richard De Haan of the Radio Bible Class broadcast and Day of Discovery telecast has stated in the *Discovery Digest,*

> It's hard to imagine Heaven without music. The lyrics of Heaven will certainly consist of expressions of worship, thanksgiving, and praise unto the Lord our God.

Now, listen to this as he continues,

> Exactly what the music of Heaven will *sound* like we can't say for sure. But of this I'm positive: when we first hear its strains, there will be no suggestion or reminder whatsoever of the sinful, shameful and tawdry elements of life here below. There'll be no worldly sound. There will be no similarity to some of the so-called religious music we hear these days. I'm thinking of those tunes that make you feel like you were in a nightclub. The harsh, raucous, shrieking, pounding, throbbing, jangling, cacophany of the instruments. Why, even Granny is tempted to throw away her hearing aid and stuff cotton in her ears. The "beat" resembles drug culture and rock concert fare. The music of Heaven, you can be certain, won't be at all like that. And neither should ours. Let's see to it that the music of the saints below "is like to that above."

"But we'll lose our young people—we won't be able to keep crowds coming," seems to be the cry of many who adopt the "new sound" in church music. But here is an interesting thing: As I look back over my preaching appointments for the past year and a half, I recall that the largest crowds in some of the greatest churches are where they had outstanding music—all of it traditional, not the mod, "new sound." This is true both in the North and the South. The Bethel Baptist Church of Sellersville, Pennsylvania; and the Open Door Church of Chambersburg, Pennsylvania; the Berean Baptist Church at Portsmouth and the Massillon Baptist Temple at Massillon, Ohio; the Emmanuel Baptist Church of Hartsville, South Carolina; and the Grace Baptist Church of Columbus, Georgia; the Campus Church at Pensacola, Florida; and the Calvary Baptist Church, Fort Walton Beach, Florida. In all of these churches we had good meetings and all of them were loaded with young people! And surely the good music was part of what drew the crowds. None of these churches compromised on music standards! That tells us something.

In the sixties some of our fundamental churches started following the liberals and new evangelicals by having religious "hootenannies" and folk singing for the young people. Soon it was the dance-hall beat and the moaning "blues" sound of the charismatic performers they were imitating. This was in the late sixties and early seventies. Musical groups came in with their "hip" clothes, long hair on males and either mini-skirts or slinky, sexy gowns on the girls. The loud, blaring amplifiers were set up. The "performance" began. You had but to close your eyes and it was easy to imagine that this was a swinging supper club, not a church! The new wailing and moaning was accompanied by the beat of soft rock. At this rate, how soon will even our (otherwise) fundamental churches be tolerating hard rock? Then will it be acid rock, punk rock or. . . ?

Some even now are tolerating young women on the platform "performing" in slacks and other male attire. The males look feminine in both hair and styles. Soon fashion will dictate that the mini-skirt return. Many of these religious entertainers grab their microphones, sway and gyrate to the beat of the gospel jive just as their counterparts in the nightclubs do. There is the forced, artificial smile, the boys and girls billing and cooing over one another, as their bodies sway in sensual fashion. Where will it all end? Is this consistent with Bible teaching on separation from sin and worldliness? To ask the question is to answer it.

"Music Hath Charms"

Melvin Munn from Washington in *Life Line* said back in the sixties, "It is well known that music can be used to charm snakes. Not so well known, music can be used by snakes to charm people." "Madness in Music, a Red Weapon" was the title of another provoking *Life Line* message as we were warned about the misuse and perversion of music. Herbert A. Philbrick, telling the truth about the infiltration of the communists, wrote a book, *Your Church—Their Target.* He explained that the reds were using folk-singing to reach the hearts of American youth. Soon, of course, as we now know, the folk singing was just the head of the camel in the church's tent.

In the *Saturday Evening Post* for April, 1978, a Mr. Paul Baker wrote on the "Rock of Ages." And was it the lovely Lord of the Bible he described as such a Rock? Oh, no, it was the rock beat of sensual music that had invaded the church. "Drowned out in the sixties by the seductive beat of rock-and-roll, the Church rallied its forces, borrowed the beat and won back the youth." But what kind of churches won what youth back to what? Churches with no militant, Bible message, preachers who were afraid to preach against sin, or charismatics who had learned that if they embraced the world and traded their holiness for "charisma" emotionalism, they could remove the "stigma" of the old Pentecostalism. So many denominationalists and others who had lost their evangelistic fire (if they ever had any) decided to join in with the upbeat trend of the new charisma. The result has been the nightclub sound, the effeminate long-haired male performers, the sexy performance, all in the name of Christ, they say. And some have the audacity to say that this modern new dress of the Old Pentecostalism is actually a spiritual revival!

Even some composers we had trusted swung over to the new beat. "Ralph Carmichael began introducing guitars and drums into some of the religious music he recorded," writes Paul Baker. Carmichael had a rough time as traditionalists balked about the "worldliness" of it, but soon with the help of Billy Graham in a movie, "The Restless Ones"; with the aid of a composer, Ray Repp, injecting folk music into the Catholic mass; and with

Southern Baptists releasing Bob Oldenburg's folk musical, "Good News," the mod performance of religious pop music got underway in earnest. Baker applauds the new religious sound "all the way from ballads to hard rock!"

As a God-fearing, Christ-honoring, Bible-preaching pastor, this is surely not what you want in your church. But a little compromise goes a long, long way, as we have observed.

Billy Graham, speaking at Great Britain's SPREE '73 said, "I am sure that many of you are finding it difficult to adjust to the music of the present generation. Well, I must confess that it took me several years and five teenagers before I made the adjustment." The music of SPREE '73 was "tailored to speak for Christ to those who have been reared on the loud beat of rock." But are we supposed to *"adjust"* to sin, to worldliness, to compromise? Or are we to *stand*? You know the answer.

A Pentecostalist (and this is unusual) warns in *Blu-Print* of the dangers of rock gospel music,

> More and more it is becoming obvious that rock gospel is half way to hard rock; and unless there is a turning back to God, we Pentecostalists are going to have to cope with demonic power which will dominate our singing. . .contemporary music in the rock vogue is dangerous. Biblical separation must be applied to our choirs, to our singers and to all our music. It is significant in this day when all-night sings are in vogue, that deeper Bible preaching is becoming more scarce. Unless we separate our music from that of the world, we ourselves shall surely become more worldly. It is my firm conviction that a demonic spirit is working through this music and is wielding a controllable power which is going to destroy its adherents.

I also refer to my book, *The Truth About Rock Music:*

> *Many of the records and tapes in "Christian" bookstores today are contemporary or gospel rock. Obviously they sell what they do to make money, to get in on the "gospel boom." Some store managers or sales people even admit that they personally do not like the stuff, but that is what* sells—*that's what the public wants.*

"Ear Pollution"

Julian Thomas, minister of music for Pastor Gary Coleman at

Garland, Texas, has spoken of *ear* pollution being just as bad for us as *air* pollution, as he describes the assault of rock music on our ears in grocery stores and many other public places. At least we ought to be able to escape the blast of such sounds when we go to church.

"More deadly than heroin," Adam Knieste, music therapist, says about rock music. "It is not a harmless pastime but a dangerous drug on which our children are hooked. It can change balanced individuals into mentally disturbed people."

"Pop music is *sex* and we have to hit the teenagers in the face with it," said a popular rock-and-roll singing "star," and rock band leader.

The Baptist Bulletin speaks of a group of doctors researching a federally-funded project who determined that there is a direct relationship between rock music and premarital sex. The article by Donald LaRose describes the many young people who have listened to "religious" rock on the "Christian" radio stations and who have soon graduated to the dance floor and out into the world to be ruined by sin. I'm personally convinced that there is nothing that has harmed and demoralized the spiritual lives of our churches so much as the wrong kind of music being substituted for the music that brought blessing and inspiration to the saints in days and years gone by.

The "New Sound" Is Confusing

N. A. Woychuk of Bible Memory Association warned us at the beginning of this drift about "The New Song and the New Sound," and how it is confusing Christians. People who want to give the young people this "new sound" in gospel music endorse the folk-rock and the "pop" in religious music, saying, "the 'way-out' young people can be best reached by the music that is rocking this world. That's where the action is, that's where the crowds go. This is the kind of music that grabs hold of their ears."

"But is this what our young people really want?" F. M. Hechinger, Education Editor of the *New York Times* says in his book, *Teen Age Tyranny,*

American civilization tends to stand in such awe of the teen-age segment that it is in danger of becoming a teen-age society with permanently teen-age standards of thought, culture and goals. As a result, American society is growing down instead of growing up. This is a creeping disease—a softening of adulthood. It leads to immature goals in music, art and literature. . . . The fault is not with youth. The errors are those of an adult society. Teenagers behave in exactly the way they have been brought up to behave.

Then states Dr. Woychuk,

They [young people] need to have leaders and parents who are willing to be unpopular with them sometimes and who will steadfastly lead them according to those unchanging precepts God has given us in His Word.

The message of salvation, expressed in the words of Divine revelation, is always relevant—for every age, for every generation—and does not have to be garbled or watered-down in the language of the unregenerate crowd. Music for the young people of this generation does not have to be in a depressive mood and with the intoxicating beat.

Mr. Frank Cook of HCJB, Quito, Eduador, writes,

I believe we are mistaken if we think that they want the Christian message in the same music forms that they like in their secular world. . . . To use, therefore, their music forms is to identify with their negative life, their frustrations, rather than to bring them assurance and real freedom!

Dr. Woychuk concludes, "Our Lord did not adopt the philosophies of the Greeks to reach the Greeks. He did not acquire the ways of the Romans to communicate with the Romans. He did not fall in line with the traditions of the Hebrews to please the Hebrews." How true!

Good Music Standards

Back in 1972, when I was a Florida pastor, we had a singing ensemble from the Southeastern Bible College in Birmingham, Alabama, for an evening of music. It was tastefully and beautifully done. They had traditional music, the great hymns and heart-touching gospel songs. I was so impressed that I wrote to their music department to ask them for their music standards. One of the paragraphs of these standards read:

We recognize that there are some contemporary musical practices which are worthy of use. Conversely, there are many which are not appropriate for use in sacred music. Therefore, contemporary idioms shall be carefully scrutinized before their use shall be permitted in any part of the college's music program. Rock-and-roll music shall not be part of the college's music program or life, especially when its presence is readily apparent in what is now being called "Christian" folk-rock. SBC does not want to be known as an institution which features the sounds of the world: (The continuous "thump" of a swing beat; the delayed beat of the jazz syncopation; the delayed vibrato of a sensualistic holding note; the lush harmonies or disharmonies of dance media; the frantic chug-chug of gyrating motion; the empty religious sentimentalities of word and thought content.)

Again,

While recognizing the fact that music must communicate to the hearers, we do not accept the popular concept that in order to reach today's youth with the gospel, one must adopt the current trends in music.

The director of the music department of this institution also sent along an excellent treatise on "The New Church Music." He describes the religious "go-go" music of the day and calls the adverse, electronic amplification of such modern jive as "musical dystrophy." As he describes the association of the rock beat with drugs, illicit sex, death, fornication, sexual looseness, the pill, do-your-own-thing permissivism and amorality, along with kill-your-parents ideology, he reminds us of the religious and musical "howlings" of which Amos wrote (Amos 8:3).

But, "this is just a way of reaching teens," they say. But remember, that the whole idea behind using such music is that some Christians are trying to tell the unsaved teens that Christians are not so much different from them: "See, we dress like you, we act like you, and we even sing the same kind of music as you."

Since I am not a composer and musician but a preacher, I have asked some successful music men, topnotch educators, and church leaders for a statement on music. I asked them to comment on the dangers facing today's church music, must we compromise in music? Do we really win the world by imitating the world in music? And a word to distinguish between the world's religious music of "the new sound" and the traditional gospel music which we believe God has blessed and will continue to bless. Here they are just as they were given to me:

> Do we really win by imitating the world? This is what many are doing in church music today. However, there is no need for this since God has planned that music should aid people in worshiping God. God cannot be worshiped through carnal music. Some say that we need this "new" type music to reach the unsaved. If we "reach" them through worldly and (carnal) means it will take worldly means to keep them. May God help fundamentalists to continue with tried and proven music. There are many old and new songs that fall into this category. Remember that the Antichrist is to be the instigator of "change"!

R. Gene Payne, Singer,
  Choirmaster, Pastor
Friendship Baptist Church
Raleigh, North Carolina

Statement By Dr. Bob Jones III, President
Bob Jones University

In every era of church history the music used by the Church has been a valid indicator of the spirituality of the churches in those eras.

The spiritual corruption within Christendom today is marked by a de-emphasis upon the necessity of sound doctrine, sound morals, sound ethical and business practices; and it is, therefore, inevitable that spiritually debilitating music promoting unsound doctrine and, at best, light, frivolous concepts of the Christian life should have invaded us. The appeal of this music is to the carnal nature of man. It is entertaining rather than instructive and has become accepted and defended by the "best" of churches.

Within the spectrum of acceptable church music there is plenty of room for variation and taste. No one would expect a church in a cultured, metropolitan area to have the same kind of music that is enjoyed by an isolated mountain congregation in Appalachia. At the same time, it must be recognized that within the "mountain culture" there is a type of music that has no place in the worship of God, just as in the "city culture" there is music that has no place in the worship of God. Nobody has any excuse for defending the wrong kind of music on the basis of "taste."

The music department of Fundamental churches has become the Devil's playground. He may not have been able to invade the preaching, but in many cases he has taken over the music; and in doing so, his subversive designs against the people of God have been realized and it will be only a matter of time before he has control of the preacher's tongue.

When a church's music standard falls and the pastor decides to stop fighting the battle for the preservation of spiritually productive music, he will allow entertainment music to enter. That very weakness in the preacher's character will show up later in his preaching and perhaps in his morals. The character fault that allowed him to rationalize his way around the right kind of music will appear again in his personal life when Satan's temptations press hard against him or when carnal Christians in his congregation press him to be less offensive in his preaching and his stand.

Christian music is for the purpose of conveying Biblical truth. It is just as important that a song be scripturally sound as it is for a sermon to be sound. Colossians 3:16 says, ". . . teaching and admonishing one another in psalms and hymns and spiritual songs, singing with grace in your hearts to the Lord." If singing is for the purpose of teaching and admonishing, then it is incumbent on the pastor to be sure the songs are spiritual and not carnal, both in musical style and content. The emphasis here, as in Ephesians 5:19, is upon *spiritual* songs. It is time pastors diligently set about to clean up the music in their churches.

When a man allows carnal music to flourish in his church, I cannot help but conclude that his own carnality is being reflected in what he allows. A man doesn't have to "know" music in order to know the difference between acceptable and unacceptable music. If a man walks in the Holy Spirit, he is taught of the Spirit that which is holy. The Holy Spirit in a man will bear witness against that which is unholy and unclean. It is not through any lack of evidence or understanding that pastors cling to carnal music in their churches, for there is plenty that has been written and said on the subject. It is instead by his choice that it remains.

Dr. Bob Jones III
President, Bob Jones University
Greenville, South Carolina

My firm conviction is that much that is happening in the

name of church music is doing little more than to provide the average young person an easy modulation into the world. The contemporary sounds are dissonant. The words so often are meaningless and maddeningly repetitious; and instead of one being made to think of Christ and the glories of the Gospel, he winds up comparing the performer with some Hollywood character or a well-known dispenser of the Nashville sound.

I know that history teaches us that the average human ear is slow to accept change, especially in church music, and that whether we like it or not, much of what we are hearing today will be the accepted music of tomorrow; but if much of what we are hearing becomes the accepted music of tomorrow in our churches, there will certainly be a dearth of real worship in our services.

J. R. Faulkner Formerly
President, Tennessee Temple
  University,
Co-Pastor and Minister of
  Music, Highland Park
  Baptist Church,
  Chattanooga, Tennessee

I believe the basic problem of the music in a number of our churches today is that people do not realize the connection that it has with every other area of our lives. And yet the Word of God says very clearly that what we listen to does make a difference. For instance, Romans 10:17 states: "Faith cometh by hearing, and hearing by the word of God." This means that if a person listens to the Word of God, he will build up his faith. It also means that if a person listens to that which is contrary to the Word of God, it will tear down or destroy his faith. I believe the faith of many people today is being destroyed by the kind of music they are allowing themselves to listen to.

First John 1:1 is also very enlightening on this subject: "That which was from the beginning, which we have heard, which we have seen with our eyes, which we have looked upon, and our hands have handled, of the Word of life." Yes, that which we hear and see are the two things which will affect our lives most strongly. Isn't it interesting that modern educators call this same process which God put in His Word "audio visuals"? And even more interesting is the fact that they put them in the same order that God had them. Therefore, the young person who says, "I can listen to any kind of music I want to," is believing that he can violate the principles of God and not have them affect him.

The strangest thing about this whole situation is that people will accept doctrine and philosophy when it is set to music that they would not accept in any other form. I have been amazed to see existentialism, pragmatism, humanism, and all kinds of other heresies being sung by the young people of fundamental, Bible-believing churches. Somehow the music fools them into accepting all kinds of doctrine that they would not allow into their groups in any other form.

In addition to this, the Word of God teaches us very clearly that when we open our mouths to praise someone, we open our hearts to that person. Psalm 40:3 says, "And he hath put a new song in my mouth, even praise unto our God." The main reason that we open our mouths to sing praise to God, is so that our hearts will be opened to Him. This also means that when we open our mouths to sing the songs of the world, we are also opening our hearts to the world. I believe this explains very clearly why so many young Christians today have such an affinity for the world, and why the world seems to be so attractive to them. They have unwittingly opened their hearts to the world by singing the songs of the world.

I believe our answer is to be sure that our music and the words which are being set to music are Biblical in their basis and philosophy. Both the medium and message must be pure.

Frank Garlock
 Noted authority on music,
 singer, musician, composer

The central question of Christian music is simply with whom are we trying to gain acceptability and who are we trying to emulate? It seems that so much of our music is written to gain acceptability with the worldly crowd that feeds their soul on the music of this world throughout the week. When they come to church they have no appetite for the music of Heaven; so, well-meaning, misguided musicians try to make the message of Heaven more palatable by wrapping it in the music of the world. Many fundamental preachers will allow their music program to do what they would never dream of doing in their preaching; watering it down to make it pleasing and acceptable.

At our church we have tried to build an enthusiastic, evangelistic, alive music program. I want the message of each song to be so prominent that saint and sinner alike can hear the voice of God clearly enough to bring conviction or challenge to do the will of God.

All music has as its primary target either body, soul or spirit. Music aimed at body response is sensual, syncopated and accents rhythm. Music aimed at the soul is situation oriented, heavily flavored with people's problems and much attention placed on the self-life. Music aimed at the spirit of man is inspirational and exalting. This is the kind of music that makes a Christian want to shout to all the world of the greatness and majesty of our wonderful Saviour. It is this kind of music we will sing in Heaven—let's practice now.

Bradley Price, Singer
  Choirmaster, Pastor,
Temple Baptist Church,
Kokomo, Indiana

There are two (2) serious problems facing church music programs today. Both are dangerous and harmful to the work of the Lord. First, most churches have forgotten what the purpose of the music program is for the church. In II Chronicles 5, Solomon has just finished building the Temple. After the sacrifices were made, the singers and musicians took their places at the end of the altar to praise the Lord. When they had sung, the Bible says "that then the house was filled with a cloud," and verse 14, "for the glory of the Lord had filled the house of God." What a song that must have been! The whole purpose is to praise the Lord and prepare. To praise the Lord and prepare the hearts for God's message.

Secondly, many churches are using the "modern" sound as crowd appeal but they have forgotten the dangers of the *"uncertain"* sound. When we cannot distinguish between the sound of the world and the sound of the church, it is not long until we are in like situation to that of Israel in Exodus 32. When the children of Israel had made the golden calf and Moses and Joshua heard their singing, it was different. In verse 17, Joshua thought they were in battle, and verse 18, they did not know what the sound was. How sad that in our churches many people will hear the music and not be able to tell whether it is a "gospel" song or a "golden" hit.

As David said in Psalm 89:15, "Blessed is the people that know the joyful sound: they shall walk, O Lord, in the light of thy countenance." How we need a people who will stand for the right kind of music in our churches, schools and homes.

David F. Price
  Minister of Music,
Berean Baptist Church,
Portsmouth, Ohio

Some other good men to talk to would be Dr. Myron Cedarholm of Maranatha Baptist Bible College, Watertown, Wisconsin; Raymond Spaulding, Minister of Music, Emmanuel Baptist Church, Hartsville, South Carolina; Geddis Allen, Minister of Music, Campus Church (Pensacola Christian College), Pensacola, Florida; and Dr. John Reynolds, Managing Editor, Sword of the Lord, Murfreesboro, Tennessee.

Books that will give details about what is wrong with rock music both out of and in the church are:

The Big Beat—a Rock Blast, by Frank Garlock.
Christian Rock, the New Paganism in the Church, by David Noebel.
What's Wrong With Rock-and-Roll, by Bob Larson.
Rock and the Church, by Bob Larson.
Jungle Madness in Modern Music, by William Ward Ayer.
Can Rock Music Be Sacred? by Frank Garlock.

(NOTE: as the book goes to press it is being stated that Bob Larson has somewhat altered his position about rock and church music. Even if this is true the books listed above are good ones.)

Also, get the taped message of Dr. Frank Garlock on "Rock Music, Can It Be Sacred?" and write Musical Ministries, Post Office Box 6524, Greenville, South Carolina 29606, for good Choral Arrangements for Choirs, etc.

Since so many so-called Christian radio stations have gone down the drain, so many religious bookstores and music stores are selling musical garbage, and so many composers are no longer to be trusted, I would urge you to contact one of the Christian schools mentioned favorably in this chapter for information on where good music can be obtained for your choir and singing groups.

One gospel singer told me the reason why he came out of the regular rock circuit into country music and religious music was because "that is where the *money* is today." I don't care for country music so rarely hear any of it, but one lady came up to me in North Carolina after I had preached on worldly *rock* and said, "Preacher, the lyrics in the modern *country* music are just as dirty as the lyrics in the rock."

Are we to use no music, then, that is contemporary? Does it have to be *old* to be *good*? Not necessarily. But since so much of the contemporary music of today is of the shallow, upbeat, nightclub-performer type one has to be unusually careful.

Is it wrong to use music that is lively, spirited, happy and singable? Not at all. How could you find any music any livelier and happier and more spirited than the following gospel songs:

"The Meeting in the Air"
"I Want to Be There When They Crown Him King of Kings"
"I'm on the Battlefield for My Lord"
"We Shall Rise"
"There's a New Name Written Down"
"Jesus Is Coming to Earth Again, What if It Were Today?"
"Jubilee"
"Springs of Living Water"
"When the Roll Is Called Up Yonder"
"Heaven Came Down and Glory Filled My Soul"
"Sound the Battle Cry"
"The Old Account Was Settled"
"Honey in the Rock"
" 'Tis Marvelous and Wonderful"
"When the Battle's Over"
"I Have Christ in My Heart"
"Since Jesus Came Into My Heart"

All of these songs are lifting, spirited, with good tempo and good rhythm. Yet, if properly sung there will be no "beat" sound, no dance band syncopation to any of them. They are all good spiritual songs with a good message. The same can be said of the gospel choruses mentioned at the end of an earlier chapter.

Our singing *should* be happy and lively. The world has snatched even songs like "Amazing Grace" and made them into rock songs, but we need not abandon the proper singing of them for that reason. And I am certainly not suggesting that you kill your church by using only anthems and "high church" music that are stiff and staid.

Look at a good hymnal like *Soul-Stirring Songs and Hymns*, published by the Sword of the Lord Publishers. You'll find a hymn book packed with great gospel songs and good solid hymns. The same can be said of some other hymnals. But you have to watch out today. Make sure what you're getting. Some modern hymnals have had a "bleeding" and many of the great old gospel hymns and blood songs have been removed.

Stay Out of the Rut

Don't let your music man or song leader get in a rut. In many churches there are a few excellent songs that have been sung over and over again until people sing them in their sleep and they have almost lost their meaning. Even "Love Lifted Me," "Revive Us Again," "At the Cross," "Victory in Jesus," "Blessed Assurance" and "He Lives" can become commonplace if "sung to death" by song leaders who just do not take the time to pray about variety in the song service and search the hymnal for good, fresh songs that have not been used for awhile.

Some of the great (and most beautiful) hymns and songs that I seldom hear in churches might include:

"And Can It Be That I Should Gain?"
"Once for All"
"Just When I Need Him Most"
"Dwelling in Beulah Land"
"The Fight Is On"
"God Will Take Care of You"
"He Leadeth Me"
"He the Pearly Gates Will Open"
"Hold the Fort"
"Jesus Loves Even Me"
"Since I Have Been Redeemed"
"Joy Unspeakable"
"Lead Me Gently Home, Father"
"Saved by the Blood"
"Some Bright Morning"
"The Cleansing Wave"
"The Comforter Has Come"
"The Lily of the Valley"
"The Touch of His Hand on Mine"
"Verily, Verily"
"When the Mists Have Rolled Away"

And in your hymnal (if you have a sound, good one) you probably have some of the most beautiful of all songs to be used for gospel duets, if you're a lover of harmony, such as:

"Ivory Palaces"
"Only Glory By and By"
"All That Thrills My Soul Is Jesus"
"Cleanse Me"
"Close to Thee"
"Day by Day"
"God Leads Us Along"
"He Is So Precious to Me"
"Meet Me There"
"Oh, Say, But I'm Glad"
"Some Golden Daybreak"
"Sweet Will of God"
"The Lights of Home"
"The Pearly White City"
"Under His Wings"

Constantly impress upon your people, and especially upon your musicians and singers, the tremendous importance of the music program in your church for worship, for praise and for encouragement, as well as a testimony of the Gospel to the unsaved who may come into your services.

Tastes vary, of course, but there are plenty of good songs, hymns and choruses to be used without compromising. Even in a church where an appreciation for good music has never been taught it is possible for a pastor and a good song leader to gradually educate the people to love the great songs that magnify the Lord and exalt His truth.

And if you and your church are lovers of quartet singing, there are *good* quartet arrangements of hymns and gospel songs. It does not have to be the honky-tonk beat of the professional performers. You do not have to lower your standards to the "jumping for Jesus" religious jives of the theatrical crowd. Listen to the quartet arrangements of the Old-Fashioned Revival Hour recordings, the Radio Bible Class or the Back-to-the-Bible quartet. Unless they have changed recently these are tastefully and properly done, have plenty of life, and the quartet harmony is beautiful. The same can be said of the young men who go out to sing repesenting such Christian colleges as Tennessee Temple, Bob Jones and Pensacola.

To get an idea of the importance God attaches to singers and a good music program take note of I Chronicles 9:33, "And these are the *singers*, chief of the fathers of the Levites, who remaining in the chambers were free: for they were *employed in that work night and day!"*

Rock in the Church?

Admittedly, much of the sorry, shallow, cheap music used in some churches today is not "rock" music. But strangely, almost unbelievably, the rock beat is creeping in. Pastors will more and more have to face the question: "What is wrong with rock music and the rock beat?"

Jerry Rubin stated, "Hard animal rock energy-beat surged hot through us, the driving rhythm arousing repressed passion. Rock-and-roll marked the beginning of the revolution!"

Dr. David Noebel writes, "Christian rock music is as consistent as 'Christian' pot parties, 'Christian' promiscuity or 'Christian' pornography."

Dr. Ronald Sprangler, chief school medical officer in Nottingham, England, charged that teenage pop music was probably to blame for the mounting obsession with sex.

Bob Larson says, "Christian rock uses the beat and the sound which even the secular world associates with promiscuous sex."

Dr. Noebel continues, "The church is hugging to its bosom, therefore, a form of music that will not turn its worshippers to God, but to the genitals, which is exactly what the old paganism did. . .a form of spiritual fornication." And again, "Christian rock is erotic and not spiritual."

Dr. Noebel in his excellent pamphlet, *Christian Rock, the New Paganism in the Church*, gives twenty-one strong reasons why rock music is wrong whether in the church or out. Get his pamphlet from American Christian College Publication, Post Office Box 42, Tulsa, Oklahoma 74102.

The following statements were given to me by a young man who had made a study of the devastating influence of rock:

> *Cheetah* (magazine) quotes a New York musician as saying, "If the establishment knew what today's popular *music* is saying, not what the *words* are saying, but what the music itself is

saying, they wouldn't just turn their thumb down on it. They'd ban it. They'd smash all the records and arrest anyone who tried to play it."

Frank Zappa of the "Mothers of Invention" (a group):

The loud sounds and bright lights of today are tremendous indoctrination tools; it is possible to modify the human chemical structure with the right combination of frequencies. If the right kind of beat makes you tap your foot, what kind of beat makes you curl your fist and strike?

NOTE: Frank Zappa has a master's degree in music.

Paul Canter of the "Jefferson Airplane":

The new rock music is intended to broaden the generation gap, alienate parents from their children, and prepare young people for revolution."

Plato (in *The Republic*):

"The introduction of a new kind of music should be shunned as imperiling the whole state."

While addressing the legislature in an effort to ban all music with effeminate and licentious natures, Plato said, "It will destroy our nation."

Lenin (dictator in USSR):

"We'll have to change the culture of a nation if they're to go Communistic."

After my message on "The Death of the Rock King" appeared in THE SWORD OF THE LORD following the demise of Elvis Presley, I received many steaming letters from those who wanted to defend him, none, of course, on scriptural grounds. One of these letters, intended to "straighten me out" on rock, at least told us what rock in the church might lead to. Here's what he said, "I first saw and heard all this in the 1930's when my mother practically drug me to the local Holy-Roller Pentecostal Meetings. If you want to hear some 'Rock' go to one of these Spiritual Orgies. THIS is where the late Great Elvis heard it, learned it, and if you do need to judge someone—judge and condemn this influence."

Preacher, let's keep the Devil in musical form out of our churches!

Chapter Eight
Sermons Are for Preaching

"Preach the *word!*" is a command of God to the preacher. If we do not give them the Word of God when they come we have wasted their time and ours. "Faith cometh by hearing, and hearing by the word of God" (Rom. 10:17).

All of the rest of what we are saying in this book is in vain if the preacher does not give the people spiritual food, encouragement, enlightenment and exhortation when they come.

They should have become better people for having been in our services and this will not be so if they have not heard from Heaven. "Is there any word from the *Lord*?" Zedekiah asked in Jeremiah 37:17, and the burdened old prophet of God said, with assurance, "There is"! Paul could not have lived with himself except that he could say, "I am pure from the blood of all men. For I have not shunned to declare unto you all the counsel of God" (Acts 20:26,27). This was the kind of *counseling* Paul did—*"all the counsel of God"*—he threw the *Book* at them!

Prepare Yourself to Preach

Your *sermons* will prepare more easily if your *heart* is prepared. Get *ready* to preach. How? By living a holy life, by spending time in fervent prayer, by saturating your own heart in the Bible even before you think about what you're going to preach to the people.

"He walks with God," a young man said concerning his pastor, Dr. Dino Pedrone, as he drove me from my motel to the Chambersburg, (Pennsylvania) church recently. He was talking about his pastor. Another said concerning this same preacher, "He is a man of vision." Both statements are true. Needless to say this young pastor who has led to Christ and baptized thousands is a man who preaches effectively because he has first given himself to the Lord.

Be a Prime Minister!

They may not think of you as a jolly good fellow, or a great builder, or a fancy talker or a sharp administrator—but whatever else they think, make sure they think of you as a man of God! There is no substitute for that. And there's a wide open market for such men. Be a *prime* minister!

"The man preaches as if God were at his elbow," was said of one Spirit-filled preacher. Never forget that. You are representing *Him*. When you preach the truth it is God's truth. You never have to apologize for that! Give them what God says. "Speak. . .all the words that I command thee to speak unto them; diminish not a word," God told Jeremiah (Jer. 26:2). Notice, "diminish not a *word*"—don't water it down, don't soft-pedal the truth, don't spread cool whip on the cancer of sin.

Now, they didn't like it. They were ready to kill Jeremiah after the sermon and "all the people were gathered against" him, but he had been faithful, and had stayed true to his calling as a preacher. God hasn't called us to win popularity contests—he wants us to be prophets of God!

Right here let me hasten to say that while you are to be fearless and faithful you are not to go into the pulpit roaring like a bull, with a chip on your shoulder, determining to make everybody just as mad as possible. Don't be obnoxious. Don't try to see how nasty you can be. Make sure that they have fallen out with your *message*, not with *you* because you're so stubborn and hard to get along with.

They may say, "Oh, me," instead of "Amen," but as long as they know you told the truth, as from God, and that you did it faithfully because you love them even as you love God, they will usually tolerate the message. We are to preach the burden of the Lord with a burdened heart. "Did not our hearts burn" as He spoke? they asked about our Lord. If *our* hearts burn, so will *theirs*.

Be a Perfectionist in Your Preparation

Spend the time necessary to get a message from God, prepare and arrange it to make it effective, cry over it, pray over it, pad it with good illustrations, garnish it well with barbs that will stick and open the wounds of sin. Then be sure you have lubricated it so with the balm of Gilead that the healing transformation of God's grace and the cleansing of His blood will bring about the complete cure as the message comes to a close.

I know it is possible to get a message so correct, so polished, so "finished" and precise, that it will be "sounding brass" and "tinkling cymbal" when it is delivered. However, this should be no excuse for our laziness. It is possible to prepare a good, well-outlined, clear, adequately-illustrated message and still have the liberty of the Spirit and the power of God in preaching it.

It is even possible to have a beautiful and poetic message and still have power along with the oratory. Thomas DeWitt Talmage, R. G. Lee, Bob Jones, Sr., and B. R. Lakin are a proof of that.

But I wouldn't try to be flowery or oratorical if you are not naturally so. And most successful preachers have become so by practice, experience and maturity. You do not get these out of a book. Be natural, be genuine, be sincere, and God will mold you into the style of a preacher He wants you to be.

But study *words* along the way. Read much. Read the sermons of good preachers. Wallow in Spurgeon, Guthrie, Meyer. Learn how to use words. "A word fitly spoken is like apples of gold in pictures of silver" (Prov. 25:11). If you please your hearers with the way the message is delivered, they may more readily accept the sharp thrust of the truth they have heard.

Listen to your own tapes sometimes. You'll find your voice is not as pleasing as you imagined, your delivery not so profound, your illustrations not so compelling, your outline not as magnificent as you thought. Then as you weep and pray and wait before God, you may do better the next time you enter the study to prepare for the pulpit.

Be preparing the messages all week. Don't wait until the last minute—not even until the last day or two before Sunday, if you can help it. Emergencies do arise, of course, but learn to get the jump on them. You can count on God to fill your mouth with something left-over-from-before if it really is a dire emergency, but not if you just got "busy here and there" or were too lazy and playful to get with it earlier in the week.

If you make a mistake, it is not the end of the world. Others have done so before you. Learn to laugh at yourself and don't be touchy about it if other people do. They might even learn that you're a human being, after all.

Don't try to preach another man's sermons word for word but do allow yourself to get ideas and help from other good preachers. Most of us would not have had any idea where to get sermons when we began preaching, if it had not been for THE SWORD OF THE LORD or some other good sermon paper. A popular radio preacher in Florida was heard one Sunday reading a message by J. Frank Norris which we had just read in a book the night before! A noted Bible Conference speaker brought one of the best messages I'd ever heard from the life of David and later I read the message (almost as delivered) in an old book of sermons by Talmage! At least put your own illustrations, style and arrangement into it if you're going to take another man's message and use it. As soon as you're out of the ministerial nursery you ought to be building your own messages. I'll admit that some of the messages I preached in my earlier days just seemed to fit my style so well that at this point (many years later) I'm not always certain which ones were mine and which were anothers. So I may still get embarrassed one of these days!

I have seen some of R. A. Torrey in George W. Truett. Sam Jones shows up a good bit in the preaching of Billy Sunday. Talmage frequently appears in the sermons of Robert G. Lee. So don't feel bad about getting help from others.

I have been helped by the logic of Barnhouse, the clarity of M. R. DeHaan, the wit of Havner, the tenderness of Charles Fuller, the plainness of John R. Rice, the simplicity of Bob Jones, Sr., the dynamic of Lee Roberson, the eloquence of R. G. Lee, the alliterative style of Appelman. So can we really say that any sermon is entirely our own?

Memorize Much of the Bible

There is nothing that will help you in Bible preaching any more than having memorized great portions of Scripture. I learned 1500 verses of Scripture in three years after I surrendered my life to Christ. And when I started I didn't even plan to be a preacher! When you can snatch hundreds of verses from your memory without having to look them all up, it will save you time, it will saturate your messages with truth, it will bless the people, and it will give luster and authority to everything you say. Turn cards over in your pocket constantly with verses typed out on them. You'll be amazed at how many will later turn out to be sermon outlines.

Not only Scripture, it will help your preaching to memorize good poems, sharp quotations, pertinent illustrations. Study words and study people. Read much. Go soul winning. Stay red hot for God during the week and you will preach hotter sermons on Sunday.

Preach every time you get a chance to preach. Even if it is just a handful of people at the rest home, the jail house, or the school Bible club, every time you preach you get some more exercise in this wonderful art. Take advantage of small opportunities and God will open up larger opportunities.

Use alliteration if it works out but don't spend all day trying to strain out an alliterative outline just for the sake of having a polished-looking message.

Titles Help

Use good *titles* for your message if God gives you one. But, if you know what you're going to preach, go ahead and develop it— the title may come in the eleventh hour.

Titles are good for use in advertising your messages. Dr. Lee preached on "The World's Greatest Love Story." His text was John 3:16. Talmage had a sermon on "The Sin of Borrowing Trouble" from the text, "Sufficient unto the day is the evil thereof." When I would preach on the rapture back about the time the astronauts were first scampering around in space, I called my message, "The Space Walk in the Bible."

A message on retribution I named "The Boomerang."

For sowing and reaping, how about "The Backlash of Sin"?

My award-winning message on procrastination was one from the words of Pharaoh who cried, "Tomorrow." People do not always remember my name or my face but they remember the title of the message, "One More Night With the Frogs!"

"How to" sermons are popular. I just saw one recently in THE SWORD OF THE LORD by Torrey on "How to Be Unspeakably Happy." Dr. Jack Hyles is famous for his messages on "How to Win Souls." Who of us have not preached on "How to Have a Happy Home"? People are interested in "How to Understand the Bible," "How to Be Spirit-Filled," "How to Know the Will of God." You'd better be sure you really find out what the Bible teaches on these subjects unless you have lived long enough to have found out by experience.

Some of my most effective messages were from great tragedies and current events that took place right around us. So many of these open the door to the unfolding of Bible truth. Sermons like these draw crowds—and they are easy to advertise. They keep people interested.

"What Killed Marilyn Monroe" was the topic of my Sunday night message shortly after the death of the Hollywood sex goddess by an overdose. That was the title—my subject was *sin*!

"The Crime of the Century, or The Man Who Was Born to Raise Hell" was the topic of my sermon after Richard Speck, the wino, killed eight nurses in Chicago in a bloody orgy. The sermon was on drink, sin, lust and judgment.

"The Body in the Deep Freeze" made a good sermon subject after an Arizona "scientist" assured us he was going to freeze someone and bring him back to life many years hence. This made possible a good exposition on death and afterwards.

"Hurricane Faith" was the name of one of the storms lashing Southern shores. How easy to turn that one into a message on the power of faith in our lives.

"P.O.W.'s Home at Last" was a message on deliverance from the prison house of condemnation. But it was timely and up to date.

"Skimpy Skirts and Hippie Hair" (later made into a book) dealt with the wierd, mod fashions that invaded our society in the early seventies, and what the Bible says about it. The book is still opening the eyes of people.

"The Fatal Fall of the Silver Bridge" was a message on the tragedy in the Ohio River just before Christmas one year. God used this warning about sudden death.

"How to Know God Is Not Dead" attracted attention after certain religionists decided to celebrate the decease of the Almighty.

These messages were a blessing when preached and many of them later appeared in print. So the work and research and study for them was worth while!

Plan and Use Series of Sermons

Especially for Sunday night interest I found the use of a sermon series very helpful. Great Texts of Scripture, Bible Heroes, Strange Texts, Epitaphs of the Bible, Sermons on the Second Coming, How Bible Prayers Were Answered, Women of the Bible, Christ in Prophecy, Mysteries From the Bible, Courtship and Marriage, The Victorious Life, Stories of Success, Nighttime Tragedies—these compose just a few of the series of messages I preached when in the pastorate.

Usually a series for one month or six weeks will suffice. Seldom would I go on to or beyond two months in a series lest the people become weary and lose interest.

Expository preaching—preaching through a book in the Bible—is another way of keeping things going, either on Sunday morning or Sunday night, and you may be able to go longer than two months on such a series. This is also true for Wednesday night studies. But watch your people. If the crowds begin to diminish and interest lags, I would abandon or postpone the series and move over into greener pastures. You *ought* to do *some* expository preaching, however. It will do you a lot of good as well as help your listeners, if you study and dig it out well. The use of good commentaries will help on this. Books of sermons by

Spurgeon and others who squeeze the juice out of Scripture portions will come in mighty handy here.

One good thing about expository preaching is that you already know where your subject matter will be for the next Sunday night and do not have to spend most of the week trying to decide what to preach on. Even with this type of sermon, though, I'd be careful to find a highlight, discover what you're attempting to do in this message, and find a good title for each message, too, if you can. Give a brief preview of the next Sunday night topic. Whet their appetites. Don't let interest wane. Keep your own heart excited about it. If you're not thrilled with what you're unearthing in the treasure house of the Bible, your listeners are not going to be.

Study Where It Is Quiet

Get away from noise and distractions. Few pastors can produce much of anything in a church office with the secretaries buzzing around and the phone ringing. Get your wife and/or secretary to realize how important this study time is for you and train them to help you guard it with their lives.

Make notes as you go. Keep track of things. Mark illustrations. Underscore and clip. File things properly. You may set aside and file more illustrations than you'll use for next Sunday but it is good to have too much material than not enough. I was still reducing excess material and eliminating illustrations at 10:50 on Sunday morning. Many of those illustrations will go better the *following* Sunday. Don't try to say everything you know just because you had planned to use it now. It will keep. You can use it later unless the Lord comes first. Then I have a good idea Heaven will do just as well without it, anyway.

Pray as you go in your study. Never cease to be conscious of the Lord as you work on your message. "Except the Lord build the house [or the sermon], they labour in vain that build it."

Get up and walk around sometimes while you're studying. Get some fresh air, gulp down some clear, cold water, keep the cobwebs out of your brain. If you get too groggy and sleepy even a 10- or 15-minute nap stretched out prone on the carpet may bring you back to life again. Better to sleep a few minutes to stay fresh during the preparation than to have the congregation fall asleep during the delivery. I worked for hours in my study on Saturdays. I expect several of my Sunday sermons were saved because I walked around every hour or two changing the hose locations on my lawn sprinklers. Just that little bit of fresh air and exercise brought me back to my study chomping at the bits and ready to go again.

Use Your Dictionary and....

Look up words. Watch out for correct pronunciation. Use a self-pronouncing Bible. Observe. Make notes. A good Webster's unabridged dictionary, a Bible dictionary, your concordance, Roget's Thesaurus of words and phrases—all of these are important to the preacher and his sermon. Even a Rhyming Dictionary I have found helpful. Any good bookstore should carry these.

U. S. News and World Report and other news magazines will help when you are preparing messages on events in the news and/or prophetic themes. You will also get some good illustrations from the daily paper. Items I use in my column for THE SWORD OF THE LORD come from the daily news around us. Some city newspapers are better than others for the news. *The Chicago Tribune,* the *Atlanta Constitution,* the *New York Times,* the *Wall Street Journal,* Washington papers, the *Cleveland Plain Dealer,* the *Tampa Tribune—these are some of the papers that seem to me to be newsiest.*

For illustrations, use not only the papers and news magazines but such Christian papers as THE SWORD OF THE LORD and other spiritual papers and magazines.

Our Daily Bread from the Radio Bible Class, Box 22, Grand Rapids, Michigan 49555, will have a lot of good anecdotes but so many of our fundamental churches use this for the devotions of their people now that they may appear secondhand to many of the people if you use them much. There are good books of illustrations, of course, but I would not use too many of these, some of which are from the distant past, unless they are tremendous illustrations. Events from right around us today may be more pertinent, and they will be fresher.

The Bible, of course, is full of illustrations and the more familiar you become with it the more of these choice morsels will jump out at you. And remember, the Bible is its own best commentary.

Develop Your Terminal Facilities

Don't be so bound to your message that you cannot whack some of it off if you see that it is becoming abnormally long. It is a good thing, indeed, to think ahead of time about what part of this sermon is really dispensible. (You may want to bury it on the spot!)

Someone has said that a "Reverend" Jones became known as the *Neverend* Jones.

The late Senator Hubert Humphrey was known for his long-windedness. His wife reminded him, "You know, your speeches don't have to be eternal to be immortal!" That's a good thing for the preacher to remember. It is better to quit when they wish you would go on than to go on when they wish you would quit.

Some who have the least to say talk on the longest. In fact, it is true that you may have to study longer to develop a short message than to come up with a long one.

Spend time in preparation. Either "rise up early" or burn the midnight oil, whichever suits you best, but an unprepared preacher need not wonder if his congregation soon wearies and wanders off to find pasture elsewhere. If you spend the time necessary to prepare well, you'll not have to be so concerned with having a message that is too long or too short.

"Be Instant, in Season, Out of Season"

This is what Paul, that master preacher, commanded. Preach the *Word,* remembering that all of the Gospel is in the Word but not all of the Word is in the Gospel. Many congregations say that all they hear from their pastor is the "Gospel," meaning that they do not really get fed on many of the meaty and strengthening truths of the Bible. Some pastors evidently feel that they are safe if they are known as "gospel preachers," and glory in the fact that we just preach "Christ and Him crucified."

Now, while Paul told us to "preach Christ and Him crucified" he did not say that was *all* we were to preach! "I determined not to know any thing among you but" did not mean that he ignored the rest of the Bible. He just used all of the Bible to preach Christ. And, by the way, it *takes* all of the Bible to exalt Him!

Preach the whole counsel of God. "Go to the pulpit with your suitcase packed" was the advice given by an old preacher to one of our pastors. In other words, don't be intimidated. Don't be afraid to preach the truth. Don't look the congregation over to see who's there before deciding to preach against sin. They all need it! "Be not afraid of their faces: for I am with thee to deliver thee, saith the Lord" (Jer. 1:8).

"Cry aloud, spare not, lift up thy voice like a trumpet, and shew my people their transgression, and the house of Jacob their sins," Isaiah was told by the Lord (Isa. 58:1). Preach against sin. "*Their* sin," not just the sins of Ezekiel's or Isaiah's day. Some pastors who think they really preach against sin simply hit the liquor business a glancing blow once in a while or raise their voices occasionally about gambling or organized crime.

Since few of your members are in the liquor business, probably, and since it is likely that none of them are engaged in organized crime, you have missed the boat entirely. "Shew my people their transgression": lust, greed, covetousness, envy, jealousy, gossip, profanity, slander, pride, worldliness, immodesty—these are just a few of the sins of His people.

God's people need to "turn from *their* wicked ways" before God can bring revival and heal our land (II Chron. 7:14). We have long-haired males in the choirs, taking the offering and working with the young people in some of our churches today simply because a lot of preachers were sissies when it came to crying out against this feminine trait and worldly addiction back when the Devil's crowd first popularized it. The same thing can be said for jazzy contemporary music, immodest fashions on the girls, women members coming to church in slacks and jeans, church members who frequently go to the theater or dances, deacons who smoke, and a lot of other worldly compromises. People are human and all of them have a deceitful and wicked heart by nature (Jer. 17:9), so Christians are just not going to clean up, separate their lives and live above the world unless we preach against sin and instruct them in righteousness!

You can get plenty of help on these subjects by keeping your tract rack and lobby tables full of good literature. Be sure your Sunday school teachers have high standards, too, as well as your youth workers. Gradually, you can grow a good spiritual congregation who will fight for your convictions because they have become *their* convictions, too. Have in good evangelists who preach the truth and your people will soon learn you are not the only "nut" in the country. From papers and magazines like THE SWORD OF THE LORD and others you can indoctrinate first your own heart and then the hearts of the people. Of course, the Bible is the best book on separation and Christian living in print. Make much of the great truths of Scripture. Be sure you memorize such verses as I John 2:15-17; James 4:3,4; Galatians 1:4; II Corinthians 6:14-17; II Corinthians 7:1; Galatians 5:16; Ephesians 5:15-18; Ephesians 6:12; Philippians 3:18,19; Colossians 3:1-6; I Thessalonians 5:22; Titus 2:12-14. They may not take to your Bible preaching against sin just because you say it, but it is mighty hard for honest people to argue with Bible verses like these.

Now, of course, make sure that you preach the truth in *love*. Don't rant and rave, but do preach passionately with fervent love for God and the people, "Serving the Lord with all humility of mind, and with many tears, and temptations" (Acts 20:19).

Keep your equilibrium, maintain your own steadfastness, be consistent, "Be instant in season, out of season." In your patience, possess your soul. Use common sense in dealing with your people. Keep their confidences. Use illustrations both from the Bible and from life around you about what sin does to people and they will more readily accept your honest and heartfelt preaching against sin.

Maintain a sense of humor. Smile. Balance your preaching against sin with helpful messages on the Christian life. Encourage and comfort your people, too. Just negative preaching will boomerang on you. We are to be separate *from* the world but we are to be separated *unto* the Gospel of God (Rom. 1:1).

Get your members working for the Lord and winning souls and most of their worldly habits will fall off like leaches off a sick dog when you pump him full of medicine.

Not to preach against sin is to disobey God, to dishonor and neglect much of the Bible, to weaken the influence of the church, to defeat the spiritual lives of your people and to make the next pastor's work much harder after you are gone. Many a man has had an uphill battle and often a church split because he comes in and preaches the truth of the Word where his predecessor had refused to preach against sin and lead his people into separated Christian living.

"Be not afraid of their faces," but don't go around with a chip on your shoulder, either, expecting the worst out of the people you pastor. If you straighten them out in the flesh they'll be more warped than ever! Do preach the Word, reprove, rebuke, exhort with all longsuffering and doctrine. (See II Timothy 4:2.) Let the *Bible* straighten them out!

Do Some Character Preaching

Preaching on the characters of the Bible will make it possible for you to say many things to your people from the lives of others. Clarence Edward Macartney was a master at this kind of preaching. He has many books of sermons on the men and women of the Bible. Get them. Your people will see the sin of adultery in the life of David, pride in Saul, worldliness in Jezebel, compromise in Lot, inconsistency in Samson, hatred in Cain, arrogance in Haman, covetousness in Gehazi.

On the other hand, the characters of the Bible will teach many positive lessons as they behold patience in Job, wisdom in Solomon, obedience in Abraham, godliness in Enoch, faithfulness in Noah, dedication in Esther, industry in Nehemiah, purity in Joseph, courage in Daniel, faith in David, boldness in Elijah!

In addition to Macartney, you will find helpful books on Bible characters by Massee, Baxter, Rice and Lockyer, among others.

Poetry in Sermons

How much should poetry be used in sermons? It depends on the sermon, the preacher and the kind of poetry. Poems, just to say the message had a poem in it, will probably be of little effect. The poem should be used to drive home a point, to give luster to what is being said, to climax the sermon or a certain part of it— never just to let the people know how many poems you happen to know.

Some preachers can memorize and quote poems with great feeling and emphasis. Many can say them only in a sing-song manner. A few preachers can read them with real blessing and success. Others read poorly and the poem would be better off left out entirely.

Then a poem should be used appropriately. Dr. Walter Hughes is remembered by many for his use of a long epic poem about a little girl who caught a street car thinking she was on the railway to Heaven and that Jesus had paid her fare. He used the poem with much expression and feeling to illustrate his great sermons on salvation.

"The Touch of the Master's Hand" I have used with results in preaching on surrender and the will of God. "I Met the Master Face to Face" is a good one in a sermon (or to finish one) for young people on consecration. Dr. George W. Truett was a master at fitting a good poem into the right spot. Many of Dr. R. G. Lee's messages were interspersed with appropriate poems in just the right places. Study how those men used poetry effectively. Louis Banks and W. L. Watkinson handled poetry well if you can find secondhand books by these old masters.

One would need another chapter or perhaps even another book to fully go into the use of poems and to give many of the poems themselves. If you do plan to use poetry, it would be advisable to read poems until you find it easy to do so. Practice putting expression in the right place. Memorize them well and then repeat them until you can say them with real feeling and with proper expression. Some people do not like poetry anyway, and will not be impressed at all unless the poems really say something and unless they fit into the message so well and are quoted with such intense feeling and expression that they really pack a wallop when they are used.

The poems of Frances Ridley Havergal, Martha Snell Nicholson and Annie Johnson Flint are among some of the best to use in sermons. The poetry in some of the hymns from our hymnals is excellent for quotation. Edgar A. Guest wrote some that have a good message and are encouraging. The songs of the Wesleys, Fanny Crosby, Isaac Watts, John Newton and B. B. McKinney have poems that lend themselves readily to quotation in sermons. The black poet, Paul Lawrence Dunbar, wrote some good ones. Some of those by Lowell and Longfellow are excellent for this.

James Gilchrist Lawson has an excellent book of *Best Known Religious Poems.* Dr. John R. Rice and the Sword have compiled some excellent books of poems, many of which are good ones to memorize and use. Some of the best hymns for memorizing will be found in the book, *Soul-Stirring Songs & Hymns,* published by the Sword of the Lord, Box 1099, Murfreesboro, Tennessee 37133.

The Delivery of the Sermon

There's a man in the world who is never turned down
    Wherever he chances to stray;
He gets the glad hands in the populous town,
    Or out where the farmers make hay;

He is greeted with pleasure on deserts of sand,
    Or deep in the aisles of the woods;
Wherever he goes there's the welcoming hand
    For the man who delivers the goods!

—Author Unknown

Deliver the goods and there will always be a congregation that wants to hear you preach. No matter how much you know and how studiously you prepare it, the spiritual meal still has to be served up!

Learn to stand on your own two feet and slug it out with the Devil. Stay close enough to your microphone that they get all you say. Some preachers lower their voices at just the wrong time and the "punch line" is lost. Don't rear back so far or skip around on the platform so much that the thrust of what you say never reaches your listeners. I've been in meetings where it was evident people were straining to hear what the preacher had to say. In other meetings, I've seen people almost shielding their ears and flinching as the message was thundered at them with such volume and with such intermittent hollers and screams that they were soon exhausted from dodging the verbal assault upon their ears.

Be careful not to develop habits that take the minds of your people off what you are saying. It is terribly easy for a preacher to get into mannerisms that offend. Rubbing your nose, adjusting your glasses, pounding the pulpit, twitching your ear, scratching your head, clearing your throat, all of these may be necessary sometime, but any of them can become distressing and distracting if done constantly. I am so grateful for a wife who kindly lets me know if I begin to get into any of these obnoxious habits. You very likely will develop some kind of "characteristic" unless your wife or some trusted critic keeps you straight.

I have prayed before many a sermon that the Lord would not let me do anything to make the people think of me instead of the sermon; also, that I would not say something foolish by mistake. Be sure and read Spurgeon's *Lectures to His Students* to really appreciate this matter of gestures, habits and mannerisms.

Outline your message for effective delivery. This gives the listeners some pegs along the way to hang your points on. It also makes it easier for you to keep track of what you are saying. But don't make your outline so long or so cluttered that it merely adds to the confusion. If you have twenty points to emphasize, it probably will be better to whittle them down somewhat and fit about three-fourths of them under four or five headings. They'll remember the four points better and still get the impact of the other sixteen things you wanted to tell them!

Thumping the pulpit can especially be hurtful if you have a microphone built into it or sitting on it. People will be flinching not so much from what you say as from the "thump" that accompanies it to their ears. Vance Havner has suggested that many preachers hit the pulpit the hardest when they have the least to say.

Repeating yourself too often is another boring habit to get into. Some points need to be re-emphasized but don't overdo it. On the other hand, if you use characters in the Bible or different verses along the same subject to say it for you in a variety of ways, you have driven your point home effectively.

Let the use of your hands be a natural thing in your preaching. To constantly wave your arms, point your finger or brace yourself on the pulpit like you are doing push-ups will soon become tiresome to the congregation. Yet, there is a proper use of the hands which will quite naturally illustrate your points as you go. To stretch out one hand (or even both) sometimes, with the palm upward is a complement to "Come unto me, all ye who labour and are heavy laden." To gesture downward vigorously may well accompany, "Depart from me, ye cursed." When describing the storm on Galilee, it is natural to look up into the clouds and you may have your listeners examining the ceiling for streaks of lightening, too. When quoting, "As far as the east is from the west, so far hath he removed our transgressions from us," it is easily demonstrated with a sweeping movement of the hands in those directions.

When not using the hands naturally in this fashion, it is probably best to keep them in front of you on the pulpit or simply at your side to avoid getting into the habit of jingling keys, wadding up your handkerchief or some other bothersome custom.

There are a few men who seem able to use certain gestures as their own trademark. Dr. Bob Jones, Sr., cupping his hand to his mouth when he wanted to clinch a point, Billy Sunday picking up a chair as if to clobber the Devil, Dr. John R. Rice tilting his head in your direction as if he could read your soul by looking between his glasses and that lock of hair, Jesse Hendley preaching Hell out of the side of his mouth. If something like this becomes you and can be used on occasion for God's glory, well and good. But, I'd be sure that it comes naturally for you and is not something theatrical that may simply cater to the flesh. It is probably best not to try to cultivate gestures.

Put *fire* in your sermon. There is no substitute for the breath of God—for the power of the Holy Spirit. "Who maketh. . .his ministers a flame of fire." Someone has suggested that if you cannot get fire into the sermon, it is best to put the sermon into the fire! Seek God's power afresh for every message. John Knox cried, "Oh, God, give me Scotland or I die!" And God almost gave him Scotland!

Look at your people when you preach to them. Eye contact is important. Make each member or visitor feel that you know they are there and are preaching to them. Make it a point to look around at different parts of the auditorium even if you are not conscious of who is there at all. The young people will be less likely to misbehave if the pastor's eyes travel in their direction every little bit. If you look in one direction all the time, the snoozers will get into another part of the building so they can sleep without being noticed or disturbed. If you preach to the ceiling or the floor, it will be no wonder if your listeners conclude that you certainly did not mean *them* when you were calling sinners to repentance.

Stand up straight. Don't slouch, loll, droop or lean on the pulpit. You are an ambassador for Christ. Your posture should match the dignity of and the importance of your message. Don't be stiff like a statue, but do stand erect as one who speaks with authority because you speak for God.

And remember, what people know about your life outside of the pulpit will largely determine their respect for you *in* the pulpit. One man who did not like the message of D. L. Moody, nevertheless said, "I like to hear him for he is the most desperately-in-earnest man I've ever known."

The Devil has a hard time stopping an humble man. Our pulpit prowess may well contribute to pride if we're not careful. Remember that humility and spirituality go hand in hand.

"Humble yourselves. . .under the mighty hand of God, that he may exalt you in due time" (I Pet. 5:6). If we take care of the preaching and praying, God will take care of our praise and promotion.

And, as we've said before in other chapters: Make sure the sound is right and make sure the air is right. If people do not hear you loudly, you will not be effective. And if the air is too cold, too hot or too polluted, many people will be thinking not of what you are saying but of their own discomfort.

To help you as a preacher, I would suggest the following books:

The Preacher and His Preaching, W. B. Riley.
How to Improve Your Preaching, Bob Jones (especially good on voice and speech).
Preaching Without Notes, C. E. Macartney.
We Prepare and Preach, C. S. Roddy (Moody Press).
How to Work for Christ, and *How to Bring Men to Christ,* R. A. Torrey.
Why Our Churches Do Not Win Souls, John R. Rice.
Spurgeon's Lectures to His Students.

Chapter Nine

How to Get Them Down the Aisle
and What to Do Next

The invitation should be given with the earnestness of a lawyer pleading for the life of his client or a fireman snatching a child from the flames of a burning home. It should be presented intelligently and sanely—yet with such fervor and heartfelt concern that no listener can doubt the sincerity of the preacher or the urgency of the Lord's call to the sinner.

Of course, the invitation may be varied, depending upon the type of the message given and the people who compose the congregation. One would not grab the microphone and cry for sinners to repent and escape the wrath to come after speaking to his faithful saints at the midweek prayer service. Too often, though, I fear, the opposite mistake is made: that of appealing to the congregation in general for various "decisions" while lost souls are sitting there under conviction and "ready for the reaping." This would especially be true in the Sunday services.

On Sunday morning, the pastor is torn in many directions. There are lost people present who need to be saved. There are backslidden folk who need to be brought back to fellowship. There are unaffiliated people who ought to "line up" in the church and get busy for God. There are people who need to make a decision to start tithing and supporting the work. There are Christians doing little for God who should be challenged to start winning souls! How do you work on all of them at once? It is not easy.

First, in giving a successful and effective invitation, make sure that your people understand that this is the most important part of the entire service. Dr. R. G. Lee has been quoted as reminding listeners that they would not want him to rush into the operating room while a surgeon was performing surgery on their dearest loved one and jar the arm of that doctor. Even so, members of his congregation were to understand that this delicate surgery-of-the-soul at the invitation was most sacred and serious and not to be "jarred" or distracted by noise, confusion, interruption or any other bungling.

People must be trained to realize that the invitation time is no time for putting on coats, fixing hair, gathering up Bibles, whispering to loved ones or gathering up the kids for a hasty exit. This (the invitation) time is sacred, vital, crucial. This is the climax of what all of the Sunday school and preaching effort has been about for that day.

The invitation is to the church and preacher what the drawing of the net is to the professional fisherman. It is his life work, his superb pleasure, his agony and his ecstasy. At the invitation, we enter into some of the fellowship of the sufferings of Christ. Here our people are to yearn, pray and plead with God for souls while the preacher pleads with men for God.

One noted British preacher and writer has stated (in a book for preachers I've just finished reading) that he does not believe in nor practice the public invitation! Yet, while I am aware of the fact that sometimes the invitation is abused, what better time to plead for the souls of men than immediately after the preacher has presented his case and poured out his very soul?

Yes, carefully, prayerfully and very intelligently the invitation should be given. Christians are more likely to decide on the spot to resolve to win souls and live a dedicated life than they are when they get home and someone has flipped on the television set while others in the household are dishing up refreshments from the galley.

Sinners are much more likely to make a decision then and there in the sacredness of the church, among Christian people, after a compassionate message, than they are after going out into a cold, critical and carnal world.

Second, be sure that your workers are also trained to give their best at this crucial time. Piano players and organists should be immediately available, near their instruments, not sitting in the back of the auditorium or jammed in with their friends in the middle of a pew. In far too many churches, the musicians make a grand parade down to the instrument when the pastor winds up his sermon and the invitation is about to begin.

The musicians should have a seat right near their instruments so they can quietly and inconspicuously slip into their places as the pastor has people bow for prayer before the invitation. If the choir and musicians do go down from the platform for the sermon, say on Wednesday or perhaps even on Sunday night (not always a good idea), then be sure the musicians sit near the front and as near their instruments as possible so they can move quickly into place without distraction. If the pianist has a steady boyfriend she likes to sit with, and the organist is married, then let the men come down and sit with them near the front rather than your musicians parading back through the throng.

Personal workers should be situated in such a way that they can see the pastor and know immediately when he needs them at the front. Some personal workers have to be dragged out for service when they could have been "watching" and praying. It is a good idea for the personal worker to be at the front almost as soon as the prospective convert is. Some pastors prefer to have some of the personal workers start making their way to the front as soon as the invitation song begins. This way they are there immediately, ready for service as the pastor needs them. These will, of course, be workers already chosen and trained by the pastor for this important work.

Third, keep the flow to the front. One advantage of the personal workers' starting to move at the beginning of the invitation is that, psychologically, the movement is already right and sinners find it quite easy just to move out into the flow of those who are going forward to deal with others. That way the sinner cannot feel that he is all alone and that every eye in the congregation is upon him. He may even think that some of those going forward are making the decision he should be making and his resolve to go forward may be increased and made easier.

It is always best to keep any movement toward the front. For this reason, it is best to have Christians who come for rededication or for some other reason to stay at the front for the closing prayer. If they move back to their pews after a prayer, there is confusion, the psychology is bad and some people begin to watch the people who are going back to their seats (perhaps even with a "wonder what she's been up to" attitude!) instead of praying and helping in the invitation.

Of course, when the Holy Spirit is working mightily and there is great conviction and good response, it may be wise to let a new convert or a newly-reclaimed backslider go back into the congregation if they're going back to get a lost loved one or backslidden friend to come forward, too. Be sensitive to the leading of the Spirit in this. Ordinarily, though, it is best to keep all of the traffic moving toward the altar.

Fourth, be sure your song leader is at your side as the invitation starts—not parading down from the back or climbing in from the wings as I've seen some of them do. He should have a hymn picked out for the invitation unless the pastor has instructed him otherwise. Many preachers prefer to pick their own invitation songs. Usually, this is best unless you have an unusually wise and spiritual music man who is so "in the Spirit" that he can almost read the pastor's mind in such cases. The leader will have the hymnbook open at the right number so the pastor can tell the people what page to turn to. This makes it unnecessary for the music man to say anything at that critical time. In some cases, the pastor has been pleading for souls with a burdened voice and suddenly the song leader boisterously blurts out, "For our invitation tonight, please turn to page four hundred and thirty-six in your red hymnal. That's four hundred and thirty-six. Everyone sing out on this good song!" By that time, the sinners are finding consolation in their hymnbooks and watching the song leader instead of the man of God who has brought God's Word to them. Thus, they may get sidetracked. The less said the better at invitation time, especially by anyone other than the man who has brought the message.

Don't let the song leader change hymns during the invitation. If a change is to be made the pastor (or whoever has been preaching) will be the one to make such a decision. Sometimes, when no one is moving on "Just As I Am," you might find it best to switch to "Almost Persuaded" or "Where He Leads Me I Will Follow." But the preacher should make the decision on the switch.

Fifth, the ushers should be alert to keeping everything as orderly and quiet as possible at the doors during the invitation. Sometimes ushers will get up as the invitation begins, swing the doors open, stack up hymnals, put away their bulletins, even (foolishly) let children or others in to find their parents or friends. This should never be. This is surgery time and everything should be centered on the decisions that are to be made down at that altar.

Choir members should be very reverent also at this critical time. They should never be putting on their wraps or whispering to others at the invitation. Some pastors find it best to have the choir do all of the singing on the invitation. In this way, sinners do not have to look up a song number, they are not distracted and they have no hymnal to "hang onto" when they should be coming forward.

Sixth: Be sure your decision cards and sharp pencils are at the front where they are immediately accessible to the personal workers. The clerk or personal workers should not have to thrash around looking for cards. In a larger church, it is best to have one leader over the personal workers to designate who is to help who and to see to it that each personal worker has decision cards, perhaps on a clipboard. A good tract for new converts should be available or better still a booklet on the new Christian life and how to live it. (The author's *Truth About the Christian Life* is a good one for this.)

Seventh: It is usually best to begin the invitation with an appeal to the unsaved. Then after two or three verses of the hymn, one can appeal to Christians who need to make decisions. If the pastor or evangelist knows that most of the people are already professing Christians, he may want to begin the appeal to them after the first or second verse. As long as people are coming forward on one good hymn, I would stick to the same hymn. If, after two or three verses are sung, no one is moving, it is sometimes best to change to another hymn. After one or two verses, if no one is coming forward, I frequently have the people bow their heads to sing softly on the next verse, urging the people to pray, and in some cases reminding the Christians that they may need to speak a tender word of encouragement to that lost loved one or friend, offering to walk down the aisle with him or her. Most people are not embarrassed if someone gently speaks to them while heads are bowed and people are praying. I would keep on singing as long as people are coming forward. If no one comes after several verses are sung, and you feel you have delivered your soul and done all you can, then there is nothing to do but leave the rest up to God and conclude the invitation. Even then you can remind the people that if they would like to stay behind to talk about it that you would be happy to stay and help them.

Eighth: Be sure the people are not confused about what the invitation is for. Make it plain that they are coming to receive Christ or to confess Him publicly if they already have been saved. Remind would-be converts that if they do not fully understand what to do that you have trained personal workers all ready with an open Bible to help them. If your invitation is for church membership, be sure and let them know exactly what you want them to do. If your appeal is for Christians to come to get rid of their backslidings or to commit themselves to become soul winners, be sure and say just what you want them to do. Some people are confused about what the preacher means by his multiple invitations.

Ninth: Be sure the people are personally dealt with and that no one is neglected. Usually, they can be helped right there at the altar by a worker who knows what he or she is doing. If there is a problem case and the person needs a good bit of help or has many questions, it is usually best to have your worker take them into a small adjoining room for further assistance and prayer. Some pastors prefer to use such "inquiry rooms" for all of their personal work instead of having it done at the altar. However, if this is done, I'd be sure the personal worker leads the person to an immediate decision for Christ, gives them assurance and brings them back to the front, if possible, before the service is over. In this way, the pastor can question the new convert, present his or her name, and have the people rejoice with them over their decision. If the person has not been brought into full assurance in time for this, then he or she should be presented at the next service. This gives great encouragement to the people, it strengthens the new convert, and it makes it easier for someone else to make a similar decision.

Most people who come forward under conviction after a plain gospel message delivered in the power of the Spirit, do not need a lot of instruction right then, they just need to have someone help them clinch their decision. An effective evangelist taught me this years ago. Just get them on their knees at once, get them to pray and ask God to save them on the spot. Usually they will do so and then they are ready for a bit of explanation and a verse or two on assurance.

Sometimes people have personal questions and problems in which they need additional assistance. But, let them be shown that to trust Christ first for salvation and thus, become His child, will make the solution to the other problems much simpler. A new convert will understand more Bible in a few hours after he is saved than he could have learned in years before he was saved. So get them to truly trust Christ and claim His salvation as quickly as possible.

When people come forward (unless you know them personally and are sure that they are already saved), I would assume that they are *un*saved and coming for salvation. After preaching a sermon to the lost, I would take the person coming forward by the hand and say, "You want to be *saved*, don't you?" If they say yes, I would sit or kneel with them and say, "Now you know you are a sinner, right?" "Yes." "Do you believe that Christ died for sinners?" "Yes." "All right, will you, right now, the best way you know how, just receive Christ as your Saviour? If you will, give me your hand on it." They will usually give you their hand. Then I say, "Let's bow together. I'll pray first." Then you can pray something like, "Dear Lord, we thank You that Mr. Brown [or

Mrs. Smith, or whoever] has come to trust the Saviour. Help him to understand right now that he is lost but that You died to save him, and that You offer him eternal life now as a free gift. Hear his prayer and save him, Lord, right now, we pray." Then I would say to the sinner, "Now *you* pray. Just start your prayer, Dear Lord Jesus. Then *tell* Him you know you are a sinner and that you are taking His Son, Jesus, to be your Saviour right now. Bow your head for the prayer." If the sinner does not start praying at once, you can help him (or her) as follows: "If you will take Christ as your Saviour and you want to settle it right now, I'll help you with your prayer. Just say these words to Him with your eyes closed,

"Dear Lord Jesus, [ask the sinner to say the words right after you and give him time to do so] I know I'm a sinner. I believe you died for me, and I trust you as my Saviour. Come into my heart. Save my soul. And help me to live for Thee. In Jesus' name, Amen."

After the sinner has prayed that prayer, I immediately say, "You believe God answered that prayer, don't you?" If the answer is "Yes," I then say, "Right! He did. And if He did hear your prayer, what did He do for you?" "Well, I believe He saved me." It is good then, to ask them how they *know* that God saved them and give them some assurance from the Word so they can know that their peace about the matter results not from their feeling, their prayer, or their counselor, but from what *God* says in the Book.

Now, the above would be a simple way to do it if they have just heard a clear message and they already know how to be saved and are under conviction. If, on the other hand, the message has been to Christians, or they are new in church and have not yet had the plan of salvation given to them clearly, they will probably need a personal worker to give them the simple plan of salvation from Romans.

I would usually say, "Now there are just three things you have to know to be saved. First, that you are a sinner," and give him Romans 3:23, with perhaps also another verse or two from Romans 3. "The second thing you need to know to be saved is that Christ bore your penalty and died for your sins, so you do not have to remain lost forever." Show him Romans 5:6 and 8, or perhaps Romans 4:25, explaining that "someone has to pay the debt of sin, either you, the sinner, or Christ, an innocent substitute who bore our sins for us." If dealing with a Catholic, it is also important here to stress that He rose again since they are used to thinking of a crucifix, and we want them to know that Christ not only died for our sins but broke the bars of death and rose again, and that He lives today to save those who trust Him. "The third thing you need to know to be saved is that you can have this salvation, this eternal life, right now by simply receiving it as a gift from God," and I show him Romans 6:23. Then, "If you will receive this gift from God and trust Him to save you, will you give me your hand on it right now?" Then proceed to pray with him as above.

It is best for the pastor or some trained leader, perhaps an assistant, to double-check the convert before he or she gets away from the church to make sure they do not still have doubts. They should go home absolutely certain that they are now new creatures in Christ.

Make Much of Each New Convert or New Member

When a person comes to be saved (or to join the church), he or she should be gladly and enthusiastically welcomed by the pastor and by the people. Never leave them sitting at the front alone or making their way out among the people with no one to rejoice with them or encourage them about their decision. Once that person knows he has been saved and his name is presented as a new convert, I would publicly state how thrilled we all are at the salvation of our new friend. Give his or her name and probably the address. Other Christians in the church probably live near this one and can give encouragement and help. Let the pastor publicly say a word or two about the joys of the Christian life and how good it is going to be to have Mr.___ or Mrs.___ to serve the Lord here with us now. Or he can give a cheerful word of encouragement to read the Bible daily, pray daily and get busy for God in an earnest effort to win others.

Next, the people should come down to the front of the church (either before or after the benediction) and welcome the new Christians (or the new members). Don't let your people get the bad habit of going on out to their cars and ignoring the new Christians who have just been saved. This is so important!

Sometimes churches never know what happened to the people who came forward. Everything is handled quietly by personal workers and no one ever knows who got saved or who came back to the Lord. It will greatly encourage your people to work, pray and win others if they can see that God is saving people in the church and that the visitors they bring will be given proper help and friendship when they make their decisions. People will go away from the service rejoicing in the salvation of sinners and the goodness of God. If the new converts are being dealt with in an inquiry room and do not get back out to the service before the benediction, then let the new Christian be welcomed by the pastor and the other personal workers and staff members before he leaves the service and then be presented so that the whole church can rejoice with him at the very next service of the church.

If your church does not receive them for membership immediately upon their conversion, they should still be welcomed by the people and given all the encouragement possible with the assurance that they will be baptized and/or taken into the full fellowship of the church shortly. Don't leave them dangling or turn them loose for the cults, charismatics or liberals to start working on them.

Be sure you have the names, addresses, ages and other information on the new converts so that follow-up will be made easier.

Let the people know why the various folks have come forward—whether for salvation, rededication, membership or whatever. This encourages both the church members and the new converts, new members or reclaimed ones, as the case may be.

If the new converts have come to be saved and are willing to go on and be baptized and become a member, I would present their names for membership at once. Don't let them have time to get cold and get to wondering whether your church is the one they want to join. Instead of saying, "Do I hear a motion that so and so be received upon his profession of faith," why not just say, "If you rejoice to receive these dear people who have just been saved, please indicate it by a hearty 'amen.' " Or it could be by the up-lifted hand. To wait around for a motion and a second, and then a vote, sometimes makes the new Christian feel that the people are not too enthusiastic about receiving him.

If they are coming forward for membership in the church on statement or by transfer of letter, then the clerk or some personal worker should have already jotted down all the information the pastor will need as to which church the new member is coming from, etc.

In any event, make sure they are truly saved, even if they are coming by transfer of membership. Many church members are not sure they are saved and need to be dealt with before you receive them.

Don't make the new convert make a speech. Once in a great while a brand new Christian may ask if he can say a word from the overflow of his heart. Usually, though, they would be scared to death to have to get up and make a talk or give a testimony. This does not mean that their decision was not genuine. Remember, they are "babes in Christ." Babies cry but they don't talk much when they are first born!

If sinners who visit your church observe that the new converts are put on the spot and made to get up and give a speech or testimony, some of them will never make a decision—at least not in your church! Later on, when they get their spiritual eyes open, they will also probably get their mouths open, too, and will be able to participate in "testimony time."

Follow Up the New Converts

Be sure that they are pursued and properly brought into the Sunday school, the training program of the church, new members' class, soul-winning sessions and other things that will help them meet other Christians and grow in grace and knowledge. Try to have someone pick them up for prayer meeting the next Wednesday night. Be sure they get into the right Sunday school class the following Sunday. All of this is important.

A further word about the invitation: Use appropriate songs. When preaching to Christians and you are pressing for a decision for consecration, then it is hard to beat "Have Thine Own Way" or "Where He Leads Me I Will Follow." However, if you are preaching to the unsaved or if you know that unsaved are present, you probably will want to start the invitation with "Just As I Am," "Only Trust Him," "Pass Me Not," or "Why Not Tonight?" If you need to go from one of these into another as God is blessing the invitation with decisions, then "Almost Persuaded" is a good one to climax the appeal to the lost.

Choose your personal workers very carefully and train them well. There are some people in every church who are eager to help and who feel well qualified but who might not make good personal workers. Don't let them be long-winded people. Be sure they understand that the work is to be done effectively and that their job is to get them saved and sure of it—not give them a whole discourse on systematic theology. Don't let them try to explain all about separation, sanctification and the second coming before they bring them back out to present their names. New Christians can only understand a little bit at this crucial time. The first and most important thing right now is to be sure they are saved, and if there is time, give them a bit of instruction on baptism and the importance of going on with the Lord and coming to church consistently. The rest will come later.

In some cases, it may be well for the same person who dealt with them to do some of the follow-up work. Wisdom will direct.

CHAPTER TEN

Ushers—
The Pastor's Task Force

Most church ushers have never been taught the importance of their task. Many churches are getting only twenty-five percent or, at the most, fifty percent of the work the ushers could be performing. Why not use those men to the fullest of their potential?

Ushers can make or break a service. How important, then, to see to it that they are properly trained.

Choose Your Head Usher Carefully

It may be best to elect a new head usher or chairman of ushers every year until you find the right man. When "Mr. Right" has been located, then I would hang onto him and use him as long as possible in this important position.

Do not select your head usher because of his rank, popularity, status or good looks. These may be somewhat important but much more goes into a good head usher than that. Neither would I allow the church to pick your head usher simply upon the recommendation of a nominating committee. Your head usher is (or can be) just as important to the pastor as your assistant pastor, music director or youth leader—perhaps more so.

If the ushers themselves choose their leader or "head honcho," be sure that you are in on it and let them know he should be approved by you, as pastor. Make it clear that this man is really an assistant to the pastor and, as such, must be answerable to the pastor. Therefore, he has to be a man who is in full accord with the pastor, loves the pastor and would die for him if need be, to be sure the services are conducted like the pastor wants them.

1. The head usher should be a likable man. The men should

like him and he should like them. He must be agreeable, flexible and cheerful. He must be kind, considerate and intelligent.

2. The head usher must be a firm man. He has to adjust to situations, and be flexible if the pastor wants some change in the procedure. Yet, he must be resolute and firm in his determination to see that things run smoothly and orderly. He cannot be intimidated by his ushers or by members of the congregation.

3. The head usher must be a consecrated man. Just because he is a hail-fellow, well met, in the business world, does not qualify him for this important position of leadership. His dedication to Christ and to his church and pastor must be foremost in his life. His is a great position of honor and trust. He must feel that it is just as important for him to be there and to be prepared as it is for the pastor to be in the pulpit and be prepared.

4. The head usher must have some leadership ability, as others will be working under him. Yet, he must be a humble man, not proud and haughty about his position.

5. The head usher should be a well-organized man. He must realize that things have to be operated smoothly, sensibly and with reverence. Yet, many times there are things that must be done with great haste. His crowds usually come within just a few minutes, and they go out even faster! Offerings must be taken quickly, yet with reverence and dignity. Emergencies can arise. Problems can develop. Men can let him down. People can expect the impossible from him. So he must be a well-organized man.

6. The head usher should also be an even-tempered man. He needs to be patient, calm, gracious—even when things are going wrong and people are giving him a rough time.

7. The head usher should have a well-trained assistant who can do things as *he* does in case he is ill or is called out of town on an emergency or is away on his vacation. But, I would not have a head usher who is away too much.

Train Your Ushers

Together, the pastor, with his head usher, should have special training sessions with the other ushers. It should be made plain to the men before they are selected or elected as ushers that attendance at these training sessions is mandatory—that it will be impossible to serve as an usher if the training is not taken. You can have some refreshments, you might even want to have a meal for these men before the training period begins. But, after the meal or the social hour is over, I would get down to serious business with them. The pastor should be present at these sessions to inspire and instruct the men and to be sure that the advice given them is just what he wants them to have. However, it is good for the pastor to let the ushers know that he has confidence in the head usher and respects his leadership.

It will probably be necessary to have two or three nights for the training of the ushers. If it is to be done in one night, then I'd let them know they were in for a long session and I would also be sure that they had instruction sheets to study and/or a good book or booklet on ushers and ushering to read and become familiar with. I recommend the pamphlet, *Guidelines for Church Ushers*, by Lindsay Terry, published by the Sword of the Lord, Murfreesboro, Tennessee 37130.

All the Kings Men—Ready and Alert
to Help the Pastor

Ushers are the pastor's task force and many times also his peace corps. They have been selected as ambassadors of Christ to serve in the most important business in the world. They are expected to cooperate, labor and sacrifice in order to serve in this great soul-winning business.

The ushers must be alert to problems, to noisy children, to temperature, yes, to every situation. They must come early and stay late.

They must be ready for rush, blush, and lush—yes, and even for "flush." In one small church the boys' restroom was just off the little vestibule and there was no door between the vestibule and the congregation. When boys would go out to the restroom and leave that door open, the entire congregation was treated to the musical sounds of an exceptionally loud toilet gurgling and surging during the pastor's message. An alert usher, of course, should have made sure that the restroom door was quickly and quietly closed after the youngster departed.

Some embarrassing things may happen. An old drunk may stagger in. This has happened more than once in my revival meetings. In one place, two drunks came in while the ushers were giving out visitors cards and before we knew it the drunks had made their way to a pew near the front, all prepared to help the evangelist with his message. A head usher should have remained at the back with perhaps an assistant—then the drunks could have been intercepted in the vestibule. As it was, several ushers had to come down and escort the noisy intruders through an exit door. Sometimes it is pretty difficult to get people like that out of their seats once they were rooted there!

Ushers, guard those *doors!* In one country church, the main door was left open and an old dog came loping down the aisle. We want someone to come forward, of course, but we would prefer that they be two-legged individuals. In recent years, some churches have even been robbed by intruders. So the ushers need to be very alert as to who comes through those doors.

Be alert throughout the service. People may get sick and need assistance. Small children may have an accident and need to be quickly removed to the restroom. People may be getting so warm that they are about to faint. Ushers should be alert to this though perhaps only one man, or two at the most, would actually take care of the thermostat.

The usher should realize that in this work he is just as needed and just as important as the Sunday school teacher, the choir leader, or the organist. When men see this, they will then realize why they should be trained, why they should be there early and why they need to remain behind to be sure that everyone is out of the building before it is locked up! I think that in most churches the ushers have never been made to see the importance of their work. In some churches, they do not even *have* ushers—just some men selected at random to take the offering. Thus, there is no one to meet, greet and seat the people. And, of course, there is no one there to be the pastor's task force when he needs one.

Dress for Success

Ushers should dress as befitting representatives of the King. Their suits do not have to be fancy or exquisite, but they should be neat, clean and proper. People will respect the office of the usher more if they look like men of stature and responsibility. The ushers should wear a suit and tie. Their clothes should not be garish or outlandish. The tie should not clash with the suit. His hair should be cut like that of a man and he should be well-groomed and as sharp looking as possible. It is good if all the men choose to wear the same color suit (black, navy, gray, perhaps) especially on Sunday morning, and a boutenniere or an usher's badge may further identify them.

The usher should be especially careful of his breath. His teeth having been thoroughly brushed, he may, in addition, use mouthwash and then have a small breath spray handy to use at times during his time of duty. He should be careful to use an effective deodorant. His choice of cologne or shaving lotion should not be cheap, offensive or shocking. His shirt collar and cuffs should be immaculate. His shoes should be shined. And, of course, he should wear a smile.

In some churches where the weather is very warm and where there is no air conditioning, it may be permissible for the ushers to agree on spotless white shirts and ties, especially for the night-time services, if the pastor agrees, and if the people are not offended by such informal attire. This less formal garb is sometimes rather expected in vacation resort areas and in extremely warm climates. However, once while on vacation, the head usher met us in shorts, the men had hair-dos like women, and the women were in slacks or midriffs! That's carrying the informality too far—even in a resort town!

People are going to respect the usher more, children will realize this is somebody important if they have to be disciplined, and the general appearance of a well-groomed usher will contribute to the effectiveness of his position.

Station Your Ushers Properly

In some churches, the ushers cluster in the lobby and talk to one another or wander around aimlessly, or walk up and down the aisles as if to display their importance. The usher should have a post and should stay close to this spot except when he is actually seating someone or performing one of his several duties.

Ushers should never spend time gabbing with one another. They should not talk at all after the service begins. Some stay out in the vestibule and carry on their own little service while the pastor (or evangelist) is pouring his soul out on the inside. These things should not be. The head usher or his assistant may have to sit in the vestibule during the sermon. In a large church it may be necessary to have two men out there. The rest of the ushers should remain seated at or near their post, ready for any eventuality. The usher should worship, should sing, should listen to the sermon. He is a sinner saved by grace and needs spiritual food just like everyone else.

If one or two men are assigned to the parking lot, let them check their respective areas periodically and return to a place where they can listen to the sermon without being conspicuous. If a parking lot check is needed frequently, then some special men should be chosen for this who can take turns so that no one man has to miss much of the message very often.

One usher at the head of each aisle is usually enough to keep on duty once the service begins. In some cases, it may be all right for the usher to sit with his family during the sermon providing there is another usher at the head of his aisle. Usually there is not a need for as many ushers at the end of the service as at the beginning, though there should be several men to cordially bid farewell to the people as they leave and let them (especially the visitors) know that they were appreciated and that "we'd like for you to come again."

Ushers should have bulletins, visitors' cards and any other such things with him at his post. He should know where the spare hymnals are. He should be alert to every need of the parishioner.

Probably the most important part of the usher's task is to meet, greet and seat the people. To do this, the usher must be at his post.

Friendly, but Not Affectionate!

The usher should be friendly and cordial. He should not be mushy or overtalkative and he should be very careful not to overdo the handshaking bit. Don't clamp down hard on the hand of a man who may be ill, aged or infirmed. Do give a firm handclasp to other men but it does not have to be a bone-crushing grip!

DO *NOT* SHAKE HANDS WITH A LADY unless she extends her hand or in some other way indicates that she expects you to shake her hand. Some women do not like to shake hands, especially with a man. I have been in churches where visiting women had to go through a whole assembly line of men and get her hand gripped (and hurt) by every one of them. Needless to say they did not have to worry about her coming back to that church very soon.

Be very careful about touching people. Even most men do not like to be gripped on the arm or slapped on the back. Never touch a woman unless it is to assist a cripple or help an aged woman to her seat or down the steps. Don't pat a woman parishioner on the shoulder or arm or feel that you must show her affection in any way. The lady may not like it, her husband may resent it, and it doesn't do your image as an usher a bit of good!

As people leave the building, it is a good thing for an usher to shake hands with the men he seated and let both the men and ladies know that it was a pleasure to have them at church and that he hopes he can seat them again very soon. However, if the visitors (or members) are rushing on out and it is obvious that they'd rather not be intercepted for another handshake, then just let them get on by with a friendly word to "hurry back to the service tonight."

Be Ready for a Change in Plans

The pastor may change his routine or he may forget and have the visitors' cards passed out sooner (or later) than usual so the alert usher must be ready for any change in the usual order of things. Always be sure you have plenty of visitors' cards handy. In too many churches the ushers go back and scramble around looking for the cards after the pastor already has the hands of the visitors in the air. I've seen visitors sit with their hand in the air until I'm sure they had cramps, waiting for an unprepared usher to try to find his visitors' cards.

Don't Leave the Vestibule Deserted

While some ushers gather in the lobby and neglect the service, it is far more often that they leave the vestibule empty and there is no one there when they are really needed. In one Southern church, I saw a young lady come in after the service was underway. In fact, the sermon was just beginning. It was obvious that the lady had had an unexpected delay and was embarrassed at coming late. The ushers were all in the auditorium sitting with their families. The pastor was sitting down on the front row instead of remaining on the platform where he could survey the situation. The poor girl stood in the lobby shifting from foot to foot. It unnerved my preaching somewhat. I wanted to stop the sermon and holler to one of the ushers to get her a chair or show her to a seat. I finally managed to concentrate on my sermon but it was only when the girl cleared her throat during the latter part of the sermon that the usher finally "came to" enough to get the poor lady a chair.

In another church, a sick lady was bending over in the vestibule with her head on a table. She had found a chair but there was no usher handy to offer assistance or get some lady to take her home or into the ladies' room. If the head usher or an assistant had been in the vestibule, this would not have happened. (Or, if the pastor had been sitting on the platform with me, he could have seen what was happening.) Even with the pastor on the platform (where he should be), it is still best to have a good usher back there to take care of such matters. If the pastor has a communication phone up on the platform, it is still distracting for him to have to ring up the head usher and carry on a conversation during the sermon and it should not be done unless absolutely necessary.

Should Ushers Also Be Teachers or Deacons?

I think at least two or three of the ushers might well be

deacons. Then, if the problems that relate to ushers are discussed in a deacons' meeting, it is quite easy to relay this information. If the head usher is also a deacon, the matter will work even better. In some cases, an usher might also be a teacher, but, he ought not to be a long-winded one since it will be necessary for him to rush from his class to his usher's post. Also, there is the matter of meeting his class visitors and prospects which he could not readily do if he was running to a post in the church for his usher's appointment.

Should an usher sing in the choir? Again, it would be very hard for him to do this and be a good choir member as he would not be back there to rehearse if he was faithful to his usher's post. Also, he would have a difficult time getting back from the choir loft to the usher's post at the end of the service. So, the answer is probably "no" to this one.

Use an Ample Number of Men for the Offering

I have been quite surprised that some churches skimp on the number of men used to receive the offering. There should be two men for the choir, two on each side of each section of pews, and, of course, as many as needed for the balcony, if a balcony is used. Some churches use only two men to serve two sections. This means people have to do a balancing act and pass the plates over their shoulders to worshipers behind them to get the plate heading back in the right direction again. There should be at least one usher on each side of every section for sure. In smaller churches, it may be reasoned that since there are only a few people to serve, or the crowd is thin, that the church can get by with using an insufficient number of ushers. But, this is poor reasoning. Where the crowd is small, there is all the more reason to have enough ushers to pass the plates since the people are likely to be farther apart from each other. Also, in a small crowd, people are more likely to give if the plate is actually passed to them since they do not like to be conspicuous in a small group by getting up and reaching over someone to get their offering in the plate. So, use plenty of men.

If the church is large and there are many people to reach, then it will be best to have even more men per section (and additional plates) and let two men (per section) begin at the front while two other men (per section) begin half way back. In such cases, just be sure you know exactly where the crowd was divided so some rows are not skipped or others may get a double dose of extraction! This has been known to happen.

Be sure that some men are left in the vestibule for emergencies or late comers while the other ushers are taking the offering.

In fundamental churches, of course, not too much can be done about the size or type of men as long as they are clean, well-groomed and consecrated men. However, where possible, the head usher might concentrate on trying to have men of approximately the same height in the same aisle. Sometimes there will be a Mutt and Jeff situation with a long, lean one walking along beside a short, tubby fellow. With a little thought and foresight, this might be corrected.

Too Young or Too Old?

Again, there is no hard and fast rule about age. However, it is best to use men who are old enough to be mature, serious men of some dignity. If a young man has been in the church for a long time and has proven himself as a good, solid and dedicated man, then there should be no reason why he should not serve as young as 20 or 21. I would not use a silly, flippant type, however. Never use a fellow who will be giving the girls the eye or who just can't wait at the end of the service to rush off with the young people before his task as an usher has been completed.

By "dignity" I do not mean that he has to glide around like he has ballbearings in his knees. But, he ought to be a man who is mature enough to take his position very seriously and who can be counted on to be just as dedicated to his post as the middle-aged veteran usher would be. He should not be childish, flippant, stubborn or boisterous, regardless of his age.

Middle-aged and older men can be used, too. Some of those men make the best ushers. But, before a man becomes slow and decrepit or aged and senile, of course, he should be replaced by younger and more energetic men. The pastor and head usher should be thinking well ahead of time on such matters.

Men of Esteem, Well Respected as Christians

Do we even need to mention this? Surely a man who smells of tobacco or has his pack of "coffin nails" showing through his shirt or coat pocket should not be ushering in church. Nor should a man ever be used who drinks any kind of intoxicating beverage. That's all you need! Let your prospective convert see an usher in your church who had been seen the week before tipping a beer can at the ball game or coming out of Buster's Bar and your sermon has been ruined for the week!

If he is the kind of church member who frequents the theater or goes to the Christmas ball or the country club shindig, or who belongs to some questionable club, he has no business attempting to serve on the pastor's task force in a good, Bible-preaching church where the pastor preaches what the Bible has to say about worldliness. Many people feel it best to give the worldly Christian a job to do in the church to get him to the services in hope that he will get "straightened out" under the preaching. But this is unscriptural and faulty reasoning. The man should become consecrated and dedicated before he is given such a place of high honor in the church. The pastor does not have to be mean about this. But, if he faithfully and lovingly preaches the Word about worldliness (and there is plenty in the Bible on this), he should be able to grow a band of men whose hearts God has touched and who will be happy to serve the Lord with gladness. God says, "Be ye clean, that bear the vessels of the Lord" (Isa. 52:11)

Seat to the Front When Possible

The ushers should attempt to fill the front part of the auditorium first if at all possible. There are some people who will always sit in their usual place come fire, storm or snowy blast, but some people will be cooperative and at least this is a start. As other people come in, the usher must use great tact and carefulness in asking the people who are sitting near the aisle if they would be kind enough to move in to the center of the pew to accommodate the new arrivals. Some people will not budge, of course, and the usher cannot make them do so.

Except Mothers With Babies

When a young mother comes in with a baby, or a tiny tot who from all appearances may be the noisy and disruptive kind of child, it is best to try to seat them near the back of the auditorium. Be sure and inform the mother that you have a well-staffed nursery and that she is most welcome to put the baby in safekeeping during the service. Show her where it is or get some lady you can trust to escort her to the nursery. If you have a tod-dlers' nursery, too, or a "church" for the little tots, it is good to try to get "Little Master Mischievous" situated, too, before the service begins.

If the baby or tot is not taken to the nursery (some parents refuse to do so), then do not hesitate to offer assistance again if the child cries out or in any way is disturbing after the service is underway. A ladies' brigade (perhaps an usher's wife or a deacon's wife) can best do this for the usher, offering to help the embarrassed mother find the nursery.

Guard the Balcony

Ushers should keep small children and amorous teenagers out of the balcony unless they are accompanied by their parents. Don't use the balcony at all except as a last resort. People will come forward more easily from the main floor than they will from a balcony. Very few converts come out of the balcony. A rope or some other obstruction should be placed across the entrance to the balcony to keep people from going up until the balcony has to be used as an overflow. I have never seen young children pay attention if they are seated in a balcony. And most teenagers who sit in the balcony are either laughing, talking and scribbling, or they are making love. So keep the balcony off limits if at all possible.

Observe Children Going Out to Restrooms, Etc.

Keep an eye on a child or teen who goes out during the service.

If the restroom is on an open court or down a long, lonely hall-way, it is best if some trusted man or woman can go along in that general direction. Some strange things (and some tragic ones) have been going on in recent years. Some teens slip out to meet their girl or boyfriends and skip church. Some small children will play along the way and even get lost or sidetracked. It *has* happened.

IMPORTANT: If a child goes out (or even an adult) toward the end of the message or near the invitation time, I would surely have some folding chairs and seat that one near the usher's post or in the vestibule rather than let him traipse back through the congregation to his seat and ruin the pastor's closing remarks or his invitation. It is sometimes wise for a pastor to let his congregation know ahead of time that small children will be held at the back if they go out near the end of the sermon. Then, the usher will not be blamed for doing his duty.

If an evangelist is in the church and having a special Sunday school service, the ushers should also be on hand to seat late comers to Sunday school (or early comers to church) at the *rear* during the message so they will not distract and cause confusion.

Don't Rush People Out

Some ushers start locking doors and switching off lights before all the crowd is gone. Don't rush people. They need the fellowship. Also, sometimes people are lagging behind because they have a spiritual problem and need the pastor or some good Christian to help them. They should not be herded out just because the usher (or custodian) is in a hurry. I've been talking to a new (or prospective) convert on more than one occasion when some eager beaver started turning out the lights on us. *All* of the ushers do not need to stay until everyone is gone but at least it should be understood that certain ones will be there as long as needed. A well-organized head usher can arrange this so that no one man has to stay until the "end of the tribulation" at every service.

Some Closing Impressions

Usher, be on time at your post—at least 15 minutes before service time. During special meetings even earlier if the head usher or pastor so directs.

First impressions are important. Make sure you conduct yourself in such a manner as to make people want to come again. Be cheerful, kind, considerate and courteous at all times.

Ushers should not be either proud peacocks or slovenly sloths. Dignified does not have to mean "stiff." Be alive. "Folly is set in great dignity," Solomon says.

Remembering names will make you a popular usher. Try to cultivate this. But, don't call men by their first names unless they are your personal friends or relatives. And I'd never call a woman by her first name—at least not in church in front of other people. If you have forgotten the name of the family, just play it cool and pretend you know them anyway. The name will probably come to you later. Or you can ask someone.

IMPORTANT: Be sure you have flashlights or lamps handy in case of a power shortage. The head usher will also want to be sure a bright light with good batteries is available for the pastor in a hurry in case of an emergency. Know where the telephone is and who has the key to the office where that phone is located. Ushers should always have speedy access to a phone. This might prevent such emergency from becoming a catastrophy!

BE SURE that all doors leading out of an auditorium are *unlocked* while the crowd is there. This is good for many reasons, fire being perhaps the main one. P.S.: Be sure those doors are locked again before everyone leaves the premises.

Make sure envelopes are in the pew racks if this is part of your job. In many churches, the pastor tells people to use the envelopes in the pews when there are none in sight. Perhaps a custodian or a secretary could check this on Friday and again on Sunday afternoon. But an alert usher can double-check to make sure things are adequately prepared for. If different kinds of envelopes are being used, building fund, missions, revival, etc., then it is obvious that a variety of envelopes should be available.

How a Pastor Can Help His Ushers

Brag on them sometimes! Let the ushers know you appreciate them. And let the people know that these men are your trusted task force, and that their job is important.

Have some social life for (and with) the ushers. "All work and no play. . ." you know.

Advise your men if changes in the routine of the service are anticipated. Try not to "surprise" them too often. If they do make a boo-boo, don't scold them publicly for it.

Once in a while, have some special recognition of ushers, either individually or as a group.

Be sure your staff members show them the proper respect and train your people to do likewise. These men can go a long way toward making your services successful!

If babies are in the congregation, the pastor should very clearly announce that there is a nursery for the babies and tots and that the little ones will have excellent care there. This helps to get the usher off the hook if he has to escort a mother and a crying baby out of the service. If babies are whining and restless even after my announcement about the nursery, I would sometimes say in my prayer before the sermon, "We thank Thee, Lord, for those who have helped to make this service a blessing: the choir, the ushers and those dear ladies who are keeping the *babies* in the nursery so that we may attend upon God's Word without distraction." Usually by then the parents get the idea and use the nursery.

Other helpful booklets on ushers and ushering may be obtained from some Christian book dealers.

Chapter Eleven
"Daily and in Every House"—
How to Visit

Why, when, on whom, and how should a pastor visit? These are vital questions.

I once visited a church where the crowd was small and the service discouraging. "Our pastor is a good man," someone remarked later, "but he doesn't visit. Only if someone *asks* him to will he go." No wonder the crowd was small and the church was dying.

Pastor, if you want a growing church, lead the way yourself in constant and consistent visitation. I heard a great man who has a tremendous church reply to the question: "What is the secret of your success?" The answer simply was "Prayer and visitation." Victory through visitation is the secret of the growth of many a church.

There is no substitute for visitation or personal calling. Eighty-five percent of business deals are finalized through personal solicitation, we are told. D. L. Moody said that of all the thousands saved in the Moody crusades, he did not know of a single one who had not first been approached or visited and dealt with on the outside.

As I look back on the many hundreds who made decisions in the churches I pastored, I can think of almost none who came forward unless they had first been invited, witnessed to or dealt with on the outside either by the pastor or some of the concerned members.

There are all kinds of visits: pop calls, get-acquainted visits, soul-winning visits, sick calls, hospital calls, shut-in visits, jail visitation, calls on prospective members, trouble calls and newcomer visits. A church can have programs of visitation for young people, men, women, the Sunday school, bus visitation, etc.

Calls can be made effectively or poorly. Your church visitation program can be a failure or a success. Let me share some of the things we learned in visitation and some things I have observed in churches around the country.

First, we will deal with the pastor and his own visitation plan, and then we'll talk about an effective visitation program in the church.

Pastor, you cannot be a success at soul winning or building a church by sitting behind a desk and expecting others to do it. Perhaps people would come to hear Spurgeon or the Apostle Paul if they did not visit but most of us are not Spurgeons or Pauls. In this day and time, I wonder how much of a church even *they* could build without visitation!

1. Why Should the Pastor Visit?

To keep his own heart hot, to maintain the pulse of the people, to inspire others to visit, to show his concern, to keep the right contact with his sheep, and to win the lost who are all around him.

2. On Whom Should the Pastor Call?

He will call on his members. Chapter one of this book suggests a plan for getting a visit made to all members of the church. Some people will need more visits than others, but he should get into the home of all of his members at least once. It is best if this be done in the first few weeks of his pastorate.

The pastor should visit the backslidden before they get into terrible trouble and become hopelessly disinterested in the church. The Sunday school teachers and deacons should also take a big responsibility with these.

Sick calls will be made. If people are seriously ill, injured or hospitalized they should be able to expect a call from the pastor. He must use wisdom about visiting those who may have a contagious disease. In some cases, a doctor should be consulted about this. I do not think members should expect the pastor to come running because they are sick with a cold or if they have the flu. In the latter case, a phone call or a card from the pastor should suffice. If the person with the flu is alone or a shut-in, then, of course, someone from the church should be willing to brave the home of the sick person with soup or fruit or whatever is needed. In most cases, though, such people have relatives or loved ones who should take care of them.

I have had to visit sick people who were blowing and snorting when it just could not be helped, and I do not know that I ever caught the illness. I believe the Lord will take care of us in such cases if the visit has to be made and there is no one else to do it. And in hospitals I have come in contact with almost every illness known to man and the Lord preserved me. But, I did not foolishly rush into every situation and I attempted to avoid contact with the flu, intestinal disorders, etc., when at all possible. After all, a pastor is not going to do his congregation much good at the next service if he is flat on his back with the flu. People should not expect a pastor to needlessly expose himself to such contagious illnesses.

If hospitalized, of course, our members have a right to expect the pastor to be interested enough to visit them or to have someone on the church staff visit them. Usually, they want the pastor, himself. I do not think it necessary for a pastor to visit the ill person in the hospital every day. Sometimes I did do it every day because I'd find myself going back to see someone else in the same hospital who was going to have surgery and, while there, felt it best to pop in and see how my other sick sheep were doing. Thus, I got a reputation for visiting those sick in the hospital almost every day. As the church grows or if you are in a large city, this is very hard to do. People should not expect it. But, I would surely keep in touch. If you cannot visit them, some other staff member can do so.

In the case of ladies, you can have some lady in the church pass along the concern of the pastor while she is visiting; "Pastor Brown wanted me to be sure and let you know he is praying for you and asked that I let him know how you are feeling today," is one way to do it. Or perhaps the church secretary can make a phone call if the patient has a bedside phone.

Troubled members and those with special problems may need to be visited. Sometimes they will request a visit. If not, the pastor can phone or visit to see if he can be of help in the time of difficulty.

When people have had disasters or accidents, we should show concern with a visit.

Unchurched Christians need to be visited before they drift or before the cults or other false religionists get to them.

Prospects who have visited your church need to be visited and enlisted. There are many saved people out there needing a church home. If they have visited the church or if it is otherwise known that they are interested in your church, you need to get there quickly.

The sorrowing, those who have had a death in the family, can often be helped and won at a time when their hearts are tender. Of course, the wise pastor will tread softly here if the sorrowing family goes to some other gospel-preaching church.

Lonely people, widows, senior citizens, elderly folks without families to care for them can often be visited and won to Christ. And be sure and visit your own shut-ins!

Newcomers to the city or community need to be visited quickly after moving in. Names can be secured from the Credit Bureau bulletin in most cities. A small fee will furnish this information each week. In a city or good-sized town, you may need a hired staff member or a consecrated volunteer worker just to take care of keeping up with the names of such prospects. Sometimes, the power company or gas company may give you the information you need about newcomers. Often, though, in this case, we found they simply listed all of the homes where power (or gas or water) had been turned on, which sometimes meant that we were visiting people who were chronic "movers" and had simply moved again from across town or from down the street a short distance.

Jails, penitentiaries and reform schools also may be possibilities for soul-winning visitation. In some places, this is easier than in others.

3. When Should Visits Be Made?

It is not the same for everybody nor is it the same in every place. Near an Air Force Base, an army or navy installation, or a large industry you may discover that people have such hours that will find thousands of people at home by 4:00 or 4:30 in the afternoon. This would mean an hour and a half or two hours of good visitation time BEFORE SUPPER, often before dark.

Shut-ins, elderly folk, retired people can often be visited in the late morning or early afternoon.

Great numbers of people, of course, can only be visited at night.

Hospital calls can be made in the morning after patients have had their baths and are fresh and rested, in some cases. Others, it will be best to visit in the afternoon. A pastor can usually get more accomplished in his visiting the hospitalized if he can get there *before* the stream of visitors comes in at the appointed visiting hours. Most hospitals will allow a "clergyman" this privilege. It is important that you do not abuse the privilege. Make your visits brief, be very sensitive to the feelings of the patient, the requests of the nurses, etc.

Self-employed people can sometimes be visited briefly on the job but I would exercise great care in this. A man working at a work bench for an employer is not going to be able to take time out to talk with you nor would it be proper for you to expect him to. Even for a brief pop-call and invitation to church, I would check with the boss to make sure it was all right. On the other hand, where a man is his own boss, operates his own business and can be found watching over his store, waiting for customers, it may not be difficult to have a minute or two of his time during working hours. Be careful, though. Don't cause the man to miss a sale or anger a customer because you are in there talking to him, or her.

Bus children and other prospects for the bus routes can usually best be visited on Saturdays. The children are home and many times their parents are. Also, if the visit is made on Saturday and they promise to come on Sunday, the day is so close that it is almost impossible for them to "forget" to be ready.

Be careful about visiting too late in the evening. After 8:30 or 8:45, I'd begin to look for signs to indicate whether I should ring that doorbell or not. Many people have already turned the light down low and are in their night clothes by then. Others wouldn't care if you came an hour later. But be careful.

Teens and other young people can be visited after school or in the early evening. Catch them before dark, if possible, and before they are sprawled out in the living room watching television. Teens can also often be found available on Saturdays or on Sunday afternoons.

4. How to Visit

Plan your visiting. If I had two hours to visit before supper, I would jot down the names of the people I wanted to see most. I then put their names on a card with a mental map in my mind. Perhaps two were on the east side of town, three on the north side and one on the west side and I live on the south side. In that case, I'd make a circuit of visits, catching one after the other, to conserve time and gasoline. Or maybe I had ten visits I wanted to make and three hours to visit. I would make my little card map again but put a star or a dot by the ones I was most anxious to see. Then, if time ran out or if I was delayed for an unusual amount of time at one place, I would try to catch the "star" visits on the way back to my home or the church, saving the less important calls for another time.

Usually I had far more names with me than I ever would have time to visit. Then, if several were not at home, I still had other names so that the trip was not a washout.

Prepare for your visiting. Be sure you have a supply of tracts, church cards, a map of the city, your visitation list, a pen or pencil and, of course, your New Testament or a pocket Bible.

Take a *flashlight,* by all means, if you are visiting at night. Why stumble around in the dark wondering which house has the number you're looking for when a flashlight would leave no doubt? By the way, be careful how you shine flashlights at houses and on people's front porches. Some people may think you are an intruder or a thief. Be careful. Don't end up in the obituary column.

Pray about, and on, your visitation. Ask God to bless you and not let you "beat the air" in your calling. Ask Him to open up the conversation and to bring conviction. Pray for wisdom about how long you should stay and what you should say.

Be brief. I'm confident that far too many visits are too long. Many of your visits should be "pop calls." Use your head. If the supper is on the table or about to be taken from the stove, that is no time to sit down for a chat with the family. Dr. Ed Nelson says he knocked on all 8,000 doors when he pastored in Aurora, Colorado. This was in two years' time. (No wonder God led him to a greater ministry in Denver.) But, you may be sure that a great number of those 8,000 calls were pop-calls or minute-visits.

In my first few years at Panama City, Florida, I made from 50 to 70 visits a week. Then, as the church grew larger and there were many other duties and demands upon my time, I had to let other workers take some of the visitation load. But even then it was from 25 to 40 visits a week most of the time. Again, many of them were very short visits and some might be termed pop calls—pop in and pop out again.

To visit folks who missed a Sunday or two, you may not need more than a cheery greeting and the assurance that "you've been missed" and "hope you're not having sickness" to be assured that they've "been to Grandma's" and will be there the very next Sunday. Many times I would not even go in, especially if it was obvious that they were about to eat or were soon to go out, or were in some difficult time at the moment. In many other cases, I would sit (if at all) for only a minute or two. Of course, if they have problems you need to help them with or if you have a chance to win a soul, then I'd definitely plan to stay longer.

It is said that some salesmen talk their prospects into a sale and then talk them out of it again. I've known personal workers and church visitors to do this. It is better to leave when they want you to stay than it is to stay when they want you to leave.

You can give the impression that you are staying longer than you really are. Try not to get drawn into a long discussion. Stay off subjects that might require a history of the family tree or a full discourse on the Democratic Party or Bible prophecy. I know the books all say that you should never act hurried. But, I personally believe that people respect a preacher more if they know he *does* have a lot of work to do and many other places to go. Far too many of us, I fear, act as if we had all day and nothing to do. No wonder some people think pastors have a soft job. Also, I'm sure that a great number of people these days are busy themselves, and will appreciate it if we do not take up a lot of their time.

You'll not make a friend out of a man if you interrupt his favorite television program for long or make him miss the crucial play in the game he has been waiting all week to see. A pastor pointed out a house across the street in a midwestern city. It was within a stone's throw of the church. But, the people would not come near the church. Some zealous men on visitation night had gone to call one time. The man was preparing steaks on the grill for a couple they were entertaining that night. The men from the church said they would "only stay a moment" since they had company and would soon be dining. But, they stayed on and on, angering the unsaved man more by the moment. Forty minutes and four overdone steaks later the church men finally departed. The man vowed to his wife they would never go to that church. How much better if the laymen had greeted the man with a cheery "hello," told him they were from the church but would call again another time when he did not have company, and had just urged the man to attend the next Sunday as they made a hasty exit. It is possible the man would have come with his wife *and* the friends who ate the overdone steaks. But the unwise visitors closed the door on that family. Some pastors are said to be just as unwise and long-winded in their calling as those laymen were.

Don't make social calls on your members. If you do it for some, others will expect the same. You are not called to be a social butterfly. Now, of course, if members invite you for a meal, that is a different matter. This gives you a splendid opportunity to make an important visit while getting better acquainted with some of your members. Do not feel that you must reciprocate. Most members do not expect a pastor to have them in their home for a meal even if they feed you several times. Other members would not understand and you would make some first-class enemies. Jealousy has not been eradicated from the lives of all the saints, I've learned.

Be friendly and cheerful when you visit. The world has enough gloom. "A merry heart doeth good like a medicine." Greet all members of the family who are in sight. Take a moment with the children. Don't overlook the elderly. Comment on something that's new or nice, a car, a new sofa, a beautiful painting, the new power mower in the drive, etc. Try to include the whole family in your conversation unless you are definitely dealing with one person about his or her soul.

Be ethical. If you are visiting people who belong to other churches, it is best not to run their church down even if you sincerely disagree. Don't try to coax the members of other fundamental churches to consider your church unless they have told you that they plan to make a move or unless they live such a distance from their church that they can no longer attend. If the people are members of a liberal church or a cult, then that is a different matter. Even so, you will succeed better if you use great tact and care in dealing with the situation. If you win someone to Christ who goes to another good church, you can bid them Godspeed as you encourage them to make a profession and join their own church. If they prefer your church, they will let you know.

How long should you stay? My average visit was from 10 to 20 minutes. The visit would range from a 4- to 5-minute pop-call at the door to an hour or more if we were really winning someone to Christ. Normally, though, 10 to 20 minutes should be enough to greet the people, exchange pleasantries for a moment, visit about the church and invite them, answer any pressing questions and have a brief word of prayer. Again, if there is a chance to win souls, the visit will take longer. If people act as if you should stay longer, try to ascertain if they are just being nice or if they really have a spiritual problem they need you for. If they are just wanting to socialize, you can always say, "As much as I am enjoying the fellowship here, I do have an appointment I must keep," or, "Since I promised Brother Jones I'd stop in, I'd better hurry on this time and we can have some fellowship again another time."

Should you always have prayer? Why not? Except for the brief pop-call at the door (and sometimes even then), I think the man of God should lead in a short word of prayer. It doesn't hurt for them to know that you are on speaking terms with God. And it's the only prayer some people ever have!

Keep records of your visits. A good card file index system will keep you in touch with what you've already done, when the visit was made, what the results were, and when you should go again. Be systematic. If you have good records, you can also work these names into your church visitation program as the need arises.

Don't be drawn into gossip and idle chatter. Stay clear of remarks about others. And, if people want to talk to you about others, you can quickly shift the conversation into other channels. "An ungodly man diggeth up evil," and "a whisperer separateth chief friends" (Prov. 16:27,28). Avoid a critical spirit.

One thing more, get the victory over discouragement. You may make ten visits and have no visible results at all. Then, at house number 11, you may find a whole family just waiting to be saved and join your church. It's worth it all!

Oh, yes, and when visiting in the *hospital*, make your visits brief, cheerful and optimistic. Don't be loud or boisterous. Don't lean on the bed of the patient. Be sure it is all right to go in before entering the room of a woman patient. Don't give the nurses a hard time. Don't tire the patient. Pray for them. Leave quickly.

NOW, ABOUT THAT CHURCH VISITATION PROGRAM

If the pastor is a zealous soul winner and visits much, the people will soon be willing to receive the instruction that they should be doing it, too. If you, as a preacher, are not working hard at soul winning and visitation, then you need to repent of this sin and ask God to fill you with His Spirit so you will want to. You'll never build much of a church without it. (See Proverbs 11:30 and Acts 1:8.)

"Daily, and in every house" (Acts 5:42) "they ceased not." Keep everlastingly at it! It is not just the preachers. It is every Christian's job!

Have a census every few years, or you can call it a "religious survey" when every door is knocked upon. Or, you may just want to ask your people to knock on every door with the Gospel, leaving a tract and an invitation to church. However, the census or survey idea makes it easier on your people, they can get the needed information better, and generally you can get the people who come to the door to open up and talk more readily. Then, on that survey or census card, you have some valuable information to work with.

Keep records. If you have a consecrated and well-organized lady who will volunteer for this and will give the time to it, you are fortunate. Otherwise you will probably have to hire a worker for this. But keeping track of the visits, changing addresses, pulling out obsolete cards—all of this is necessary. Also, if you do not have records, you'll have people going back to visit "prospects" who have already joined your church, somebody else's church, or who have long since gone to their reward!

Be organized. Most people will not do much visitation if it is pell-mell, helter-skelter and voluntary. You almost have to have a regular night for church visitation, a regular day for ladies visitation and a specific time for bus visitation, or it just will not get done. Everybody's business is nobody's business.

Visit newcomers. Earlier in this chapter, we told how to get these names. If you do not have good volunteers who will do this *every week*, then it will pay you to hire someone to do it. They can make the initial contact. Then, the pastor or his workers can follow up on the pertinent ones.

Ladies will best visit in the daytime. Not many ladies are going out at night to visit anymore, not unless they are with their husbands. And there are many ladies who can be won by other ladies in the daytime. Not all women are working. It just seems that way. You have to work harder now and knock on more doors to find them. Perhaps in addition to a morning visitation time for ladies, others would visit say at 4:00 p.m. for an hour or so.

Take an attractively-printed church card. It will pay any church to print up a slick, glossy card with a picture of the church, the pastor, youth director, music director, etc. If you have more pictures than the church and pastor, you will probably need to make it in the form of a folder with 4 or 5 pages. Emphasize your music program if you have a good one, your Christian school if you have or sponsor one, your youth activities, your nursery. The card should be the proper size to fit in a man's pocket along with his tracts. A quantity of them can be carried in a lady's purse. Card stock will not bend or tear as easily as paper. And have a good printer do a first-class job.

Go two by two. While, as a pastor, I enjoyed visiting alone and could get to more houses that way, it is generally best for your people to go two by two. This gives encouragement to the people doing the visiting, it makes it possible for someone to be praying, getting the cards ready, memorizing the name of the people, etc., as the other is driving to the next house. If you visit two by two, there is someone to pray as the other witnesses. Also, the second lady can entertain the baby or sometimes intercept emergencies while the other (first) lady is winning the lady of the house to the Lord.

The same is generally true for the men who visit at night. Two by two generally works best. Sometimes couples can visit couples effectively.

Keep your Bible hidden (or just carry a New Testament) until the conversation turns to things spiritual. If people see you coming with a Bible, they immediately freeze up, hide, or run out the back door. If you were planning to shoot somebody, you would not want them to see you walking up the front steps with gun in hand. A fisherman tries to show the *bait* to the fish, not the hook.

Get the television turned off. Most sinners have a television set blaring when you walk in. What do you do? Well, if they're watching a program they've been waiting all week to see, or, if the man of the house is watching the World Series or the Super Bowl, you might as well watch it with them for a minute, invite them to church hastily, and make a speedy exit. But usually they've just got the tube on because of nothing more important to do. Sometimes you can remind them to turn it down by talking loudly and acting like it's hard for you to think with it on, or by talking softly so they realize they cannot hear you for the noise. But frequently I would talk to them above the racket of the television until the conversation got onto something serious or even onto soul winning. Then I would say, "Would you mind if I just cut this down?" Usually they will say, "Oh, just cut it *off.*" Sometimes I let my hand slip and cut it off, anyway. "Oops!" Or they may cut it off themselves. But, since the Devil wants that thing to stay on, I usually found it best to stand near the set so that I could take care of that when the conversation turned to serious matters.

Arrange and organize your areas. Try to have "missionaries" from your membership for the general areas where they live. Otherwise, you will neglect the far-out sections of your county. Put some encouraging cards along with some not so encouraging so that your workers will not feel their time has been wasted.

Leave something behind with them. Tracts, church cards, perhaps an attractive bulletin from Sunday. If you have a broadcast, be sure and point out that you do, and tell them how and when to listen in. Be sure that your church card has the *time* of services on it, and emphasize this time to the people you visit.

Visit your adults along the bus routes. So much has been written about the bus ministry and bus visitation. I think one area of neglect here, though, is the *parents* of the bus children. Many times they can be won if consecrated workers follow up on them. They usually appreciate what the church is doing to take their children to Sunday school and church and deliver them home safely again. They should be among some of those easiest to win. Prayer, patience and persistence will pay off.

What Are Some of the Problems of Visitation?

Q: Does a pastor need to take his wife with him?

A: The church did not call the pastor's wife to be their under-shepherd, they called *him.* The church does not have the right to expect that the pastor's wife should have to accompany him on all of his calling and to all of his various appointments. The wife will have all she can do if she properly manages the pastorium, takes adequate care of her husband and children, answers the phone fifty times a day, attends the regular services, participates in the activities of the church that are for ladies, reminds her husband of all the things he asks her to remember, and maintains a good testimony before the congregation and the town. It would be a back-breaking if not a killing schedule for any poor pastor's wife to have to constantly visit with her husband. Also, it would be more time-consuming for him.

Q: But should the pastor call on a woman when he is alone and she is by herself?

A: It is a sticky question but if a man lives close to God, stays devotedly in love with his own wife, and keeps moving quickly in his soul-winning endeavors, it need not be a problem. If a woman was alone when I called, I rarely went into the house and sat down for any length of time. However, if a man of God sits down in the living room, near the front door, states his business quickly and moves on, he will probably never have any difficulty with temptation or with a soiled reputation. If I had to go back to that same home a *second* time, however, I would generally either take my wife along or be sure the lady of the house had her husband or some other member of the family there with her. Otherwise, on a second visit, I would merely stand in the front door, state the purpose of my call, and be gone. If a man does this, he should never have any question as to his moral character.

If a man preaches hard against sin and then practices what he preaches, the ladies will know that he is above reproach and will stand for no foolishness. Usually, a lady will have her children, a sister or a maid around, anyway, so I seldom ever visited a lady alone. If she was scantily dressed, I visited only at the door or standing just inside the living room with the door open, stated my business and left. Since my pastorates were in Florida, I could frequently make such visits in the yard or on the front porch. All pastors are not so blest.

However, I would usually try to visit when the man of the house was home. If ladies needed another visit after the first call, I usually could send my wife or other Christian ladies to do the follow-up.

Q: But what if a woman throws herself at or seeks to entice a pastor?

A: I don't think she will if there is absolutely no foolishness on his part and if he lives completely above reproach. If his eyes are either on the Bible or on the face of the woman he is witnessing to and he is talking "in the Spirit" about the things of God, I do not think a woman would dare do such a thing. Perhaps there may be in every town some "mental case" or some woman so evil that she would attempt to seduce a preacher, but a man of God should be able to discern the situation and dismiss himself at once if such a problem arose. And, of course, he would know never to go to that house again unless his wife or other trusted workers were with him.

Q: What about bad dogs in the yard?

A: Well, the Bible does say "Beware of dogs," so I guess one should watch out for four-legged as well as the two-legged variety. Usually, a dog will bark enough that someone will come to the porch and call the beast off. If not, you might try calling out, "Hello, there," until you get the attention of the dog's owner. The next best thing would be to phone the owner and tell him kindly that you wanted to stop by for a minute but that since he had a vicious dog you wondered if he would state a time that you might visit when he would have the dog penned up. If that doesn't work, you could just make the visit over the phone.

Q: You're going up on a stranger's porch, invading his own "castle." What is the best approach?

A: Knock on the door two or three short, sharp knocks or ring the bell, and then step back a foot or two. By stepping back, they know you're not standing there right against the screen as if to plunge in or stick your foot inside when they open the door. It is an act of courtesy to stand back until he or she says, "Come in." Also, they know you're not peering through the glass at them if you step back.

Q: What is the best thing to say when he opens the door?

A: "Hello" or "Good evening, Mr. Brown. I'm Pastor Whoever from Calvary Church. Could I have a moment of your time?" would be good. If he invites you inside, well and good. If not, you might say after a remark or two, "It's a bit chilly and I don't want to cool off your house. Would it be all right if I stepped inside for a few words?" Usually then they will let you inside the door. But, if he still seems hostile or even "distant," I would not insist upon sitting down. In many cases, they will ask you to be seated, and then, of course, it is proper to do so. Take a seat NEAR THE DOOR, don't try to lunge for the most comfortable chair. In fact, give the impression that you're not trying to get too comfortable. If you take a plain chair near the door and just sit on the edge of the chair, the man will realize that you are not planning to stay forever and will probably open up to you better.

Q: What if the wrong kind of people show up to represent your church at visitation? What do you do with them?

A: Well, sometimes I've taken a fellow with me to visit who insisted on leaving his false teeth at home. He *had* teeth but seldom wore them. I usually took him because no one else wanted to take him. After a night or two of this, I told him quite frankly that he would make a better impression as an ambassador of Christ if he wore his teeth. He did so for a few weeks. Then, he'd show up toothless again. I would sometimes try to pair him up with some other fellow who wasn't the best dressed fellow, either, and send them to a section of the town where it didn't make too much difference how you were dressed. If people who refuse to dress up or look presentable insist on coming to visit, then I would not hesitate to send them to visit in a place where it could not hurt the cause of Christ. There are some bus route areas where the people are quite poor and someone like this may fit in real well there.

In extreme cases, you might just have to ask a man or a woman to please try to find some other way to serve the Lord since you had some strict requirements for your visitation teams. I did not hesitate to preach to our people that they should look their best when going out to visit. Of course, that did not mean they were expected to wear their Sunday finest on Thursday night or Thursday morning. But, they at least knew they should be dressed neatly and in proper attire to represent the King of kings.

Q: What if they ask you questions you cannot answer?

A: I would always let them know that the Bible *has* the answer to everything. I may not always know immediately where to *find* it, but God has the answer. "My preacher can help you. Come and hear him," a visitor for the church could say. If you think he is going to approach the pastor with some hard (or stupid) question, it would be good to forewarn the preacher.

Q: We visit and visit but seem not to make a dent on our town. What is wrong? How do we overcome this?

A: In the first place, by means of radio, newspaper, signs and otherwise, I'd make sure everybody in town knew about your church and could never forget it. Then, too, if a pastor will train all of his people to realize the importance of daily passing out the church cards and constantly inviting people, with no letup, it won't take long before the town will know that this church means business! Then, when you go visiting, people will already know about you. Wherever I visited, people had already heard me on the daily radio broadcast. This made it easier to visit most people. Of course, if they were rebellious sinners and hated the Bible, they were not receptive, but at least they knew what we stood for and we didn't have to waste a lot of time with them. But, I think it is vitally important for *every member* to realize that he or she is a missionary, an ambassador, a representative of that church and that no clerk, receptionist, salesman, repairman, postman, policeman, neighbor, customer or friend should cross our path without a church card and an enthusiastic appeal to "come to our church next Sunday." A thing like that will pay off!

Q: Should a pastor try to demand that all of his members come to the regular visitation program of the church?

A: Well, in the first place, his demanding will not accomplish it. Let's face it, some of our people are never going to participate in all of the things we urge them to do. We know that different people have different talents and opportunities. Also, a man who works ten hours a day in the hot sun for six days a week and then "moonlights" at something else in the evening, does not have the same amount of time to visit that the man does who works a forty-hour week and is off every night plus Saturdays and Sundays. Some of your people who live fifteen miles out in the country may not always be able to make it to the city visitation program of your church, but, they can be encouraged to work hard on their neighbors and others along the way between their house and the city limits. You need a missionary out there, anyway. There are a few people who will not make it to the organized visitation program of the church and yet are stubbornly loyal to their pastor and will invite people all along in their daily contacts with others. I've had some like this. I finally decided there was no sense in my getting all lathered up over the fact that some of these good people just wouldn't come to visitation.

I did urge my Sunday school teachers and deacons to visit and tried to insist that they do so. Some of them did better than others. Some who did not make it to the regular visitation program, nevertheless, *did* make visits and contacts at other times that suited their work schedules better.

I've had men who were timid about visiting and just froze up at the idea of going out calling who still made very good men on the building committee, the grounds committee or the maintenance crew. So why not use them where they can best be used?

I have also sometimes felt that it was absurd to insist that all people come to visit when, to tell the truth, some of them would probably have done more harm than good if they went out. Some people just do not have the personality for it. Others are so bashful they blush at their own shadow. And there are always a few people in the church who are not the brightest in the world when it comes to saying the right thing. So do the best you can, pray hard that the Lord will send those to visit who can best do it, and take what the Lord sends!

Q: How can a pastor best train his people to visit properly and win souls?

A: First, by doing it yourself. Then, some pastors successfully take laymen along with them, one at a time, until they've learned to do it, too. Other good men—staff members, deacons, Sunday school teachers—can take a man who is weak but willing, or a new Christian, and take him as his visitation buddy until he can stand on his own two feet.

Have a course in visitation and soul winning now and then and emphasize some of the things in this chapter, and in other good books.

Preach on soul winning periodically. And bring in the kind of evangelists and guest speakers who believe in and practice soul winning.

Take some of your key people to soul-winning conferences put on by the Sword of the Lord, take them to the Southwide Baptist Fellowship, and you might want to take some of your men to Jack Hyles' Pastors' School at Hammond, Indiana.

Let your people see souls being won in the services and others coming forward on Sundays who have been won during the week and they'll get a taste for the hunt, themselves.

It was said of Wesley, "He is out of breath, pursuing souls." Should this not be true of all of us?

Chapter Twelve

School Daze!

Should Your Church Start a Christian School? And What to Do if You Already Have One!

When a pastor asks me if he should start a Christian day school, I usually say, "Not if you can help it!" If you want to stay busy day and night, if you enjoy long night vigils in school board meetings, if you crave more problems than you've ever had before, if you don't care whether or not you have a day off again, if you are eager to tangle with the state and the federal government, and if you are anxious to create difficulties in your church that would tax the wisdom of Solomon, then start a private school!

Now Christian schools are doing a lot of good for a lot of people. But, I'm going to give both the pros and cons about starting one. Weigh the matter carefully. Find out for sure if God wants you to start one in *your* church. Much is involved.

Many good books and articles have been written on how to manage and administrate a Christian school, so I'm not going to venture into that field. I believe in Christian schools, I appreciate what they are doing, I frequently preach in them, and I pray for this good movement among us.

We started a Christian school in 1960 when I was pastor of the Central Baptist Church of Panama City, Florida. From 32 pupils that first year we saw the blessing of God upon the school until when I left the pastorate in 1973 we had well over 900 attending, including child care, 4-year prep-kindergarten and right on up through the eleventh grade. Since then, the school has added a twelfth grade.

Hundreds of children have made professions of faith in the

school. But since about eighty-five percent of our student body came from outside our own church membership, I'm sure we encountered almost every problem a school could run into.

God gave me some good administrators and some good workers during those years. He sent the teachers we needed in answer to prayer, though we had to work hard and pray much to get them. But, as president of the Christian school, I certainly could not give all of my time to the church any more. Even at best I had to go over to the school facilities at least once a day and sometimes more often. The principal or other workers frequently came down to my office. Many new problems had to be faced having to do with students, money, personnel, parents, standards, discipline, regulations, state controls, sports—you name it, it'll come up sooner or later, sometimes all in one day!

It goes without saying that I could no longer make as many personal visits for my church and give as much undivided attention to the flock as I did before starting a Christian school.

Before starting a Christian school, you should be dead sure the Lord is leading you to do so. If God isn't with you all the way, you've *had* it!

Make sure that your church is with you on it—at least a great majority of the people. Even at best you'll probably lose some people over the school, and you'll always have some who will be sour on the idea.

Don't make the mistake of thinking that if you start a school all of the parents of your pupils will rush over and join your church. Dr. Lee Roberson told me before we started ours that I need not expect to get a lot of new members because of my school. He was right.

Make sure that you have the support and help of your church leaders. You're going to need all you can get, and then some.

Many pastors in this country are snowed under with their schools. Some are teaching school, others are supervisors or principals—at least they're trying to be. Still others are handling the finances of the school, driving a bus, coaching a team or even doing the janitorial work. Some are trying to do some of all of the above! No wonder so many churches are struggling along at a poor dying rate!

About the time you think you've caught up and can devote your time to your church for awhile there'll be a crisis in the state and to keep some of the bureaucratic brass hats from closing in on you you'll have to start a pilgrimage to the state capital.

And if you really want to wrestle against flesh and blood, just wait until you are in a building program in your church and your school at the same time!

If there is already a good Christian school in the town to which you can send your students, then I'd think a long, long time before getting into the education business. You can cooperate with the other Christian school, send your students, help them out in their government problems, etc., without jeopardizing your own ministry in your local church.

As much as I believe in the good things Christian schools are doing, I wonder if it is worth what it costs some pastors to neglect their churches.

And, strange as it may seem, some of the strongest youth groups in some of the churches I've been in, and some of the most spiritual young people, have been youth in churches where most of them attend *public* schools. Facing what they have to face and being taught to witness and stand their ground in the public school will develop character that one does not always find in the sheltered, private, Christian schools. (Usually, where they have a very strong youth group there is also a strong youth leader or youth pastor in that church!)

Most pastors are not educators and do not know how to run a school even if they had time to do so. In churches where both the school and the church are flourishing and growing, one or both of two things will be true:

(1) Where the pastor is a very gifted preacher, a fast reader, a dynamic leader and a genius in organization, he may also have developed a good school.

(2) If a pastor is one of the rare individuals who has the temperament, the personality and the leadership ability to

manage people and time, one to whom good workers are magnetically attracted, and one who has the wisdom to know how to delegate responsibility, he may make a success of both church and school.

Even then it takes the kind of leader who doesn't mind hard work, welcomes problems, is not afraid of a crisis, develops sermons and lectures easily, likes people and can get along with almost every kind of person God ever made.

If you, as a busy pastor, are going to start a school, plan on getting up early and staying up late. Forget about days off and free time—at least until you are large enough in your organization to have an excellent principal, good supervisors and efficient secretaries. Also, you'll need a good visitation man or assistant pastor to help with your church visitation while all of this school business is being developed. I hate to sound pessimistic, but starting and maintaining a successful private school is anything but easy.

I'm sure that many pastor-educators feel that the time they give to the education business is worth it all, and that if their church never grows to any extent because of it, that the school more than compensates for that. Perhaps they are right. But, many real preachers, who know beyond all doubt that they are called to preach, become frustrated and overworked in their efforts to run an educational institution, too.

My only mixed emotion about the Christian school movement in America is that, in many places, it has taken the strong Christian young people out of the public schools (removing the salt), and leaving the public schools with no real testimony for Christ and no parents who will stand up for much of anything. Even if some try to effect much of a change they have so little support because the stronger Christian parents are all over in their secluded Christian schools and are not in a position to help fight the battle.

Many Christian leaders feel that at least every town should have a Christian school, but that does not necessarily mean that every church in that town should have a Christian school!

ADVANTAGES OF HAVING A CHRISTIAN SCHOOL

(1) Your own children and teens have the opportunity for Christian training along with (sometimes) better academic excellence than in most public schools.

(2) Your church children can, for the most part, escape the drug scene and much of the profanity and vulgarity that goes on in the public schools.

(3) They can hear Bible preaching in chapel, can have prayer in the classrooms, and can escape the lie of evolution and the stench of humanistic and atheistic teachings.

(4) They can learn history from the patriotic and conservative viewpoint and, thus, be taught the things that truly made America great.

(5) If your school is a success, is well run, pays its bills and creates a successful climate for real academic excellence, it will impress the community with what you are doing and more people will become interested in the ministry of your church. From time to time you probably also will win some families who will join your church.

(6) If your school is successful, you will attract students from many churches and homes where there is no strong evangelistic emphasis and thus, you will have the joyful privilege of winning a great many of these children to Christ.

(7) Some public school situations are much worse than others. In many school systems, the textbooks are vile, the required reading matter vulgar and the philosophy of "situation ethics" and the so-called new morality are such that it becomes mandatory that a Christian school be started somewhere in the community. On the other hand, in some communities, particularly in the country and small towns, there are still a number of Christians and other people with good character teaching in the public schools. Some public schools are better than others, and for some reason, some schools have not yet been tampered with as much by evil, humanistic forces and by government agencies as have others.

My children went through public schools without being

scarred. They stayed clean, kept their testimony and still have a good time living for the Lord. They did not attend theaters, dances or proms, they made good grades, dressed properly and did not pick up bad habits. However, I know that in the past few years with the hippie dress styles, unisex emphasis, racial chaos, rock music influence and the drug scene, it is much worse now than it was fifteen and twenty years ago. Frankly, I'd hate for our little grandchildren to have to attend a public school today!

So What Does a Pastor Do if He Starts a Private School?

If there is no Christian school handy that you feel like you can conscientiously support and send your young people to, then you may feel compelled to start a school. What do you do?

First, I shared the matter with our church. Next we contacted Dr. Arlin Horton at Pensacola (Florida) Christian School and learned all that we could from him about the Christian school procedure. He and Mrs. Beka Horton have spearheaded this movement and are seasoned veterans. They know all the angles and have had great experience. We also studied some other Christian schools and picked up all the information we could.

Then, we visited the local superintendent of public education and told him what we were planning to do. We told him we intended to use what we (conscientiously) could of the public school curriculum and that we would give our students everything they needed to get a well-rounded education and to graduate knowing everything they ought to know.

I contacted the presidents of some outstanding, fundamental Christian colleges and inquired about getting an administrator and/or teachers. I read the books and pamphlets that were at that time available about the Christian school movement.

We met with twenty-five of the people in our church who were most interested in a school and formed a corporation, getting our local attorney to draw up the papers. We made sure that he cleared things with the state office of education so that we were doing everything in a legal and proper way.

We made our plans and established our goals. We determined that our school would major on the following distinctives:

(1) The Word of God. We would teach the Bible and seek the salvation of all of our pupils.

(2) Academics. We determined to give our children the very best education possible.

(3) Patriotism. We would teach our children from the historic and conservative point of view in order to make them not only good Christians but good citizens.

(4) Manners. We were determined that our children would be properly trained here.

(5) Character. We would instruct our children morally, instituting proper discipline and instilling Biblical moral values.

Where to Meet?

Next, we determined that we'd need classrooms that could be used exclusively for the school, that we would have to have a small office and, of course, restrooms. Sounding out our own people and putting "feeler" ads in the paper, we projected our possible enrollment for kindergarten and the first grade. We raised some money among our own people and a few other interested parties and talked our church into deeding a choice part of our church-owned property to put up our first school rooms.

By now we had our charter from the state and our congregation was well aware that we were going to start our Christian school. We ran ads in the local paper several months ahead, stating our intentions. We also printed attractive circulars and had our young people hit several thousand doors with information about our school. At that time, we announced that we would have kindergartens and an elementary school. We could not, at the time, be sure that we would ever go on into secondary education, much less high school.

We put up two classrooms of block construction, building them large enough so that no state snooper could ever tell us the rooms were not adequate. We made sure they had plenty of windows, doors, lighting and heating facilities. We checked with local health authorities to be sure we had enough of everything that would be needed in the restrooms we constructed. We built a tiny office.

Our school began in 1960 with thirty-two pupils, twenty of them kindergarten kiddies and twelve of them in the first grade. A young lady was employed who had graduated from a Christian college to teach first grade. She also was acting-principal. A capable and dedicated lady from our own membership became our first kindergarten teacher. My music director and assistant pastor served as principal for a time after the first year.

I was assured by Dr. Horton at Pensacola that some of his best teachers were Christian college graduates who had not had education courses. In fact, there were very few young people available in those days who were prepared or trained at all in the field of education. We set out, as Dr. Horton had done, to train our own on the job. Many of our best teachers in those earlier years were young people we brought straight to the field and put to work teaching fresh out of college. Since then, of course, as the Christian school movement has grown, there are many schools with education courses and great numbers of young people are being taught and trained for their school positions later.

The second year we added second grade, adding on another room and working on plans for a bond program to build still more rooms. We were soon into that.

From our original corporation, we had selected a school board to work with the pastor and the principal. As pastor, I was also president of the school. At first I called and directed all school board meetings. Many times, however, the principal and school board needed to meet briefly on some matter after prayer meeting or at other times when I was tied up with my church, so we hit upon the idea of selecting (each year) a chairman of the board from among the board members. It was his duty to moderate the board meetings and they could thus go ahead and get started (with the president's approval) when I had to be tied up somewhere else. I did not, however, make it a point to skip school board meetings or let the men go on and make important decisions without my being in on it.

At our corporation meetings once a year we re-elected the school board, sometimes adding a man as we needed him and as the school grew. The board then later met and selected their own chairman. By now we had a full-time principal.

Later, we borrowed the plans of another successful school (I think we actually *bought* them at a good price) and proceeded to construct a fine pod of air-conditioned rooms that had already been proven to be adequate and functional. We thus made sure that our halls were big enough, that the building was safe, that we had adequate restrooms, that the kitchen would be large enough for future expansion, etc. By that time, we had several hundred students, our school was paying its bills and making a good impression on the town, and we could now approach the local banks for financing—which we did. We had one of these fine bankers on our advisory board.

By now we were advertising in the papers, on radio and with attractive, slick and colorful brochures. Our school was well known and God was blessing it! Twelve years later we had nearly 1,000 students—from child-care on up into high school.

PROBLEMS IN HAVING A CHRISTIAN SCHOOL

What Are the Answers?

Q: Can you just use teachers from your church?

A: Not unless they are qualified. Of course, in child-care and prep-kindergarten we did use some teachers who did not have college degrees. With the pressures from the state, it is becoming more and more necessary to use qualified (and in most places certified) teachers.

Q: Where do you get trained teachers?

A: I went *after* them, visiting colleges early in the year or sending my principal. Many times in February I'd hit the schools again, and, because I was a preacher, could get a chance to speak in chapel and then interview prospective teachers. *Now* the competition is so keen that there are many others after the education majors, too, but at least there are a lot more of them to interview. Also, you can contact other large schools who may know of teachers looking for a job, and you can advertise for them in Christian periodicals. I really think most of ours came to us in answer to prayer!

Q: Is it best to have the school separate from your church?

A: We thought so, but now many schools are being put back under auspices of, and even the budget of, the church since there is so much government interference.

Q: Can't you just ignore the government agencies and state troublemakers and run your school to suit yourself?

A: It is not quite that simple. I do think, though, that the less you tangle with them the better. And don't take any government help or get tied up with them in any way that they feel you owe them something. Don't agitate them unnecessarily.

Q: When you bring teachers from other towns and states to teach in your school, is it best to make them join your church or should they be free to go to the church of their choice?

A: We tried to let them be free about it at first and it didn't work. If teachers do not attend your church, then they do not understand entirely what you are doing and they may not adopt your philosophy. Dignified, conservative-type teachers from a Bible church up North (for instance) may not take to the fiery, evangelistic preaching of a Southern, soul-winning church. But, if they attend all of the services of your church, they will soon learn what you are up to.

Q: How do you finance your school?

A: Tuition, mainly. Find out what other schools charge and then weigh the matter in view of the pay-scale and standard of living for the area where you operate. You can make money off child-care or nursery-care if you handle it right.

Q: But aren't churches having a lot of trouble trying to operate day-care facilities? I thought the state was giving them trouble.

A: That is true in some places. You may have to call it "Three-Year Prep School" or something like that. We made money by having a four-year prep kindergarten. You could also have a *three*-year one. If the word "child-care" facility or "day-nursery" is frowned on, then call it something else. And rig it up as part of your school, or church, as the situation suggests.

Q: Why can you make more money from the day-care and kindergarten?

A: Because you don't have to have college-bred teachers, necessarily, and you do not have to have expensive textbooks and other equipment that you have further up in your school. And with drop-in kiddies, you can charge by the hour.

Q: How else can you finance your school?

A: By running buses and charging for this service. Also, you may make a little bit off your lunchroom. You *should* if it is run right. We would also stage a big bond program when we had some real building to do.

And don't let your parents get away with getting behind with their tuition payments. Have a deadline for payment and stick to it, say by the 10th of the month. Give them an ultimatum on pastdue bills, and mean it.

One plan is to let them pay by the year in advance and finance it through the bank. They pay the finance charges, of course, and you'll have to knock off a bit of the yearly charge for such payment, but it will give you some operating cash at the beginning of the year when you need it most.

Another plan would be to arrange for them to finance it on their Master Charge or Visa cards. This keeps you from being left holding the bag on slow accounts.

Then we would have an annual fish fry or a Halloween Festival and things like that to finance certain big projects. We had candy sales and let the children sell the candy to finance the several thousand dollars it took to send our teachers, supervisors, principal and board members to the annual Christian Educators meetings. These meetings do a lot for the staff and for the teachers. They learn much and they pick up some good pointers. Then it is a nice break for them, too.

You may also be able to get interested churches to put your school in their budgets for a monthly contribution. This helps. Most fundamental churches are glad you have a school and will want to help.

Q: But you say you "made money" off child-care, yet a private Christian school is a "nonprofit organization." How do you figure that?

A: By "making money" I simply meant that we took in enough money in child-care and kindergartens to help to finance the upper grades. We actually never had any surplus. We never made money that anyone could spend on themselves! It was just that in the overall layout we could help finance the upper part of our school with the money we made on the lower part.

By the way, another reason for starting kindergarten and day-care just as young as you can is to feed your first grade. The larger kindergarten we had the more first grades we soon had. One year we had five or six kindergartens and a couple of prep-kindergartens going on at the same time. And that was in addition to child-care. Most of our elementary pupils had already been in our kindergarten. And a lot of our kindergarten kiddies had started out in our child-care program. That's the way it works.

You can also help finance your work by having something like a "Four Hundred Club" with 400 of your family members pledging a certain amount to the school (above tuition) to belong to the club.

Also, we would have a big annual spring extravaganza at the city auditorium or somewhere like that. It was patriotic and exciting. It involved all of the kids. We advertised it big. The students and faculty really worked on it. It was a top-rate production with stage props, back drops, good music. You can charge for tickets. Students can compete in selling them. You can also sell refreshments at the production. All of this helps with your financing.

Q: How do you get your parents to cooperate, especially those who do not attend your church?

A: We had a Parent-Teachers' Fellowship meeting much like the PTA in public schools. Put the kids on the program and the parents will attend. Many of them will, anyway. Let them know what you are doing. Take time for the parents. Be sure your teachers are ready to greet them and talk to them about their pupils after the initial program in the auditorium is over.

Q: How do you make a school really "succeed" in the eyes of the public?

A: Produce quality education! And keep your school in the news. Some of the ideas for making a *church* succeed (in the chapter on "Making a Joyful Noise") will also work for your *school*. Work out the publicity with your principal and supervisor. When your school gets big, you may need a public relations man to handle this. Or you will be greatly blest if you have a principal or a supervisor who is also a good publicity man.

Q: What do you do about *standards* in this day when morals and customs are so lax?

A: Draw you up some good sensible and scriptural rules and stay with them. Let your teachers know what you and the principal demand. Be sure your principal and supervisors are 100% in agreement with you on the standards. Don't hire a principal if he does not agree with you about such things as good music, short hair on boys, modest attire on girls, etc.

Q: What do you do if boys insist on wearing their hair too long?

A: Send (or take) them to the barber shop! If they don't want to abide by the rules, give them their walking papers.

Q: Even if the boy is a good athlete?

A: Especially if he is! The athlete will influence the other kids more than the average run-of-the-mill student. Don't be afraid of rules. The best of the winning football coaches have had them. Military academies have standards. So do the marines. There is no use having a private school and calling it a Christian school if you do not have standards.

Keep some good literature going in mail-outs to your parents often. You'll have more trouble with parents, generally, than with pupils. If your parents do not all attend your church and hear strong Bible preaching against sin, then you have to send it to them. Keep them posted on humanism, the new morality, situation ethics, immodesty, drugs, sex education, rock music. Make them glad they have their children in your school.

Q: How do you get parents who are unsaved or worldly to agree?

A: They won't all agree. But they must subscribe to it and be willing for their kids to be brought under such discipline if they send them to your school. Have them sign an agreement. That gets you off the hook. Let the parents know that the schools that really succeed (like Pensacola Christian, Bob Jones, etc.) are the ones with tough standards.

Q: How do you avoid church-school conflicts?

A: You don't altogether. There will always be problems. Do your best to keep the school before your church graciously, kindly and tactfully. But don't just preach school, and announce school, and talk school so much that your church members get sick and tired of hearing about the school. I would certainly keep school announcements to a minimum in the pulpit.

Q: What about teachers that are more concerned with the school than with the church and do not really endorse the church program?

A: I'd not *have* a teacher who did not endorse the church program. Train your teachers. Let them know that this is a church-related school and that the church is the mother of the school and that you consider the church most important. When I was at Massillon (Ohio) Baptist Temple for a revival, I remember that Dr. Cummons, the pastor, was reminding his schoolteachers to go *easy* on the homework for the pupils so they could come every night to the revival. This is as it should be. I've been in some churches where the Christian schoolteachers seemed to really pile it (the homework) *on* during revivals in the church. Train your teachers.

Q: What do you do if parents in the school and church begin to renig and rebel about the standards in your school?

A: Don't ever let it get to first base. Stick to your standards. Remind the school kids that you cannot have as rigid rules for voluntary pupils who simply attend church on Sunday—and especially unsaved ones you're trying to reach, but that you *do* have rules for your school and they'll have to understand this.

Don't ever start giving in and letting the bars down. If you do, you're sunk!

Q: Do you ever get to the point where the pastor can just take his hands off and let the principal and school board run the school?

A: Not entirely. If you have a godly, firm, powerful leader for a principal, one who loves the pastor and would die for him, you might be able to *almost* turn it all over to him. But not altogether. Even at best you'll have to retain your place as school president and keep your hand in the thing. There will be times when parents will just have to talk to you. And you can't ignore them. Especially is this true if parents who are members of your church feel that they are not being treated properly at the school. You just *have* to get to an understanding in such cases. There is nothing to be gained by letting things fester and sour in your church because of the school. If it is *your* school, you can't let it get away from you. Keep your hand on it. But use your head. Don't try to tend to everything. Don't meddle. Let your administrator do his job.

Q: What do you do if young people from your church feel that the kids who go to your Christian school are getting preferential treatment? How do you reconcile the two?

A: Well, it is always a problem. You've got to work hard at keeping your school kids from developing a pious, holier-than-thou attitude. And then be sure that you have something good going on for the kids in your church so they will not feel that the school kids have all the breaks. Wise youth leaders can help a whole lot with this problem. If your youth director is not also affiliated with your school, then he at least ought to work closely with the school leaders. Try not to have conflicting programs with your youth. And keep your school from scheduling things that will interfere with your church, especially during revivals and Bible conferences in the church.

Let me say also that it is vitally necessary that your Christian schoolteachers, staff workers, supervisors, all of them, be faithful to all of the services of your church and be active! This will keep down a lot of trouble. It will help keep your teachers spiritual and it will prevent heartaches before they develop.

Q: If your school is under your church, is the school board made up of deacons or who?

A: That depends on what the pastor and his leaders agree on. If it is the deacons, though, I'd be sure that it is understood that a working "board" or "council" chosen from the deacons will actually tend to the business of the school. A whole lot of men cannot possibly take the time to learn about and get themselves involved in all of the activities of the school. You'll ruin some good deacons if you bring everything to the deacon board that goes on in the school!

Three men, or at the most five, could be chosen by the pastor to work with the pastor and principal. Even then, most of the school work would be left to the principal and his supervisors. Ninety-nine out of a hundred deacons would not make good educators and we need not expect them to be.

Delegate authority, let your administrator administrate but work closely with him. Then pray without ceasing that God will keep the whole thing together until the rapture!

Q: Was your school an A.C.E. school?

A: No, ours was a regular traditional school. But some small churches would not be able to *have* a school if it were not for the A.C.E. program. I think in many situations it is working well.

Q: Can a school just meet in a regular church building?

A: Not too well unless the church was built with that in mind. Rooms should be large, well-ventilated, well-lighted, with large hallways and plenty of restrooms. Most churches do not have this. You might get by with it just as a temporary expedient. Some states have tough laws about room size, etc. Then, too, you have the problem of teachers complaining on Monday because the Sunday school pupils messed up the desks and blackboards on Sunday. You have janitorial problems, too. It is not easy.

If you do try to combine, be sure the school kids are taught to pick up after themselves carefully. Keep the grounds clean.

Monitor the restrooms very carefully. Otherwise, you'll have problems with your church people.

Q: What do you think about just restricting your school pupils to students from your own church family?

A: Some schools are going to that, hoping to eliminate difficulties. As churches get worldlier, it is becoming harder to get some parents to cooperate and allow a Christian school to discipline their children. But there are problems. Most schools would never be able to make it financially if they restricted the student body to their own church members. I don't think *we* ever could have done so. And it would be hard to get and pay teachers.

Then, too, you cheat yourself out of winning a great host of kids to Christ who come to you from worldly churches. And if your church-school situation is a strong one (as it should be), you can instruct and indoctrinate children from other churches who in turn may some day take the Gospel to others. In this way, we are obeying the Great Commission. With all of the problems, I'd say if you're going to have a school, get everybody you can in there who will be willing to abide by your discipline and regulations. If we can get the Word of God into enough of them, who knows? We may be able to turn this thing around one of these days!

Chapter Thirteen

Facing, Solving and Avoiding Problems

You're going to *have* some problems if you serve God. But, try not to manufacture your own! Spurgeon said we have a trouble factory inside and if we don't get enough from without, we make our own. This is often true of preachers.

"All who will live godly in Christ Jesus shall suffer persecution," Paul tells us in II Timothy 3:12. Jesus said we are blessed when people say all manner of evil against us for righteousness' sake (Matt. 5:10,11). But, often our troubles come on us, not because we are so right or so righteous but because we are so stubborn, impatient or hotheaded. Those kinds of troubles we can and should avoid.

Even at best the man of God will face problems and they are too numerous to even begin to list them all. But many of them will fall into one or more of the following categories:

(1) MOUTH PROBLEMS. ("What will this babbler say" next?) Or, "They say and do not." The human tongue is an unruly evil, full of deadly poison, James reminds us (chapter 3). Either *my* mouth as the pastor, or the mouths of others, create many problems.

(2) MONEY PROBLEMS. Either the pastor's personal finances or the finances of the church have led many a man of God into troubled waters.

(3) ME PROBLEMS. "The Big I." Diotrophes loveth to have the preeminence. Some preachers have a tendency to lord it over the people. Others have men (or women) in the church who want to run it all or at least be at the center—if not the head—of everything.

(4) FEMALE PROBLEMS. Some preachers, far too many of them, have been deceived or trapped by temptation into becoming involved with a woman.

(5) DEACON PROBLEMS. How to get the right ones. How to secure their help and love instead of their enmity and disdain.

(6) STAFF INFECTIONS. What to do with staff members who get out of kilter, or who are not fulfilling their duties.

(7) OPPOSITION. How to handle it.

(8) PERSONALITY CLASHES. All of us are different. Some people are not going to like us no matter how winsome we try to be.

(9) FELLOWSHIP WITH OTHER PASTORS AND MOVEMENTS.

(10) WHEN YOU ARE CRITICIZED, WHAT DO YOU DO?

(11) WORLDLY MEMBERS AND CHURCH LEADERS.

(12) THE PROBLEM OF LOSING YOUR YOUNG PEOPLE.

(13) DIVISION—WHEN PEOPLE LEAVE THE CHURCH.

(14) WHEN BUSINESS MEETINGS GET OUT OF HAND.

Now some of these problems will be dealt with somewhat in other chapters in this book. I'll not take time to try to cover everything that ever may come up in the pastorate. If I did, the Devil would invent some *new* problems tomorrow.

But, I am confident that most problems can be faced, dealt with and solved. And that many, many other problems can be avoided. Crises can be met in the strength and wisdom of God. It is not necessary to become defeated and remain discouraged. We preach that there is victory for our people in the Lord. So there is victory for the preacher, too.

We are going to look at the fourteen problems I've just enumerated. But first, let me share a splendid outline by my brother, Norman Pyle, on avoiding problems. It is far *better* to avoid them, if possible. I asked Norman if he would make some suggestions for this book. He is an outstanding pastor. He has been through building programs, church problems and heart-breaking traumas of more than one variety. He has remained solid and true and steadfast as pastor of the Bible Baptist

Church of Atlanta, Georgia, now for over twenty years. He is an excellent preacher and a very devoted pastor. His people love him. He has a fine, loyal congregation and his business meetings run smoothly.

Here are his suggestions on how pastors can avoid many of the problems we bring on ourselves:

(1) *"Stay in Crete."* He refers to a great message by Dr. Jack Hyles on that theme. Paul wrote to Titus and told him to stay in Crete. I have just read the message again in Dr. Hyles' book, *Let's Hear Jack Hyles.* Instead of running from problems and seeking another pastorate when trouble comes, God would have many a pastor to stay put and remain "in Crete," as Paul advised Titus to do (Titus 1:5). Dr. Hyles suggests that the preacher, even in the midst of problems and difficulties, should "stay in Crete" because the preacher needs the training and blessing that God has for him there; because Crete needs him, and because God needs him in Crete. It is a good message. Don't think you have to *run* every time difficulties arise.

Dr. John R. Rice said, in referring to the pastors who always want him to recommend them somewhere, "Why don't you get the *Lord* to recommend you? Then maybe you won't have to *leave!*"

(2) *Develop a blind eye* and a deaf ear. Here, my brother refers to the famous and outstanding message by Spurgeon to his students. Don't see and hear all of the trifling little picky things that the Devil wants to use to upset you. Keep one blind eye and one deaf ear for such things.

(3) *Don't expect your wife* to have the same dedication to the ministry that you have. This, of course, is not to say that your wife should not be spiritual and consecrated. It is to say that God did not call *her* to pastor your church, He called *you.* Some pastors allow their churches to demand too much of the pastor's wife.

(4) *Get your priorities right.* Distinguish between God and the church. Just doing "church work" does not mean that your own personal life is what it ought to be. You need the Bible and prayer and devotion and soul winning for your own heart—not

just because you are a pastor. Don't read the Bible only to get sermon outlines and ideas. Read it for your own soul!

(5) *Differentiate between preferences and convictions.* Even though you would die for your convictions, you need to learn to "give" a bit where the problem involved is just a matter of preference.

(6) *Make your deacons your friends,* not your competitors!

(7) *Hold the ministry in respect, but be able to laugh at yourself.* Too many preachers are too touchy and too easily offended. You are human, have you forgotten? Maintain your sense of humor. I think Norman gives good advice here—don't be too proud to laugh at yourself.

(8) *Admit when you are wrong.* It does not undermine your leadership. People will appreciate your honesty and humility in the matter.

(9) *Share your problems* and pains (personal, family, etc.) with the people, as wisdom directs, instead of trying to hide them. Let them know you are human. If they know you love *them,* they will love *you* and pray for you when they see you're treading some rough waters.

I hope these thoughts from Pastor Norman Pyle will help you to avoid some difficulties that you might be prone to bring upon yourself. Now, let us take up the fourteen problem areas that are most likely to arise in the life of a pastor, remembering that, when possible, it is far better to *avoid* having the problem than to try to unravel it later.

1. MOUTH

"Mouth" is the first one. "Set a watch, O Lord, before my mouth; keep the door of my lips," David cried in Psalm 141:3. What a wonderful prayer to pray at the beginning of every day. "Study to be quiet," Paul advised in I Thessalonians 4:11. People who say what they think should think! If you think ahead and speak advisedly, you will more likely keep your big number ten out of your mouth.

Don't promise with your mouth what you cannot be sure you

will do. Say what you mean and mean what you say. Someone has declared that those who think by the inch and talk by the yard should be kicked by the foot. Some people just talk and ramble and wander around in their speech until they are bound to say something wrong. Conversation does not have to be going on all the time. "Be *still* and know that I am God," the Lord says.

Ask God to guard your lips and control what you say before you meet your family or your public. Make notes on what you will announce and say in the pulpit. Learn to get your brain and your mouth on the same wave length.

You do not always have to commit yourself to every word of idle chatter or gossip that comes your way. Don't repeat anything until you are sure it is true—and then don't repeat about 95% of what *is* true! Careless words, like falling leaves, are awfully hard to pick up again.

Don't let yourself be drawn into the criticism of others.

Always tell the truth and you'll not have problems trying to remember what you said.

Find something good to say about people in your membership if you have to say anything at all about them. When your critics or enemies hear that you have been saying good things about them, they may not be your enemies long.

If you find yourself becoming angry or keyed-up, try counting to ten before you say *any*thing—better still, spend ten minutes in prayer. One pastor admitted to his congregation that he was as mad as a hornet. I think that was one admission he might have kept to himself. "Let not the sun go down upon your wrath" (Eph. 4:26).

Boast of another person and not on yourself. If you have done something worthwhile, it will soon be applauded by others and it will sound much better coming from them than from you.

To keep loose tongues from running wild in the flock, I'd preach now and then on "the tongue is a fire, a world of iniquity" (James 3:6), or on "how great a matter a little fire kindleth!" (James 3:5), or "a lying tongue hateth those who are afflicted by it" (Prov. 26:28), or "a fool also is full of words" (Eccles. 10:14).

There are many other verses to add to these. You can soon throw the fear of God into your people about this gossip business.

When naming sins such as lust, drinking, evil thinking, rock music and drug abuse, be sure and include malice of the tongue, filthy communication out of your mouth, lying, gossip, back-biting and slander. They do just as much damage if not more. Teach your people what God has to say about the tongue. Search it out in your concordance.

Keep some good tracts and booklets on the tongue handy and be sure they circulate among your people. Keep your people busy winning souls. And soak the place constantly in prayer. People who are truly praying for others are not preying on others.

2. MONEY

"Money" is the second one. Be very careful about your own finances. Don't get in over your head. Learn from chapter six on how to get better offerings and then it is likely your own income will increase. Don't let yourself become money-minded, but do train your people to understand that God's servants are to "live of the gospel" and that the laborer is worthy of his hire.

Pay your debts if it kills you. If you ever have to put off a pay-ment, be sure and explain to the person you owe that you are in a bind and will make it up very soon. If you promise payment by a certain date, be certain that you keep this promise.

Learn the difference between faith and foolhardiness. If there is a definite need, you have a right to claim the promise from God and expect Him to supply that need. If you wait on God about it, He will show you whether you should buy it on time or wait until you have the cash in hand. While waiting on God about it, He may delight to send it in an unforeseen manner. It may even be a gift to you and then you won't have to make payments. But, don't go around with your hand out expecting people to give you things or give you a discount on everything you buy just because you are a preacher. Business people resent this even if they do give you the discount.

When I moved to one Florida city, I had to go to an eye specialist. After serving me, he said, "Now do you want me to give you a preacher's discount?" I could tell he was a bit exasperated. I said, "No, Sir, you just tell me what I owe you." I paid the regular price but it was never high and I always had good rapport with that doctor after that. It was obvious that other preachers had poor-mouthed him for a discount.

On the other hand, there will be many blessings that will come your way because you are serving the Lord. There are some merchants who really *want* to help God's servants. In this case, I would respectfully accept what they give you and thank them for it, but never act like you expect it. Just praise the Lord for all He provides for you. Let them know that you accept it as unto the Lord and that you are sure God will bless them for it. Then pray a blessing upon them when you get where you can.

By the way, if you are generous with others, then, according to Luke 6:38, others will be generous with you. Pastors who give all that they can are generally those who have the most themselves. I have observed that the pastors who are happy to see an evangelist or a missionary get a good love offering will be those who will most often prosper themselves. "He that soweth bountifully shall reap also bountifully" (II Cor. 9:6).

Don't let yourself get tangled with the finances of the church. Keep out of the money end of it. Let others count the money, wrestle with the budget and sign the checks. Don't go around checking up on what everybody is giving or is not giving. You'll soon get dollar signs in your eyeballs. And you may soon be accused of spending money that doesn't belong to you.

The pastor does have a real responsibility to teach the people how to give and to give them intelligent opportunities to do so. In chapter six I have dealt with this rather fully. Beyond that, you'll be smart to stay out of the money business. The love of it truly is the root of all evil, and worrying about it will only stifle your faith and produce premature ulcers.

3. ME

"Me" problems we usually bring upon ourselves. "Before honor is humility," Solomon tells us. I praise God for an old lay-evangelist who worked me over good when I was a young preacher starting out. He embarrassed me, humiliated me, called me down and aggravated me until I sometimes almost despised him. Yet, I knew he was a spiritual man and a soul winner so I let him help the Lord "break" me. He sensed an ego and a self-sufficiency in me that he knew had to go if God was ever going to use me to any extent. So he worked on me and gave me very little peace or privacy until God had taught me some valuable lessons about humility, brokenness and the crucifixion of the self-life. Along with that, I received the booklets of McCall Barbour on victory, death-to-self and how-to-die-daily from an old uncle of mine who was a chaplain in the prison system up East. Those earlier days of training, coupled with my Scofield Bible and the weekly arrival of THE SWORD OF THE LORD, had much to do with my effectual service for the Lord in those early days. And I still need these truths put to practical use in my life today. We never get to the place (in this life) where the "old man" does not have a mean habit of coming down from the cross.

Don't be a dictator, but don't be a pipsqueak, either. Self (the Big I), is evident in either case. Some pastors start out to "lord it over" the flock (see I Peter 5:3), while others are so afraid to assert themselves that they end up being trampled by the deacons or others in the church. Read carefully what the Bible has to say about the duties and responsibilities of the pastor or bishop or elder in the Bible. Then serve the Lord in all humility of mind while at the same time remembering that you are God's undershepherd and that you stand or fall to your own Master, even Christ.

Do not forget that, even as God has so designed a civilization that has kings and presidents over countries, governors over states, principals over schools and a man as the head of each home, so God has ordained that a pastor should be over each flock of believers. The people need to be taught and trained to respect those 'who labor among them and are over them in the Lord and admonish them, and to esteem them very highly in love for their work's sake' (see I Thessalonians 5:12,13).

If you want them to respect you, though, you have to give them something to respect. If you are humble, pure, earnest, prayerful, dedicated, conscientious, and loving, then they will take your leadership over them even when God has to give you a holy boldness and make you a mighty weapon in His hand at times.

They ought to respect you and love you even if they hate you!

While you are young, you must tread softly. Keep in mind that there are many things you will yet learn and that some of the older saints may have some insight that God has not yet given you. It takes time for the cream to rise. Giant preachers, like oaks, grow from little nuts. As I look back on some of my sermons (and some of my pictures), in my early days in the ministry, I wonder how on earth the people even *stood* me back in my twenties and thirties. And yet, at the time, I thought I was pretty mature!

The bigger a man's head, the easier it is to fill his shoes. "Pride goeth before destruction," Solomon said, and it was never more true than of the minister. Someone has well said that pride is a peculiar disease, in that it makes everybody sick except the person who has it.

When you are sure that you have been to the cross yourself and learned that you are just an instrument and not an agent of God's, then you are in a position to grapple with the "Big I" people in the congregation.

Preach the truth of self-abasement to your people. Remind them that with God, the way up is down, that we win by losing, and that we gain by surrendering.

Preach on such verses as Galatians 2:20, Luke 9:23,24 and John 12:24 often enough that your ego-maniacs in the congregation would be pretty well exposed if they got too high and mighty. But, be patient with them. For some people, it takes longer than others to be led back to the cross and see that not only did Christ die for them there but they died with Him there.

Gradually, grow a congregation of soul winners. If people are busy fishing for men, filling the buses with prospects and laboring in the Sunday school and other areas of the work, they'll have little time (nor inclination) to try to run the preacher and the program of the church. Hunting dogs growl at and pick at one another only when they're away from the field and have nothing else to do but get lazy and sassy.

For those who try to be the big cheese in everything, it is good to have a democratic change of officers about every year. Don't let any one man feel that he has a monopoly on being Sunday school superintendent, chairman of the deacons or the financial wizard. Let it be understood that the treasurer is to help count the money and sign the checks, not control the spending of it.

With proper instruction from the Scriptures, the women of the church should learn that they are not to teach men, nor to usurp authority in church matters (I Tim. 2:10-12).

4. FEMALE PROBLEMS

Stay very much in love with your own wife and don't be afraid for the congregation to know that you are in love with her and intend to keep the honey in the honeymoon. Never embarrass your wife or play her down before the people in any way. Thus, you will never give any other woman the impression that all is not well inside your own home. There should never be any question in the minds of any member of the congregation but that the pastor and his wife are devotedly and happily in love with each other.

Avoid physical contact with women or girls in (or out) of your congregation. Some women are more affectionate than others and will be inclined to hold on to a pastor's hand or press up close to him while engaged in private conversation. It is a good idea to withdraw your hand as quickly as possible after shaking hands with a woman. It is not necessary to pat her on the shoulder or put your hand on her waist when helping her to the door. If a woman is in tears and emotionally upset, she sometimes falls into the arms of a pastor or counselor. In such cases, just ease her into a seat and disengage yourself immediately. Then have prayer with her and keep the conversation on a strictly spiritual plane.

Most Christian women are naive and completely innocent when they hold onto your hand or lean on your shoulder. Just be sure that you keep your own thoughts and hands where they belong and get on with the prayer or counseling!

Once in a great while there may be a love-starved woman who really will long for the touch of a man's hand on hers and may encourage more than just a handshake. Watch out for such temptations. If a woman or girl persists in showing affection, then it is best to turn her over to your wife or at least call your assistant or secretary or someone else into the office.

I fear that much counseling being done by pastors today is consuming far too many more hours than it should and that instead of two or three hours of counseling the whole thing should have been wrapped up in ten minutes or so of letting the lady tell her story followed by some definite words given to her from the Word of God and an earnest prayer. Don't let your Bible-teaching and soul-winning ministry be consumed with counseling. Long counseling sessions have sometimes led to temptation.

If a woman (or anyone, for that matter) continues to ask for counseling, then I'd let an assistant "assist" or eventually send them to a regular psychologist or psychiatrist if they are not taking your advice and letting the Word help them. The book of Proverbs, plus regular, consistent church attendance and service for the Lord (following honest confession) is what most people need who come for counseling.

Remember, that most people are having their troubles because of *sin*. The blood of Christ and the Word (and will) of God is what most of them need. And it does not take days (or even hours) of counseling to present that truth to them!

If you have to see the same lady more than once or twice, then it will be best to have your secretary or wife in on the conversation. If the woman brings her sex life into the discussion, then it will be best to advise her to let your wife or some other trained, capable and spiritual lady be the one to talk to her. Also, you can usually help her by putting the right kind of books in her hand.

If the lady or girl begins to tell you that her husband is not satisfying her or giving her the attention and affection she needs, then that is the time to let your wife assist you with the counseling. Stay out of situations that might develop into something unsavory or that might lead you into temptation.

Don't make a practice of visiting ladies alone unless it is just a pop-call to the front door. If you're going to have to stay any length of time, it will be best to be sure your wife or assistant goes with you or that someone else is home when you call.

Don't offer a ride to ladies you see waiting for a bus, even if you know them real well. It is said that one noted pastor even refuses to pick up his own daughter on the street and take her home from work. Perhaps that is a bit extreme, but at least he is "avoiding the very appearance of evil." If you are forced to offer a ride or take a woman to the hospital, it will be most wise to have someone else along for the ride.

Young teenage girls sometimes get a "crush" on a young pastor or youth worker. Do not encourage this at all. Be nice but stick strictly to the business of serving the Lord.

Be careful with your eyes as well as your hands. Many women are not as careful to dress as modestly as they should. "Let thine eyes look right on, and let thine eyelids look straight before thee," Solomon wisely advised (Prov. 4:25).

Stay "clean through the word" (John 15:3) and "keep thyself pure" (I Tim. 5:12).

5. DEACON PROBLEMS

I think we'll take a separate chapter for the deacons. But, be sure you have standards (written out) for your deacons and do emphasize the spiritual qualification for deacons. Teach the Word lovingly but firmly so that the members of the congregation realize that this is not a time for selecting friends, relatives or popular figures in the church. Deacons should be good men who are "full of the Holy Ghost and wisdom" (Acts 6:3). They should be chosen and elected with great care and much prayer.

As my brother, Norman, suggested, "Make the deacons your friends, not your competitors." Teach and train your people about what the deacons should do and be when all is going *well* in the church; don't wait until some of the deacons are giving you trouble. (See chapter 15.)

6. STAFF INFECTIONS

Many pastors say that their headaches increase when they

begin to hire staff members to help them. This should not have to be. In some cases, pastors spend so much time trying to keep their workers working and helping to solve the problems they cause that they might be better off without help.

Now, in the first place, we preachers need to examine our own hearts and be sure what we want these helpers for and just what we ought to expect of them.

When my last (and longest) pastorate grew to about 400 or 500 members, I found it difficult to cover the ground, make the visits, keep up with the hospitals, do the daily radio programs and prepare all the sermons without help. The first helper we hired was a good secretary. Before that, I had used volunteer ladies to do my letters. The church also had used a volunteer lady to do the financial secretarial work of the church. But, there comes a time when a growing church almost has to take on some staff workers. Most pastors will need a secretary if they want to get very much done. Someone needs to be at the church to answer routine phone calls and keep up with the many things that begin to need attention in a growing church.

A good custodian is also a necessary person to have on the premises, especially when the church gets to be any size.

Some pastors have problems by hiring someone in the church to do these jobs (secretary, custodian, etc.) just because they are members and need an extra paycheck. In the case of a secretary, the pastor should hire someone who can do the work he needs done, one who can spell and type (fast), and is well-organized and neat, and one who can keep her mouth shut. It is usually best to get someone who has been trained for the job of a church secretary.

In the case of a custodian, it might or might not be a member of your own church, but it should be a man who does not mind taking orders and who can do a multitude of things and is not afraid of work. A good man from the deacon board may be the best man to work along with him but he should, of course, also be accountable to the pastor.

The pastor should have the authority to hire and fire his staff members. Those hired should understand from the outset that they are responsible to the pastor.

There should be a work sheet or job description printed out for every worker employed. They should know what their duties are to be. It should be understood from the beginning if they are to work a strict 40-hour week or if there will be hours that will be demanded of them over and above, simply because they are working for the Lord.

To just leave it loose and say you'll work "all day" and then expect work from them every night, too, often leads to frustration and misunderstanding.

Most church secretaries, assistant pastors, music directors and youth directors are going to be needed at night and on Sundays for many of their duties in addition to the time they'll spend working in the office and on the field during the week. A loyal, consecrated, hard-working pastor may put in 60 or 70 hours a week. His workers and assistants may have to work 50 to 60 hours, too, but they should know this and know approximately what and when their hours of work are. In such cases, you should see that these workers have a day off and some evenings to themselves when you don't "hold the whip" over them.

Many hired assistants and workers become confused and ineffective, not because they are lazy and irresponsible but because they get too many irons in the fire and meet themselves coming back from other jobs they probably did not even know they'd have to be responsible for when they came to work for you. Instead of just assuming that your helpers will do anything you tell them to do, it would be good to call them aside and ask them if they can work such and such into their schedule, and how they feel about it. To have them doing the work happily and agreeably is much better than just being faced with extra duties they must turn out by neglecting something else or doubling up in their off-hours.

No matter how important we feel the work is and how enthused about it we may be, it is well to remember that no hired helper brought in is going to feel the same heat of enthusiasm about the work that you do. You have to stay on top of the whole project while the music man or youth man you employ is going to feel the keenest responsibility only for the particular task you bring him in to do. After a man has been with you for many years, you may see that he has something of the same heartbeat for the whole church that you do, but don't expect too much too soon.

As our membership moved on up into the 700, 800 and 1,000 bracket, we had to not only have help with our school but with the music and the youth. When the membership stood at 1,200, 1,400 and then 1,500 we had to have two secretaries, a music man, youth director, visitation leader, etc. Most churches will discover the same thing. Some may even need more workers. But, try not to hire so many paid employees that you find yourself paying for work that ought to be done by the members. Don't take from your people all the joy of serving the Lord. The visitation man, for instance, should not be expected to do all the visiting. Your members need to be doing some of it and they need to be learning to win souls and build up classes, bus routes, etc.

Don't let your youth man be the only one who works with the young people. Your people need to take some responsibility, they need to help finance some of the projects and the young people themselves need to feel tied to the church, not just to a hired youth man. The youth director or youth pastor needs the help of members for transportation, chaperoning, fixing refreshments and other things.

What About Double-Duty Workers?

Many churches are looking for combination men. We had a youth director who also worked at visitation at one time. Again, we had a music director who was assistant principal of the Christian school. On more than one occasion, we had a music man in the church who also took care of the music in our school. At another time, we had a combination music and youth man. How does it work?

Well, if you want to get the very best out of a music man and if that is his field and his calling, he will probably work best just in music. If you have a school and a church, too, his hands will probably be full, especially if you have several choirs, plus trios, quartets, instrumentalists, etc.

A youth-and-music man will have divided attention and mixed affections in his work. His duties will conflict at times. And some men might have trouble quickly adjusting to the serious work of an adult choir on the evening of the day that he has been out romping with the kids.

I'm sure that many music men would say that the music is enough to keep them busy all the time. This probably is true if you have both a church and a school or if your church is unusually large with many choirs and a varied music program affecting different age groups. But, if your church is small or moderate in size, then I see no reason why a music man could not also do some other work for the pastor. And certainly all workers (music, youth, school, etc.) should do personal soul winning and visiting for the good of their own spiritual lives as well as for the need of the work.

Some youth workers just want to play and have a big time with the young people in the church. They need to be serious enough to take some other responsibilities, too, and to lead (by example) the youth to win souls and work in the church. And you want to be sure that the youth pastor or youth director is absolutely loyal to the pastor and is leading the youth to love the Lord, the church and the pastor, rather than just building up a little unrelated church by itself. It is best that this be understood from the start rather than trying to cope with the problem after it develops and begins to fester.

When Staff Members Become Unhappy or Troublesome

Sometimes it does happen. Try to prevent it by foreseeing the problem and maintaining a happy and relaxed understanding with the worker. But, if it does become a matter that demands attention, I would talk graciously and kindly with the worker, alone, of course. Be humble about it and be sure that you have been perfectly fair, that you have given the worker the proper job description. Pray with the worker and give him a chance to prove himself or herself. Sometimes a change of pace or a change of work duties for a time may help. Maybe the worker needs more assistance or a boost from the pastor or the members. Be sure that you have not offended or neglected your helper. Try to be a friend as well as an employer. But don't get too thick. Pray with the worker and pray for him (or her), too.

There may come a time when some workers are just not fulfilling their duties and you conclude that you have done all you can to help or encourage them. In such cases, you will have to just level with them and let them know that you expect them to produce. Sadly, some Christian workers are lazy and some have come into the work of the church expecting it to be rather an easy position.

If you see that the worker is not going to be the one you need for the job, then I'd let him or her know that it just is not working out and that you will be praying with them for the Lord's will in their lives. By this time, and after several prayerful sessions, they surely know that soon they'll be making a move and they may, by now, already have something else in view. Pray hard for them and very probably the Lord will move them on without your having to fire them or do anything drastic, at all. In all of my years in the ministry, I do not recall ever having to let a worker go. But, I talked to the Lord about some of them and they found something else they would rather do right away!

Sometimes a worker will want to resign to the congregation at a regular service in order to induce sympathy and even perhaps (in some cases) to reflect on the fact that the pastor has not been the easiest fellow on earth to work with! Let it be known from the start that if the work-relation is ever to be severed, that the resignation will be made to the pastor and he will take it from there. Then the pastor can graciously (on Wednesday night) let the congregation know that Brother Blank will be answering the call of God to another field of duty over at Fairer Land and that while we deeply appreciate all that Brother Blank has meant to us here we surely want to join in prayer that God will graciously bless his new work and make it an even greater challenge.

Avoiding "Staff Infections"

Have a staff meeting, perhaps once a week, and pray with all of your workers. At this time, you can challenge them, pray with them, and suggest ways by which the work can be made to prosper. Allow them a chance to make suggestions and requests. But where there are personality clashes or personal problems with a worker, be sure you talk privately with that worker. Don't allow one disgruntled worker to affect (or infect) the others.

Keep the platform hot with strong Bible preaching and give your workers time to win souls. Set the example, yourself.

Read some good books on management, supervision and delegation. Learn to delegate and try to let the worker go as far as he can on his own as long as he is doing what he was brought here to do.

While the pastor should have the authority to hire (and fire) his workers, it is not wise to bring in someone who is disliked or alienated from your people. If very many deacons or other good people feel that a man would be wrong for the post, I'd think a long time before signing him up for the job. If a good many of your choir members feel that the music-minister prospect would not go over with the choir, I'd study the matter carefully before bringing him in. They may know something or have sensed something that hasn't registered with you yet. Don't be too hasty.

Check out prospective workers very carefully. Find out all you can about the work they are now doing or that they have done in their last churches. Find out about how they got along with people, if the pastor was satisfied with them, how they paid their bills. Sometimes a man may be an excellent man for the music or youth job but may have a wife who is totally uncooperative and who gave the last congregation fits! Or, they may be a nice couple but have children who are undisciplined incorrigibles. Try to talk to some lay people as well as pastors where they were last employed. Find out what their record was in the school they attended. Discover if they can work on their own or if they have to be told every little thing to do. Learn how well they took orders.

One of my problems was how to see what workers were really

doing and help them to do better without giving them the impression that I was breathing down their neck and "checking up" on them all the time. We do need to give our workers some liberty to prove they can do it on their own and yet we do also have a responsibility to improve the caliber of work being done and to challenge our workers to do all they can to improve. One of my school principals said that a leader does not get from his workers all that he expects but what he *in*spects. Yet, I'm sure the inspection has to be done in such a way that we do not intimidate the worker, nor discourage him. Pray for wisdom and tact in this.

Observe and read after good managers and executives in the business world. Also, look in on outstanding pastors who are doing a great job and find out all you can about how they go about it. Don't be afraid to ask questions.

Send your workers to seminars and conferences that will help them now and then. Be sure your assistant has a copy of Dr. Wally Beebe's book on *The Second Man* and try to get him into any conference or preachers meeting where Dr. J. R. Faulkner of Tennessee Temple University is speaking on "The Second Man."

Watch your own attitude and be sure there is no jealousy or ill feeling in your heart toward or about your workers. Be sure of your own dedication and ask God constantly to make you the leader He would have you be.

Read the Bible with the thought in mind about how to be a better leader.

7. OPPOSITION

How to Handle It

Some people will oppose you because they are unspiritual or mentally sluggish, but remember that some people who oppose you may have some very good reason for doing so. Learn all you can from your opposition. Let it make you check up on yourself and determine if you really are on the right course.

To your *knees*! God sometimes uses opposition to bring us back to the place of prayer. Then maybe much of the opposition will vanish or be won over.

Study how opposition was dealt with in the Bible in the lives of such men as David, Joshua, Moses, Daniel, Elijah and Paul.

Books on leadership and supervision as advised above in item #6 may give you some good counsel on how to face this opposition.

Remember it is better to win your enemies over than it is to defeat them. And it is better to keep them with you happy than to run them off mad. BUT SOMETIMES it is better for them to go away mad than to stay with you mad!

Tread softly. Some preachers are too bombastic and too impatient. I know successful pastors who do not try to just ramrod everything through, regardless of the opposition. If a thing goes over well with your deacons or a group of your people, *fine!* But if not, why not put it on the back burner and study it a bit more? Let it simmer. It may even taste different to *you* a week or a month from now.

People change. The men who opposed you last month may have just had a bad day at work or a rough session with the little woman before coming to the meeting. Their gout may have been acting up or they may have been suffering with lumbago or arthritis. Now, if you have flown off the handle and lambasted them, they'll come back "gunning for bear" at the next meeting. But, if you were sweet and gracious and asked the men just please to pray about it and wait on God with your assuring them that you surely do not want to make a wrong move, they may come back completely on your side next time. Try it!

Use the time after the opposition rears its head to study the matter more carefully. Come back next time with some new and valid reasons why your plan will work and ought to be installed. Also, you may have close friends in the church who will be happy to talk to Brother Disgruntled and explain some things to him before you meet again.

Don't resign or threaten to every time things do not go to suit you. Someone may take you up on it! Don't act like a spoiled child. Exercise the calm, strength and maturity you want the people to think you have. Prove yourself. Then, you can better prove your point.

8. PERSONALITY CLASHES

People are different. We're all cut out of the same mold—"some are a little moldier than others," it has been said. What do you do when you just can't seem to ever make certain people agree with you?

Remember, that some people never will! "If it be possible, as much as lieth in you, live peaceably with all men," the Bible tells us in Romans 12:18. God knows that some people never will live peaceably with you. In such cases, just smile and pray and do the best you can.

But most people you can get along with and enjoy it if you make up your mind to it. Rejoice in the variety of God's handiwork. There are blessings in store for you as you set out to make friends with these people and love them into fellowship with you and the Lord.

Speak well of the people, even those you do not particularly care to be with all the time. There is something good in every one of them.

Be kind to their children. Try to befriend them. Be nice.

Ask God to give you a genuine love for these people who seem not to like you.

Take time for them, listen to their complaints, show genuine interest in what they do.

Pray for them and determine you'll bend over backwards to be the best pastor they could possibly have. After awhile they may surprise themselves by agreeing with you.

9. FELLOWSHIP WITH OTHER PASTORS AND MOVEMENTS

What do we do about this? There will always be people telling you who to associate with and who to ignore. You'll have to let the Lord lead you. He'll show you what to do. But, let me make a few suggestions:

1. Be a friend to other fundamental pastors in the area. They need you and some of these times you're going to need them. It doesn't hurt to have some fellowship along the way. But, I'd not

make a practice of hob-knobbing with them all the time and consuming too much time just gabbing and entertaining. Announce their meetings and attend when you can. Don't be jealous of the crowds other pastors get. Cooperate with men who are fundamental and true to the Book.

2. Don't get too involved in civic affairs or political matters. Be a good citizen and urge your people to be. But, there are plenty of liberals and compromising denominational hirelings who will give the civic clubs all the "religious" flavor they need. Stick to the business of preaching the Bible and winning souls.

3. At the same time, you can join with others in matters of right and morality even if you do not agree with them doctrinally. I personally do not believe that I could belong to a ministerial association, especially if there were known modernists or infidels in the body. On the other hand, if that association should happen to be crusading against Sunday sale of booze or against abortion or homosexuality, then I'd be glad to boost their cause and help all I could. I could not have any doctrinal fellowship with a Church of Christ preacher or a Mormon, but if he was campaigning against television profanity or pornography in the local stores, then I'd be glad to join in that particular cause.

4. I would shake hands with a fellow pastor who was a charismatic and if I had reason to believe he was a saved man, then I could call him "brother" in conversation with him. But, I would not suggest that my people go over to his meetings. A pastor can be a gentleman and a good neighbor without compromising in doctrine.

5. You'll have about all you can do to keep up with all the activities of your local church, fight the Devil, crusade against sin, preach the Word and win souls without joining in every extra-church movement that comes along.

6. Cooperate with other good, fundamental, soul-winning pastors in youth meetings, summer camps for your children, Christian school programs, etc. There are power and encouragement in such cooperative efforts. It will do your young people good to learn that you are not the only "nut" and fanatic in the county!

7. Invite other good pastors to come and bring their people to visit when you have an evangelist or Bible Conference speaker in your pulpit. Cultivate a spirit of Christian fellowship among the brethren.

10. WHEN YOU ARE CRITICIZED, WHAT DO YOU DO?

Well, it would depend on who was doing the criticizing and what it was about. Maybe sometimes I needed criticism. If you know you are right and scriptural in what you are doing, do not let criticism bother you. Learn from it if you can. Seek the Lord about it. Be sure you are doing what God wants you to do. If you are doing right, you may be sure some people won't like it.

But don't run from the cranks and the critics if you are obeying God and doing what you know He is leading you to do. He will see you through if you trust Him. But, it won't hurt to keep sweet and gracious in all you do. Be kind, even to your critics.

11. WHAT ABOUT WORLDLY MEMBERS AND CHURCH LEADERS?

Well, all of us are going to have some worldly members. Otherwise, God would not have had to warn Christians to "love not the world" (I John 2:15). The lure of the world is strong and the flesh is weak. And Satan has his traps set for believers. If he cannot make us religious oddballs, he'll try to succeed in making us worldly.

Preach hard against worldliness and sin. Warn about Hell. Develop soul winners. Get your people on the main track. Bring in the kind of evangelists who will help you develop a spiritual people. Teach them that the friendship of this world is enmity with God (James 4:4). Keep them aware that our citizenship is in Heaven. This world is only our temporary abiding place.

Having worldly *leaders* is another matter. Try not to elect worldly people to places of leadership. So instruct your people that they would not dare do so. Have written standards for deacons, teachers, and others who would be leaders. If you don't have them *sign* them, at least be sure they have a copy of them and understand that God and the church expects them to abide by the scriptural standards or bylaws the church has adopted. If people violate their covenant, you need to talk to them prayerfully, lovingly and firmly about this, reminding them of their testimony and influence.

12. THE PROBLEM OF LOSING YOUR YOUNG PEOPLE

Get rid of the idea that preaching against sin will run all the young people off. We had as many or more young people than any church in town in my pastorates and I thundered against worldliness and sin all along. Of course, I fed the people, too. And we tried to challenge them and keep them busy. You just can't flog them all the time!

When a pastor is young, the young people will often follow their leader just because they feel he is one of their own. As he gets older, he sometimes feels himself losing his hold on them and gets frustrated or mean. Grow old gracefully, keep your sense of humor, keep apace with what is going on, don't use old, out-dated ideas and illustrations all the time. Keep the love and respect of your youth even though the years are coming between you. Secure some help from other couples in the church. Some lay-people make excellent youth workers. If you can afford to do so, it is good to employ a full-time youth worker who has been trained in one of our good, distinctively Christian Bible schools or colleges.

Don't think you have to entertain the young people all the time. Teach them to win souls and keep the challenge before them. We had a youth revival once or twice a year in addition to our other meetings. Frequently we'd have a week-end meeting with some good youth evangelist or some other man who had seen real success with young people. And we kept musical teams from good, fundamental colleges coming through our church every year.

Have a special night for youth activities. Show good Christian films. Keep them in touch with missionaries. Young people can be taught and trained to attend and get great inspiration from missionary conferences.

We developed youth singing groups and used them on the radio, on television and in meetings. Get trained youth men from Dr. Hyles' church and school (and from other such good places) to come and give your young people a shot in the arm. Have week-end or summer retreats. Winter ones, too.

Attend youth seminars or have your youth workers do so. Read books on working with young people. Pick the brain of the experts in the field.

Circulate good books among the youth. Keep everlastingly at it. They'll soon be grown and mature and will surprise you. Then you'll have to start all over again with their brothers and sisters!

And, of course, you *may* lose some of them to worldly churches. You may not be able to keep them all. But, to save and train a young person for God is one of the greatest things you'll ever do.

13. DIVISIONS—WHEN PEOPLE LEAVE THE CHURCH

When we had a bit of a rift at one church and a few people splintered off and followed a former pastor, I was reminded by a seasoned pastor in the city that it is always "good to have a splinter church nearby for your come-outers to go into when they come out!" Our church never really missed those who left. I remember (even though this was in the early days of my ministry), that on the Sunday bulletin next week the following verse was featured, "The Lord Hath Done Great Things for Us Whereof We Are Glad!" There was no split and no real problem in the matter. We kept out equilibrium and just let God work it out.

Of course, you want to try to keep your good, spiritual people with you if you can and if misunderstandings come up, I'd not just ignore it and let good people go away because they did not know the score. But, there will be some people you will be just as well off without, so don't take it too hard when they leave. God will raise up others to take their places.

When divisions arise, I'm not sure it is always an act of wisdom to get up and lambast everybody from the pulpit. Many people will never get upset if *you* don't upset them. Keep calm. Be a statesman and an ambassador for Christ. Use your head. If you speak well of them and love them and pray for them when they leave you many times they'll soon get tired of wandering and return to the fold. Keep the door to the fold open to them.

14. WHEN BUSINESS MEETINGS GET OUT OF HAND

For one thing, I'd plan my business meetings well ahead of time, do your homework, know what you're going to say, and anticipate what you may think others might say. Then, be sure you're *prayed* up!

Come to the business meeting in the right frame of mind. Don't have a chip on your shoulder. Get the bull out of the china closet.

Keep sweet but direct the business meeting firmly and go according to proper rules of procedure. Train your people to expect *Robert's Rules of Order* or some sensible method of carrying on the business meeting.

Don't necessarily encourage everybody in the church to comment on the matter that you're going to vote on. If a good, trusted deacon or some other respected man makes a motion or speaks to the motion, it probably will go over good if you don't rock the boat. People should be allowed to comment if they feel they must, but don't ask for trouble. Have the proposition explained so clearly, simply and enthusiastically that it doesn't leave much else to be said.

If people do get out of hand and blow off or blow up, then I would pause for a calm moment of prayer asking God to take control and to remind us that this is God's work and that we would not dare grieve the Holy Spirit by having friction or harsh words. Remind the Lord that we love Him and one another and that we especially need His help just now. Ask Him to help the people to realize that what we do we must do in the spirit of love and Christian fellowship, as unto the Lord. Then, say to the people that the meeting will proceed and that if people will speak in kindness and love, they will be permitted to speak, briefly.

Be sure that you let only one person speak at a time. And, be sure that *you* stay at the pulpit or podium. Never sit down and just turn it over to the people. They are sheep. They need the guiding hand of the shepherd!

God will see you through. Lean strong on the everlasting arms.

By the way, I would be sure and *have the business meeting on Wednesday nights* when your spiritual people are present, or else call a special business meeting on an off-night. If some matter of great importance just *must* be brought up on Sunday night, then I would dismiss the visitors before starting your business. But, you'll generally be safer to keep business to a time slated right after a brief but fervent prayer meeting.

ADDITIONAL WORDS ON AVOIDING PROBLEMS AND HEARTACHES

Don't allow yourself to have intimate friends in the church. There will be some people who will like you more than others do and who will be your friends. For these folk, you will be thankful but try not to show favoritism. To many people familiarity does breed contempt. It is not a good practice to have members of your church in your home for meals. You cannot have them all and others will feel hurt, left out or jealous.

Don't make social calls on friends in the church. Now, if they invite you for a meal that is different. Or, if members ask you by for refreshments along with others after a service, there is no reason why you should not go. But, don't let your people get the idea that you're getting thick with certain people.

There will be some people who will have you in for meals often enough that others will think you're getting thick anyway. Try to be as nice and friendly to those who never feed you or befriend you.

Observe the golden rule, "Do unto others," etc. It's a good one.

When your people need correcting, try to let the *Word* do it as much as possible. God told one evangelist, "If *you* straighten them out, they'll be as crooked as you are!"

Use "horse-sense"—they don't teach that in school but you know what it is. It comes with stable thinking.

In other words, use good psychology—which, again, is mostly common sense. (The book of Proverbs will help you to develop this.)

If "the High and Lofty One" can condescend to men of low estate, so can you.

Be consistent and be fair in your dealings with the people.

If you talk on and on after you have already concluded your sermon, you are probably nullifying what you said in your sermon.

Be as ethical with your people as you want them to be with you.

Roll with the punches—don't let trouble and friction get you down. Keep looking up! The Devil can wall you around but he can't roof you in.

Put I Corinthians 13 into practice in your life and ministry. Love will cover a multitude of sins (and problems).

It is amazing what *prayer* can do! It moves the Hand that moves the world.

If you're having financial problems (or even facing disaster), don't let your visitors and unsaved parishioners know it. Have faith in God. Live by Hebrews 11!

Study Spurgeon's *Lectures to His Students* and take notes in Dr. Jack Hyles' Pastors' School. But remember, you're not a Spurgeon or a Hyles. "To every man his work."

Chapter Fourteen

The Preacher's Home and Personal Life

Your ministry will probably be no better than your home life. "Keep the home fires burning" at any cost. Perhaps "helter-skelter" best describes the household of many a busy pastor. But does it have to be that way?

Sadly, there are some pastors whose wives have left them and far too many preachers' kids who have brought disgrace upon the ministry! You don't want this to happen to you.

Perhaps I should say at the outset that most of the pastors I have known personally and those I have held meetings for seem to have good homes and a happy family relationship. Also, in most cases, their children are living for the Lord. This speaks well for the Bible-believing, fundamental pastors of America.

Outside of guarding your own soul and your personal fellowship with the Lord, your home should have priority. Read I Timothy 3 again and be reminded that God wants you to consider your wife and your children very carefully, having your own children "in subjection with all gravity," being the husband of one wife, ruling your own household well and, in so doing, give a good report to them that are without. Among other things, he points out that we are to be blameless, vigilant, sober, of good behavior, given to hospitality, patient, no brawler, not given to wine or greedy of filthy lucre.

It will pay any pastor not only to search what the Scriptures say about the home, but to read good books by competent and spiritual men on the home and family life. You'll need a double dose of grace (as will your wife) to maintain a happy and successful Christian home.

1. GET ORGANIZED

You'll have interruptions and emergencies, of course, but it is still wise to organize your time, budget your activities, make plans for your play time and relaxing time together as well as for your work load. Your wife will appreciate you more if she knows that you are at least trying to make room for her in your schedule and that you consider her the most important person in the world. Make her the queen of your home, honor her and love her.

Sit down together, husband and wife, and have it understood that you are serving the Lord together and that you want to share every bit of joy and blessing you can with her. But, at the same time, you both must realize that there will be some hard times, some heartaches, some problems, some interruptions, some disappointments along the way that you must share also. If you make up your minds that you will gladly take what comes and what happens as from the Lord and as a part of your training and service for Him, then the difficulties will be much easier to bear.

Plan time with your children as well as time with each other. A wise pastor will try to give his entire membership two or three nights a week at home when there is nothing going on at church. Urge them to have at least one "family night" each week and set the example yourself. The exceptions, of course, will be during weeks when you're having revivals, Bible conferences, etc.

2. CONTINUE TO "DATE" YOUR WIFE

Keep up the romance! Have a luncheon date with her once or twice a week. Take a day off with her and just go somewhere together—just the two of you, whenever you can, once a week if possible. Take her to dinner in a really fine setting sometimes. Your work may keep you up longer than she cares to stay awake some nights, but be sure you don't make a habit of that. Stay fervently in love with each other. (My booklets, *How to Live Happily Ever After* and *Keeping the Honey in the Honeymoon*, will give you some good advice, though not written expressly and only for the preacher, of course.) Be affectionate, and show it.

After two years in country pastorates (Sunday only) and over

26 years in the full-time ministry as a pastor, plus nearly 9 years as an evangelist, I can truthfully say that my wife and I enjoy one another and love being together more now, I think, than at any time in our entire married life. It has gotten sweeter as the years have gone by. By faith we bought a motor home nearly seven years ago when I launched out into a full-time traveling ministry, so that my wife can go with me and we can "keep the home fires burning." She gets road-weary, and I know that sometimes she must long to "settle down" again and not have to move every week, but still, I can hardly ever leave home without her—though I would rough it and "batch" for a few weeks gladly to give her a rest, she nearly always decides to draw a deep breath, pack up again and launch out with me once more on the next journey. She has been a great encouragement and blessing to me in the ministry. One of these days I hope that I can collaborate with her in getting out a book especially for preachers' *wives*. She has been a dandy one.

3. DETERMINE TO BE THE BEST KIND OF HUSBAND YOU CAN BE

Never get lazy at the job. Do everything you can for her and you'll have her bending over backwards to do nice things for you. Be patient, kind, thoughtful, appreciative, mannerly, and gracious to her. Your children will profit by it, your congregation will be better because of it, and your marriage certainly won't suffer from it! Check up on yourself every little bit. Make sure you're not forgetting little things that mean much to a woman. Especially don't forget her birthday, your anniversary, Valentine's day and such special times. Open the car door for her, help her to her seat at the table, assist her with her wraps. As much as possible, be a perfectionist with her even as you would determine to be for God.

4. HELP HER TO GROW AS A WIFE AND CHRISTIAN

Don't pull her down, low-rate her or give her the impression that you think she is a failure as a wife, but, do read good books together that will help both of you grow in the husband-and-wife relationship. If she knows *you're* anxious to improve, it will encourage her to do the same. You can ask her to review pamphlets and books on married life in order that both of you can counsel better with young couples. As she reads them for others it will help her, too.

Allow her to attend a good seminar now and then for husbands and wives or for women only, conducted by some of the good, spiritual, fundamental leaders of the day.

5. IS IT THE PASTORIUM OR GRAND CENTRAL STATION?

There may be a few advantages to living quite near the church. But, sometimes people will take advantage of you and make a track meet of your living quarters if you do. Sweetly and firmly you must lead the people to realize that a pastor is human like the rest of the flock and that you are entitled to privacy in your home, indeed that you must have it if you're to be the kind of pastor they want you to be.

In one early pastorate, the pastorium was across the street from the church. People would come early for church and make themselves at home in our living room. People would drop off their children there or tell them to wait at the pastor's home after church until someone had time to come pick them up. Meetings would be announced—"the ladies missionary society will meet at the pastorium on Tuesday at 10:00" without my wife's being consulted. The ladies would prowl around and look the house over very carefully while they were there. After all, the pastorium had been paid for by the church and was their property!

These are some of the reasons why more and more pastors are urging their churches to help the pastor buy his own home. But, even if the preacher's family does live in a home owned by the church, they need to be taught that it is the home of the pastor as long as he resides there as their preacher. Even if you have to gently hurt some feelings, you must give your wife and children a house they can call their own. If you go about it kindly and with prayerful grace, the people will soon realize this.

If you live several blocks, or several miles, away from the church, you will not have as much problem with this, even if the church does own the house. But, if you really plan to stay there and make a long work out of the pastorate, it would be mighty good if you could persuade them to let you buy your own home with the church making the payments, and the down payment, too, if possible. Be sure that the vote and decision of the church is written into the minutes of the business sessions of the church and that you have a copy of them. Years later some people may have forgotten the action of the church back there when you came.

If you live in a pastorium, don't be too demanding and don't be unreasonable or hard to live with, but do let your deacons or trustees know when the house needs repairs or improvements. It is to their advantage as well as yours to keep it up. Also, be sure the proper thing is done about taxes, insurance, etc. The church should take care of these matters which is one factor in favor of the church owning the home.

6. GET SOME REST

Some preachers seem to have the notion that since the Devil never rests neither should they. But, we're not getting our instructions from the Devil, and Jesus does advise that we "come apart and rest awhile"—a good way to keep from "coming apart!" Take a day off every week, if possible. I tried to take Monday off. Many times I'd have someone in the hospital on Monday morning or other pressing matters, but usually by noon, anyway, we could get away or get off to ourselves. To *really* take a day off, leave town! This is not always possible, I know, but if you can take the queen of the pastorium and leave town early Monday (or late Sunday night) and not even show your face 'til Tuesday a.m., it will give you a wonderful miniature honeymoon now and then. Pray about it and maybe God will raise up someone with a lakeside or mountain cottage or a bungalow at the shore or a vacant condominium where you can hide away now and then for a day or so. If nothing else, go visit another pastor friend and his wife in a distant town, or, go out to dinner and just unbend and relax. You'll come back Tuesday a.m. or late Monday night chomping at the bits and ready to go again.

Once in a great while (maybe twice a year or so), I used to get on a deep-sea boat about 2:00 a.m. on Monday and wake up at 7:00 50 miles out in the gulf with the bell ringing to start fishing. Not often would I leave my wife for a day off (for she needs a day off, too), but once in a great while a man will fare well to have a day in the deep or hunting up on the mountainside by himself or with male friends.

Rest at night. Rendezvous with your wife. Help her relax, too. Don't carry the burdens of the church and the problems of other people to bed with you. Pray about the matters that concern you in the church. Take these things to the Lord and leave them there—at least until the next morning. Your sex life will benefit, you'll sleep better, and you'll wake up with renewed joy and enthusiasm as you face the tasks of the pastorate the next day.

Write down things you want to remember the next day, shove them into a mental cabinet and turn the key. In this way, you'll not have these problems in your subconscious mind when you're supposed to be relaxing, reading or enjoying your wife. Perhaps a game, a good magazine, watching the late news (or listening), a late snack, perhaps using an electric massage on each other's backs—these things will be relaxing and will help you to sleep without worrying about the problems of your pastorate at night. And, of course, pray—pray for your wife and pray with her, too. Don't let her feel that you are concerned about everyone's problems except hers.

Granted that if you have children in the home you may not be able to get away as easily for that miniature honeymoon or the evening may not be as relaxing, at least until they are settled in their own rooms, but work at it and try to get so well organized that the burdens of the household and the day do not destroy the peace and relaxation of your night. Usually there is someone in the church who will be tickled to keep the kiddies sometime for you two to get away from it all for a day and a night.

7. ENCOURAGE YOUR WIFE

There'll be times when she'll feel sorry for herself for not being able to live a "normal" life. There are times when she doesn't feel good. Sometimes she'll be lonely for friends and fellowship that she cannot quite have as a pastor's wife. Keep her conscious of how much you love her and appreciate her and what she is doing for you and for the Lord. Let her know how much her life and love is doing to make your ministry what it is.

Keep your sense of humor. Laugh together. Read the comics if necessary. Find something to laugh about. Share the humorous things that come along with her, too.

Get excited over her cooking and thank her for fixing your meals. Show appreciation for the delightful little things she fixes for you. Help her to be hospitable but don't bring folks home to eat without giving her advance notice and do not invite a crowd to dine at the pastorium without discussing it with her first.

Don't burden her down with all the problems, pains and perplexities of all the people. Some of these things you need to keep to yourself or just discuss with the Lord. If your wife is a very strong Christian, you may sometimes feel that you need to discuss serious matters with her and have her pray with you. But, if possible, I'd spare her some of the needling things that might just cause her undue anxiety.

Where possible, encourage your people to phone the church office for contacts, appointments and prayer requests. Of course, some will call the pastor's home in spite of all you do, but many a preacher's wife has a case of "weary ear" at night because she has been on the phone with "Sister Sob-a-Lot" for half the afternoon.

Help your wife when she needs it. Don't make her hound you to take out the garbage, mow the lawn or fix the leaky faucet. Lift the heavy things for her—especially if the baby has become a weighty little 2-year-old moose or when she is trying to get six bags of groceries into the house from the carport. Babysit for her and let her relax sometime, or go to a shower, a class party or a ladies prayer meeting without you. It wouldn't hurt you sometimes to bathe the baby or give her a hand with the dishes. Especially should you help her with some of the physical chores if she has to work at a job to help you make it. I hope this is not the case. A pastor's wife needs to be at home to take care of her husband and her children, but sometimes in this day of financial strain and inflation it is a fact that some women do hold down a job outside the home. Don't let that go on any longer than absolutely necessary but do help and take your share of the home duties if she is carrying a work load on the outside.

But, Pastor, there is something here to beware of! Some young wives get in the habit of expecting their husbands to do a lot of her work and to constantly be at her beck and call. Especially is this problem likely to develop if your study is in the house. Try to get your study off somewhere away from earshot. But, if it is absolutely necessary for you to have your study at home, then be sure that you have an understanding with your wife that you must have those precious hours with God for study, prayer and sermon preparation. Don't let a good wife make an errand boy out of you. You must follow your own schedule of study and visitation just as surely as she has a routine of household duties to perform. Those duties should rarely conflict if you plan things right. Don't become hen-pecked.

8. TRAIN AND CONTROL YOUR OWN CHILDREN

How important this is! Teach them very carefully at home. Encourage your wife to drill into them that "king's children are different," that we belong to Heaven, that we must obey our parents at home (there is to be no question about it), and that at church we set a good example to others whose mamas and daddies may not be Christians. Remember, that it is your duty as a father "to bring them up in the nurture and admonition of the Lord." Even though your wife will have much of the child-training to do at home, you are responsible for it, under God.

Know what your children are doing and where they are at church. If your children are roaming around outside, or running through the auditorium or throwing paper towels back by the restrooms or stepping on the feet of the parishioners as they gather to talk after church, this all reflects on you and/or your wife. Often a pastor's wife seems to be on the organ bench or taking on some other task that takes her away from her small children. She needs to be with them and if this is impossible then they need to be trained that they do not hurt your ministry by misbehavior. When they are quite small sometimes a trusted friend will help with them if your wife is playing the piano or has to be back in the choir rooms. But, do not presume too much upon the goodness of other people to accept your duties with your own children.

When your children become teenagers, they still need to be observed by their parents and you need to know what they are doing until they are old enough and spiritual enough to take their own responsibilities as children of the King and as young adults in the service of the Saviour. Don't let them set the bad example of sitting in the back of the church.

An excellent booklet for you and your wife to read and study is *Children, Fun or Frenzy*. Also, Dr. John R. Rice and Dr. Jack Hyles have good books on child rearing. My booklets, *Taming of the Toddler* and *Taming of the Teenager*, will be of value. A book list will be given at the end of the chapter.

Take your boy or boys fishing or pitch the ball with them a little bit or romp with them for a few minutes now and then. It will do them (and you) worlds of good. Then, when your children become teenagers, don't let them get away from you. That same little fellow who helped you with chores around the church when he was small will still want to help at the church or go visiting with you or help inspire the other young people if you work it right, pray much and stay with it. Don't neglect him. Keep the door open to him (or her) for consultation. Be fair with them. Be reasonable. My booklet, *The Taming of the Teenager*, can give you some valuable help on this. Be human. Be a good sport. Keep cheerful with them. Even as you discipline your children be sure they know you truly love them and want the best for them.

"Train up a child in the way he should go" (Prov. 22:6) means what it says—all the way up! Don't get soft and shirk your duties as a parent. Be consistent. Have good rules and guidelines for your own kids. Otherwise, you'll have a mighty hard time getting the parents in your congregation to pay attention to you when you preach on the home. Some preachers have become so lenient with their own children that their ministry has suffered immensely.

On the other hand, don't expect perfection out of your own children—or your wife. You'll be fortunate indeed if you have a wife who *strives* for perfection, but neither one of you are going to make it in this life.

Train your children to help with the chores as they become able. Young girls can be taught to cheerfully wash and dry dishes, pick up after themselves, make their own beds, even iron their own clothes sometimes. Boys can be taught and trained to do many odd jobs around the house and keep the yard trim and neat. Sometimes he'll profit, though, to have you work with him on it.

A preacher's wife has enough problems and burdens in the pastor's home without having to go around picking up after her children. And kids won't be as likely to get into mischief if they have plenty to do at home. Do allow them some play time, however. If both you and your wife will learn to "hop to it" and do what you do quickly, then the children will learn, too, that if they'll hurry and do their chores they can get on to something else more to their liking.

9. MAINTAIN THAT FAMILY ALTAR

Be sure that your own children know that when Daddy preaches to the people that they should pray and read the Bible together that he is not preaching something he doesn't practice. If you can do it in the morning, fine. If not, get together after supper or at some other good time for an appointment with God. Don't make it too long and don't let it be a preaching or scolding session. Do it cheerfully. Also, let your children see you reading the Bible at other times when it isn't time for devotion, just because you love the Book.

The mother can drill the little ones in the family on verses so that many, many Bible verses can be memorized by the time the child gets into school. Also encourage the memorizing of Scripture after they get into their teens.

10. TAKE CARE OF YOUR HEALTH!

Prevention is better than cure. Doctors and insurance men say that preachers are a poor health risk. Take sitting-up exercises several times a week or work out in the yard. Walk briskly or jog or ride a bicycle for a few minutes—every day when possible. Eat properly. Some preachers have a reputation for being a glutton. This should not be. Take care of the one body God has given you. It is the temple of the Holy Spirit.

I know that some Christians have become "health nuts" and perhaps have gone "overboard" on dieting and such matters, but keep in mind the apostolic admonition to "moderation in all things" and learn what you can even from the health food extremists. Read *Health Shall Spring Forth* by Dr. Paul Adolph (Moody Press), and *None of These Diseases* by Dr. S. I. McMillen (Revell). Both have some excellent advice and suggestions. I do not particularly care for the references to modern versions of the Bible in the latter book, but you can profit by the health advice from that doctor, nevertheless.

11. DON'T LET YOURSELF GET ABSENT-MINDED

Some preachers have become "numb," I guess, but many seem to be in such a dream world that they do not notice what their children are doing or hear what their wife is saying. "Take heed to thyself," Paul advised. Making notes will help. Jot down things so that you don't have to constantly be trying to remember all the things the members have asked you to do. Save some of those gigantic problems until you are on your knees. Try not to wrestle with them at home. Your wife and children need a daddy as well as a pastor.

12. CULTIVATE GOOD MANNERS AND TEACH YOUR CHILDREN MANNERS

Say "thank you," yourself, and teach this courtesy to the children. Be courteous, kind, thoughtful. Good manners mean unselfishness. Teach the children to say "please" and "thank you" and "excuse me" and the people you serve will be more likely to invite you to their home again.

We have a crude, ill-bred, poor-mannered generation on our hands in this age and it behooves the people of God to set a good example. Sadly, many young adults are coming even out of Christian schools with very poor manners.

People should not sit down at the table until Mother is seated unless she expressly gives permission to do so. When we are guests in a home, we should not sit down until the hostess is seated. Then the ordinary rules of good etiquette should prevail at the table. When dessert is served, again the hostess should be seated and begin to take up her fork before we "dive right in" to the dessert. Don't let your children slouch or "slurp" at the table.

Introduce your children or guests to the people in whose home you are visiting. Too many people just assume that everybody knows everyone there.

Express sincere thanks and appreciation for the meal, whether in your own home or (especially) in the home where you are a guest. The children will pick up good manners if Mama and Daddy set the example.

A FEW FINAL THOUGHTS

"Ruling your own home" or being "head of the house" does not mean that you are to be a tyrant or a dictator. Use "loving kindness and tender mercy" in your domain. Let your children grow up remembering that Dad was consistent, was a firm disciplinarian but ruled in love and fairness, and that he truly practiced what he preached. "Provoke not your children to anger, lest they be discouraged" (Col. 3:21).

"Husbands, love your wives, and be not bitter against them."—Col. 3:19.

You can preach against sin if you keep your own "skirts" clean.

Keep your chin up. "Be strong in the Lord." The arm of flesh will fail.

Be on time for appointments—even with your own family, unless an emergency arises.

Live above reproach. Someone has suggested that a Christian should live so that he would not be afraid to sell the family parrot to the town gossip.

Discipline yourself first—then others. Don't be lazy.

If you're too busy to pray—you're too busy!

Recommended Book List

The Taming of the Toddler, Pyle (Box 1508, Panama City, Florida 32401).

The Taming of the Teenager, Pyle (Box 1508, Panama City, Florida 32401).

How to Rear Children, Jack Hyles (Hyles-Anderson Publishers).

Children, Fun or Frenzy, Mr. and Mrs. Al Fabrizio (Box 183, Palo Alto, California 94302).

Correction and Discipline of Children, John R. Rice (Sword Publishers).

Home—Courtship, Marriage and Children, John R. Rice (Sword Publishers).

Keeping the Honey in the Honeymoon, Pyle (Box 1508, Panama City, Florida 32401).

How to Live Happily Ever After, Pyle (Box 1508, Panama City, Florida 32401).

The Act of Marriage, (on the Beauty of Sexual Love) Tim and Beverly LaHaye (Zondervan Publishers).

Chapter Fifteen

Deacons or Demons?

"How to deal with deacons" is one matter a pastor asked about when he learned I was writing this book. *"How do you motivate deacons?"* was still another question.

One Southern church has the reputation for being a "preacher-killing machine." It is said that two or three carnal deacons run off every preacher they ever get. They have no respect for the man of God.

Another pastor said he had had *no* deacons' meetings for three years. "If the men were not going to act like Christians they just wouldn't meet!" The church prospered and even doubled its income when the deacons quit functioning.

A Christian layman was lamenting the spiritual condition of his church as he talked with me in a hospital corridor. He said they could never keep a pastor because the deacons insisted on controlling how much time the pastor spent in visiting and such matters, then they started telling him what to preach. The next thing was to run him off. Now, granted, there are some preachers who seem but to draw their breath and their salary who *should* be run off! But it is clear that many deacons and churches (and some preachers) have not understood the scriptural qualifications and purposes of deacons. I have been with more than one pastor who have no deacons at all because they are *afraid* to have any.

Some of the finest Christian men I have ever known and some of the best helpers in the ministry I've ever had were godly deacons. On the other hand, in some instances, some of the sharpest thorns in my side as a pastor were deacons in the church who were supposed to be helping to lift the load and make my burdens lighter in the ministry. Deacons are not just to "hire and fire" the preacher—they are to "free" the preacher. See Acts 6:1-7.

Keep a good scrapbook if you are not most careful and scriptural in selecting deacons, for you'll be in for many a scrap!

Some pastors have trouble with their deacons because they act as a dictator and lord it over the men. Others have trouble because they allow the deacons to dictate and lord it over them!

As a pastor you should not be a tyrant or an isolationist. Neither should you be a puppet on a string to be manipulated by the deacons.

The pastor should be in charge and should be esteemed very highly in love for his work's sake (I Thess. 5:13). When he and his deacons meet it should be as it was between Boaz and his workers: "The Lord be with you" and "The Lord bless thee" (Ruth 2:4).

When one noted and successful pastor was asked if he had a church Constitution, he said, "I *am* the constitution!" Perhaps there may be a man of such stature and ability in every decade but I imagine they are few and far between, and that if most pastors said that they would soon be served with their walking papers.

Still we need to teach our people that if a nation has no head or leader there will be anarchy, if a home has no head there will be frustration, and if a church has no head there will be utter confusion. True, Christ is the Head of His church, but He is the One who has appointed the pastor (or bishop) as an "overseer." Leadership must have 'followship.'

Now, Pastor, if you would have harmony with your deacons there are some things you should first of all determine for yourself.

First, if you are a young pastor or just starting out you must tread softly. You must win the respect and confidence of men who may be older and in some cases more mature than you are. You may inherit a board of deacons that you will have to live with for awhile until the people are taught and until the congregation grows, not only numerically but spiritually. When considering a pastorate it would be well for you to ask about the deacons, what they stand for, how they respect and feel about a pastor, and what they anticipate about the relationship of pastor and deacons if you become their leader.

If you start a *new* work it will be easier for you to "grow" your own deacons and develop the kind of relationship that you feel is scriptural and proper.

The word "board" has been abused. Too many men, because they belong to a "board," think of it as a "board of directors" and thus feel they can control the pastor and anyone else who gets in their way. I would get away from calling the deacons a "board" as much as possible. It is a term of convenience and most of the time it is called a board just for want of anything else to call them.

Be an humble man, yourself. You can be spiritual, firm, consecrated, courageous, and still be a man of humility. Walk humbly before God. When your men see and realize that you truly walk with God they will respect you and be less likely to cross you. "Except. . .[it] die, it abideth alone" (John 12:24). Die to yourself, crucify the flesh, and it will not matter too much whether some deacon disagrees with you or says something offensive. "The Son of man came not to be ministered unto, but to minister, and to give his life. . ." (Matt. 20:28).

Don't be touchy, pouty or easily offended. As much as lieth in you live peaceably with all men—including the deacons. Be patient with the men. Some of them may not have had the training, background and spiritual teaching that you have had. On the other hand, some of your men may have had *more* business training, financial knowledge and practical business dealings than you have had and you may learn some things from these men that will truly help you. Don't be too proud to learn from your laymen.

Be honest but do not necessarily be too frank or candid. Some brutally frank people become tactless and cruel. Don't always say all that you know or certainly not all that you think.

Don't be evasive and deceitful, however. Have firm convictions but do not become bullheaded. Be flexible, under God, and don't be afraid to admit when you have been mistaken or impulsive.

Do teach your men that "we walk by faith" and that there are times when nothing will be done for God if we do not "launch out" and take the step of faith. To always use good business sense and be overly cautious may take God and faith out of the picture entirely. Caution *can* lead to timidity or to defeat.

Your deacons, although they are not to "rule" you, are nevertheless not just to be "flunkies" either. While Acts 6 might seem to indicate this, the spiritual qualifications of I Timothy 3 would certainly indicate that there is more to the office of deacon than that. You need men of sound spiritual sense to take some of the responsibility and burden for the material and financial needs of the church organization. Dr. Harvey Springer said, "My deacons have helped me out of trouble a hundred times for every one they have made for me." Again he said, "I have often said that I was the head of the church organization and that I was going to stand up for my rights—all of which may be true; but I realize that a man should be as eager to share his love as he is to demand his rights."

Paul said, "Wherefore, though I have all boldness in Christ to enjoin thee that which is befitting, Yet for love's sake, I rather beseech" (Philemon 8,9).

There was a man, large of stature, who in an earlier pastorate of mine, used to rise at almost every business meeting and say firmly, "I'm bitterly opposed to it." That was his song and sermon—"I'm bitterly opposed to it." He did slow us down sometimes and maybe we needed it at times, but I learned some grace and patience through my experiences there. Years later that man when he was going through some stormy waters drove a great distance to see me and in tears apologized for having given me such a rough time in the pastorate. I can truthfully say I have no bitterness or resentment whatever when I think of that deacon.

NOW WHAT ABOUT DEACON PROBLEMS?

"Here comes the *beacons*!" a little girl said as the deacons filed down the aisle to serve the Lord's Supper. Would that all such men were indeed "beacons"! What kind of men ought to be deacons? What are deacons for? How do you deal with deacons and how do you motivate them?

Acts 6:1-15 and I Timothy 3 will, of course, give you the information about what the Bible says about them. This should be taught faithfully, lovingly and clearly to your people. A church can rise no higher than its leaders. While deacons are *servants* (Gr. *diakonos*), they are usually thought of as leaders and spiritual pillars in the church. But they are not the "overseers." The distinction is made in Philippians 1:1. The deacons are to be men of honest report, full of the Holy Ghost and wisdom (Acts 6:3) and they were first appointed to tend to the "business" of handling the problems of charity and assistance to the widows who needed help. They were to tend to these menial things so that the preachers could give themselves to prayer and to the ministry of the Word (Acts 6:4). As a result of the choosing of these first deacons "the word of God increased; and the number of disciples multiplied in Jerusalem greatly, "so that even a number of the priests were saved!" (Acts 6:7). Deacons, then, are to free the pastors and evangelists to study the Word and win the lost.

Stephen was a man of faith (Acts 6:5,8), as deacons should always be. We are laborers together with God. Dr. Jack Hyles has said that all of his deacons were soul winners. Ideally, this is as it should be.

Many a good layman has been ruined by making a deacon out of a man who was not mature enough or spiritual enough to properly accept the position. He is to be "not a novice" but is to have a good report both in the church and to the outside world. He is not to be "doubletongued" (I Tim. 3:8), not talking out of both sides of his mouth. "A double minded man is unstable" (James 1:8). He is to be an abstainer from all kinds of strong drink, of course, and is not to be money-mad (I Tim. 3:8).

He should first be "proved," to be sure he is a solid, stable, sensible and spiritual man, and thus "blameless" in his task (I Tim. 3:10). Also he must have the right kind of wife (vs. 11). The deacon must be the kind of man who, like the pastor, has a good Christian home with his wife and his children under proper control and discipline (I Tim. 3:12).

He should "hold" the faith and be *bold* in the faith (vss. 9,13). In other words, he is to be sound, fundamental and positive in his faith in the Book.

Really, if a man is all that Acts 6 and I Timothy 3 calls for he will be an ideal deacon. Even at best, though, he is human (as is the pastor) and will not be perfect while still "in the body."

In one of my files I have noted that right after *deacon* comes *demon* and *devil* and it has, indeed, seemed that sometimes the deacons and the demons go hand in hand. How do we avoid this? Let's take up some questions that pastors ask:

Q: Should you have a set number of deacons, say seven men?

A: Not always. Seven was a good Bible number but they had a huge congregation before they chose these seven men. There is a danger in putting it into your Constitution that you'll have so "many" men as the wrong kind of men are sometimes chosen in order that the quota be met. I'd start with two or three good men rather than have the kind of men who will give you heartaches.

Q: Can you get too many men?

A: I'm sure you can. There is more chance that you will get some fellows on there who will be duds or who will become antagonistic and selfish. On the other hand if you have a big number of men as deacons it will prevent two or three fellows from getting the idea that they run the church. If you have half a dozen deacons and two or three give you trouble you've really got problems. But if you have twenty men and two or three are troublesome then you still have at least seventeen men on your side!

Q: What if you have a big board and they all want to have their *say* at the meetings?

A: Why encourage them all to have a "say"? If you have a large number of men it may be easier to conduct the meeting in a businesslike way. A small board, say of four or six men, may lend itself to informality and discussion of everything that is mentioned. On the other hand, a large group of men are more apt to keep quiet unless they really have something to say since they know it will prolong the meeting needlessly. Most men want to get home before midnight!

Q: How do you keep the deacons' meeting from going astray?

A: Why *have* meetings if you do not really need them? Some pastors just call a meeting when there is really something important to meet about. Then they meet to discuss that item and go home. If you meet all the time there are some men who may be ready with problems because they figure it is time to unload something. On the other hand, you might at least have a good deacons' prayer meeting once a week or at least once a month. But don't let it grow into a gossip session or a time to air grievances.

Q: What if your *needed* deacons' meeting became rowdy and unmanageable?

A: One good thing is to have a set time—say one hour or an hour and a half for the meetings. Men become tired and cranky if they stay too long. Conduct the meeting in a businesslike way. Stand at the front and preside. If your chairman conducts the meeting you should still be right there beside him and don't lose control of the podium. Have your secretary at the front also, taking minutes. Keep the meeting moving. If you have some troublesome things to discuss then be sure you have done your homework and know what you are talking about before you bring it up or allow it to be mentioned.

One successful pastor in Alabama says his meetings last one hour. They keep growing and winning souls, he says, and who wants to oppose a growing thing? He said he suggests the names of those who are loyal to the pastor and he has not been opposed for seven years. The meetings conclude with earnest prayer. He calls deacons' meetings only when he needs them.

Q: But what if other deacons or church members suggest names for deacons who are *not* loyal to the pastor?

A: Keep it before the people—I Timothy 3 and Acts 6. Also have some written rules or standards for your deacons. This will eliminate most of them. When I was a pastor we never had a large board of deacons. Maybe my standards were a bit *too* tough—I don't know. But most men refused the opportunity to even run for deacon when they read the standards. Again, it takes time, teaching and patience to grow a congregation who understands what a pastor needs to help him and the church.

Q: What are some of these standards?

A: Well, among other things, the deacon is to answer yes or no if he is in good fellowship with the pastor and feels that he could assist the pastor willingly and cheerfully in a scriptural manner. He and his wife have to state that they can and will hold their tongues and maintain a ready spirit of forgiveness, and they have to subscribe to what the church is doing under the leadership of the pastor. I'll list these standards at the end of the chapter.

Q: I have inherited some bad deacons. How can we get rid of them?

A: Teach and train your people, saturate the matter in prayer and then set up a deacons' rotating system so that two or three men rotate off the board or list of deacons every year. Then they would have to be chosen again and re-elected to get back on.

Q: But what if they are definitely doing wrong and are a reproach to the church?

A: In such cases you should first talk to the Lord, then to the deacon in question. Explain in a loving and prayerful manner that there are those who are disturbed by his behavior and that you are sure he would want to obey the Scriptures in such matters. You would like to help him and would be glad to have another spiritual man sit in with you and see if you could help him to understand what the Bible says about it. If he refuses and does not want to resign as a deacon then I would take the matter to the board at a meeting of the deacons. But do what you do lovingly, carefully, and in all humility. Unless it is a moral matter that would hurt the whole church it might not be necessary for you to even announce to the church that he is no longer a deacon—certainly not if the election of new men is soon at hand. Maybe you can thus spare the man embarrassment and win him back into a close walk with the Lord.

Q: What do you think about a board or panel of "Junior Deacons"?

A: We tried it in one church I pastored. I'm not sure it is scriptural. Still, I see nothing particularly *un*scriptural about it. You would simply be training a group of young men who have real potential to groom themselves for the task of deacon later on. If they did not prove themselves at least you'd know not to put them on as a deacon.

Q: How do you motivate deacons to get the most out of them?

A: We gave each man (or tried to) a specific area for which to be especially responsible. For instance, one man was our maintenance chairman; another worked with the custodian (making sure he was following his work sheet); another was responsible for the grounds and would call a work day (or suggest one) when the flowers, shrubbery, etc., needed special attention; another might work with the youth; another was our missions chairman; another kept tab on our buses, etc. But all of them were urged to visit, to win souls, to keep down strife, to work as a friendliness crusader, to keep up with the people, to greet newcomers.

If you keep them praying, visiting, winning souls they are not liable to be cooking up ways to give problems and pains to the pastor.

Q: What about men who want to be deacons and who are good men but they "politic" and work on people to get themselves elected?

A: The kind of man who *wants* to be a deacon so he can exercise power and get in a position of prominence is not the man you want on there! The humble man who is *willing* to serve as a helper and is thrilled for the privilege but who feels his inadequacy is the one you want. The man who is just as content if it is the will of God for him to be left off, that is the man you want on there!

Q: What about the deacon who just "blows up" and gives trouble in spite of all you can do?

A: The more he *grows* up the less he will *blow* up. He is not mature and has no business being a deacon. "Cast out the scorner, and contention shall go out," Solomon said (Prov. 22:10), "yea, strife and reproach shall cease." By that time surely the other men will be tired of the "blowups" and will assist you in relieving the man of his post until he grows up and gets his temper under control.

Preach sometimes on "Rebellion is as the sin of witchcraft, and stubbornness is as iniquity and idolatry" (I Sam. 15:23). Remind people from the Bible that the spiritual man is 'not self-willed, not soon angry, no striker, not contentious,' etc. Grow a congregation who understands what a real Bible deacon is.

A commentator said of some of the courageous scientists who went into outer space, "The more spectacular the achievement, the less spectacular their behavior." This is the kind of deacon you want. Preach sometimes on "Who is the greatest?" (Matt. 18:1) and on "Before honour is humility" (Prov. 15:33).

A deacon ought to be like a custodian I heard about in a great Kentucky church. Dr. Fred Brown said, "If I were a pastor, I would rather have that custodian working with me than anybody else's assistant pastor!" God give us deacons with the humility of a loyal custodian.

One preacher said, "Get the *deacons* to hold the funerals for you, because the Bible says, 'Let the *dead* bury the dead.' " But it should not be this way. The deacons ought to be the most spiritually alive men in the church.

Let me suggest that, in addition to having standards written out for the deacons, you also read carefully what Dr. Jack Hyles has written in his book, *The Hyles Church Manual*, about deacons and how to elect them. It is a plan for choosing the deacons only by the deacons themselves, and presenting only those chosen men to the church for election. It is a method of eliminating men who may have something about them that would disqualify them without bringing it all out in the open and hurting a man unnecessarily. There are good men who love the Lord but who for some reason might not be qualified scripturally to serve as deacon.

Following is a copy of the Questionnaire we sent out to prospective deacons in one church I pastored. You can alter it to suit your own needs and convictions. It is not perfect, but it did help many a man to ease himself out of being considered for a post he felt he could not conscientiously serve.

But your own heart attitude, remember, will have something to do with how you get along with your deacons. Consider them your "special agents." You are on the same team. Love them, pray for them and let them know that you do. And you can always learn from those who seem to appreciate you the least.

"QUESTIONNAIRE FOR PROSPECTIVE DEACONS"

Dear Brother:

You have been nominated to be considered as a Deacon. This is a serious and sacred responsibility. In order to help you determine your own qualifications for this office, the questions listed below should be answered honestly, carefully, and with the deepest prayerful regard. This is a confidential inquiry. Its purpose is to insure a minimum of embarrassment to any and all concerned, and to enable your church to make the most spiritual selection possible (Read Acts 6:1-7 and I Timothy 3:1-13).

1. Do you know that you have been saved through a personal experience with Jesus Christ?_____

2. Do you believe that the Bible is the verbally inspired Word of God?_____ Do you firmly believe in the Virgin Birth, the Atoning Blood and the personal, Pre-Millennial return of Christ? _____

3. According to the teachings of Acts 6, do you believe that the main duty of a deacon is to serve as the Pastor's helper in secular and menial duties so the preacher will not have to "leave the Word of God and serve tables?"_____ Are you in good fellowship with the pastor, are you loyal to him, and do you feel that you could assist him willingly and cheerfully in a scriptural leadership under God?_____

4. Do you want to be considered as a deacon in your church?_____ If you should be elected will you conscientiously serve to the best of your ability?_____

5. New Testament deacons were men "full of the Holy Ghost." Have you so surrendered and do you purpose daily to live a Spirit-filled life of consecrated service?_____

6. Is Christ and His church really FIRST in your life—ahead of other activities?_____

7. According to our charter our church is and must remain an Independent Baptist Church not affiliated with any association or

convention. Do you firmly believe this is the New Testament pattern?_____

8. The Bible demands "modest apparel" (I Tim. 2:9), insists that "the woman shall not wear that which pertaineth unto a man," etc. (Deut. 22:5), and that we are to "abstain from all appearance of evil" (I Thess. 5:22). Do you and your wife and children dress properly and modestly in public (for instance, no shorts, mini skirts or other scant, sexy or questionable attire)?_____

9. God's Word insists on separation from worldly practices. Do you or your wife belong to a lodge or secret society?_____ Do you go to or allow your children to go to dances, theaters, card parties, or such things?_____

10. (I Tim. 3:12) Have either you or your wife ever been divorced?

11. Are you the head of your home with your wife and children in subjection, do your children mind you respectfully, and do you have them under control?_____ (Eph. 5:22-25; I Tim. 3:12).

12. Do you faithfully attend all of the services of your church, Sundays, Wednesdays, Revivals, etc. (Unless providentially hindered?) _____

13. Stewardship is a serious qualification. Do you believe in and practice tithing (giving God at least a tenth of your income)?_____ (Mal. 3:10; I Cor. 16:1-3). Will you contribute to your church regularly through the envelope system?_____

14. Will you work with the pastor and other deacons on the basis of frank, brotherly confidence and cooperation? _____

15. Do you indulge at all in alcoholic beverages, have part in the sale of it, or do you allow it in your home? _____

16. Do you pay your bills promptly, so as to stay out of financial difficulty that might embarrass your church? _____

17. Do both you and your wife know how to hold your tongues against spreading gossip or talking critically about others?_____ Can you and your wife avoid holding grudges, and do you maintain a ready spirit of forgiveness?_____ Can your wife qualify as a deacon's wife as stated in I Tim. 3:8-11? _____

18. The body of a Christian is the temple of the Holy Spirit (I Cor. 6:19). Do you defile your body in the use of tobacco, narcotics, or any other questionable habit?_____ Do you keep yourself pure in sex matters?_____

19. Can you say that you consistently try to witness and win souls to Christ?_____ Will you support the soul-winning program of

Visitation carried on by your church? _____

20. Do you believe that the main mission of the believer is to carry out the Great Commission of Christ as stated in Matthew 28:19-20? _____ Are you fully sold on the program, promotion, preaching, music and ministry of our church? _____

21. Do you believe in the principle of majority rule in a Baptist Church? Will you quietly abide by the decision of the people in church business matters? _____

22. Will you keep the observance of the LORD'S DAY above reproach? _____ Will you work for the active advancement of your church, moving by faith to make it a great and growing church for the glory of God? _____

23. If you ever feel that you cannot conscientiously, and in the spirit of Christ, (working together in harmony and love) back your pastor, your fellow deacons, and/or the majority of the church, will you be honest and fair enough to resign without strife or discord? _____

Please sign and return to the Pastor within the next 10 days.

NAME: _____

Chapter Sixteen

How to Have a Successful Revival in Your Church

After pastoring churches of all sizes in both village and city areas, and after having served as an evangelist for another (total) nine years, I've had ample opportunity to see both sides of this matter of revivals in the church. I want to devote a chapter to the "How" of revival and then at least another chapter to problems involved—what a pastor should expect of an evangelist and what an evangelist should expect of a pastor. There are many important things we are prone to overlook.

It is gloriously possible to have successful and fruitful revivals and evangelistic campaigns in your church as well as well-attended Bible and missionary conferences. A crusade of one week (or longer) can truly "pay off" in your church. But such success in evangelism does not just happen.

It is worth the effort. If you get the right man of God to help you, and if you adequately and wisely prepare, your meetings can be gloriously effective and the results can be long-lasting.

You probably should plan to have at least one, and perhaps two, revival campaigns each year. In addition to that a Bible conference and perhaps a missions conference can be of great blessing. The revival meetings should, if possible, be of at least a week's duration. In some cases two weeks would be even better. Your Bible conference could be 5 or 6 days and your missions conference from 4 to 6 days long. To have too many long meetings during the year may wear the people out and also it takes the keen "cutting" edge off the excitement of such events.

Too many pastors, I fear, have given up on having revival crusades. Don't be afraid to plan for one and to expect real victory. Crowds will still come if proper prayer and planning go into it.

What should a good revival meeting do for your church?

1. Increase the crowds and inspire enthusiasm.
2. Fire up members who have become discouraged.
3. Reclaim backsliders.
4. Create a spirit of togetherness and fellowship.
5. Stimulate consecration, dedication and giving.
6. Bring new members into the church.
7. Rekindle the flame of family devotions.
8. Get the young people excited again.
9. Uncover new talent for service in the church.
10. Bring souls to Christ, both during and after the meetings.

Even today, with television and all of the things that take people away, many pastors have told me that they are having the best crowds—that people are coming more consistently than to any campaign yet. Many also have written to say that souls continued to be saved and that there continued to be evidence of revival long after the crusade ended. So I know it can still be done.

God has given to the church "evangelists" (Eph. 4:11), so obviously he wants these men to be used of God in the churches. I'm afraid, though, that some men have given up on having revival meetings in their churches. Why?

Perhaps some have been disappointed with a certain evangelist, or the results were not what they thought they should have been, or they are afraid they cannot keep up the pace after the crusade has finished.

In some rare cases some pastors are afraid the revival offerings will hurt their church, or some, I am told, are a bit jealous of their pulpit and actually become jealous of the evangelist who has been used of God to bring blessing to their people.

But none of the above need be true. You can get an evangelist who will bless and help your people, the results can be gratifying both during and after the meetings, money given to a godly evangelist will not hurt your own church, and after a revival your people will actually appreciate their own pastor more than ever.

Your sheep will be grateful to you that you have allowed them to hear a different voice and that they have been permitted to enjoy listening to one of God's choice servants. Most of them would never receive the blessing of being in a real revival if you did not bring the evangelist to your own church. Then, too, many people become weary enough of fiery evangelistic preaching night after night that they'll be actually excited about just hearing their own pastor again. Many say, "Well, no visiting preacher is quite like our own pastor!"

I really believe that one of the main reasons why some pastors and churches do not often have revival meetings any more is that they have been disappointed in the attendance and have actually lost faith that their people will come night after night. Too many pastors have taken a defeatist attitude—they have concluded (at least silently) that the days of real revival campaigns with glorious results is a thing of the past!

Now, granted it is harder to get unsaved adults to come to revivals in great numbers than it used to be. Young people have more distractions, people are more worldly, more sophisticated, cults and isms have brought much reproach and confusion to the term "revival." But all this means is that we have to work harder, pray more, plan more wisely, start sooner to get ready, and perhaps advertise more widely to break through the crust of indifference around us.

Some old-timers used to pitch a tent or a tabernacle and stay for a month or even two months or more until revival came. Today we are not willing to pay the price to have successful crusades. It would surely be unwise and unfair to invite an evangelist to invest a month of his time (or even two weeks) with your church if the church would not plan to go all out and believe God for real revival and do the working, praying and weeping that would be necessary to make such a crusade a success.

With our modern assets and conveniences we can notify more people, travel to more homes, advertise over wider areas, reach more people and should expect greater crowds than ever before. People now have telephones, automobiles and many other things that were not available back in the days of "great revivals."

With all of this we can have some outstanding meetings in 7-day, 8-day or 12-day campaigns. Eight days is perhaps considered ideal today, with the meeting both beginning and ending on Sunday. Of course, due to travel schedules of evangelists, it is not possible to be *just* in 8-day meetings. It would mean the man of God would have no more than 20 to 22 campaigns a year, and unless he was in large and strong churches would probably feel that he could not support his family on only 20 to 22 paychecks a year. Then, too, a good preacher will soon have so many invitations that he would have to turn down a great number of pastors if he limited himself to only 8-day meetings.

Because of this, many meetings will be 7 days (Monday through Sunday), or 6 days (Sunday through Friday). I'm not sure which is best. I used to prefer the Monday-Sunday combination, but here of late it has seemed to work better to begin on Sunday and close out on Friday. This leaves Saturday for travel which is often needed if the next crusade is some distance away. More and more evangelists are traveling in motor homes or with a travel-trailer and need ample time for the trip. Some of the meetings, at the beginning and at the end of the tour, can still be 8-day meetings.

Now if your meeting is to last from 6 to 8 days it is going to take an all-out effort to make it a real success. Begin to pray at once that God will lead you to the right evangelist for your church and then get started on the preparation for such a crusade. Make up your mind that you're going to do all that is possible to have your church ready for the campaign when the evangelist arrives.

NOTE: If you plan your special meetings a year or even two years in advance you will be more likely to be able to line up your favorite evangelist. Don't feel hard at an evangelist because he has to turn you down for a spring meeting if you wait until January to invite him!

Another important thing to remember: Spring and fall dates always fill up first for an evangelist. Plan some of your campaigns for summer or winter. Obviously an evangelist cannot take all his meetings in the spring or fall. Naturally, you'd like to have April or October but March and November may do even better. Some of my best meetings have been in January or February. When I was a pastor I often invited an evangelist to be with me shortly after the first of the new year so we'd get off to a roaring start after the holidays were over. Also we would sometimes have good meetings in the summer months. Announce your meetings for months ahead of time and urge your people to make their vacation plans so that they will be in town for the revival. Children are out of school, teens are available and wanting something to do, people are more relaxed, there is more daylight time for visitation, mothers are not having to fight the schedule of getting children up and off to school each morning. There is no reason why you cannot have good meetings in the summertime.

For summer meetings you might want to vary it by having a revival meeting one summer and the next year combine it with your vacation Bible school, using a man or a team of men who can work with children, too. Another possibility for summer meetings would be to have a family emphasis or a home conference, with perhaps a week-end retreat at a nearby camp for the Friday or Saturday night meetings. You can also have youth revivals, or have a summer meeting with some outside youth activities for the young people since they are out of school.

Setting up a tent and having a two-week tent crusade may be the answer to your summer revival plan. Bible conferences in the summertime are also a possibility, using an evangelist who is also a good Bible teacher or perhaps advertising widely and bring in two or three good Bible conference men.

Even if you do not reach a lot of lost people at the time in your campaign or conference it can still do your church a lot of permanent good. I know there are some who would say that you did not have a revival if you did not have a landslide of conversions, but remember what "revival" is—an awakening of those who already belong to God, and the saints need feeding and challenging and inspiring and firing-up just as much as the lost need converting. If they really get revived they will help you reach the lost in the months to come after the campaign or conference is over.

How do you prepare for and how do you finance such successful meetings? The answers will come in the pages that follow. There are some simple and common-sense ideas that will make it much easier than you think.

HOW TO HAVE A SUCCESSFUL REVIVAL— SOME HELPFUL HINTS

(1) *Pray about it and then line up* the evangelist God lays on your heart. If you have not heard the evangelist you may want to drive to another town and hear him firsthand. If that is not possible you can probably get a tape of some of his messages. At least, talk to some other pastors who have heard him or check his credentials by reading a brochure or some printed testimonies from churches where he has been. Don't be afraid to make some phone calls. If he has messages in print you can learn a good bit about him from these, too.

(2) You can sometimes get some of the greatest men in America if you are willing to take them in the winter or summer months. I'd rather have an outstanding preacher in January than a weak preacher at Eastertime! To have a meeting in August or in January or February puts you way ahead of the other pastors nearby who are still dragging along waiting for the appropriate time to do something!

(3) *Start at least two months ahead* to plan and prepare your people. I'm sure that if lost adults are to be won we are going to have to be praying for and working on them well ahead of the time the meetings begin. Print up your advertising from 4 to 6 weeks ahead of the crusade. Begin to get your people excited. Start training personal workers. Get to visiting the unsaved. Organize your people to line up prospects and start praying for them well ahead of time. If you start well in advance of the meetings you have time to cultivate the prospects, to show kindness, to make friends with those you want to win.

On the other hand, if you wait until the meetings are just about to start, people wonder why the sudden interest, they get suspicious, and they get gun-shy. Get the names of prospects on cards and start prayer meetings for them to be saved.

Take a census or some kind of survey of the area for several miles around your church. Christian bookstores can put you on to some good survey cards or you can print your own. Do this well ahead of time. Then get your Sunday school workers and teachers busy sorting them, visiting them, filing them.

Try to challenge every member of your church to have several people on their hearts and on their prayer lists whom they hope to win during the crusade. If each member won just one other, think what a tremendous ingathering you would have! But it likely will not happen if you wait until the day or the week before the evangelist arrives.

(4) *READ carefully* the letters and the preparation-information your evangelist sends to you ahead of time. Even if it is mimeographed material remember that is the result of the years of experience the man of God has had and he will have some good suggestions for you. Try to carefully follow his requests. If any of his ideas are totally unusable or unwise in your case it would be well to suggest this to the evangelist and perhaps an alternate plan can be followed. If the evangelist wants "Pack the Pew" used every night and you have worn that plan out so that the people have threatened to excommunicate you, then let the visiting preacher know ahead of time and something else can be done that may do just as much good. In some cases, I'm sure the pastor has not carefully read my information letter and other materials and then time is wasted and some good ideas are neglected that could have helped the meeting substantially.

(5) *Be enthusiastic* yourself about the coming meetings! Get so excited that it cannot help but be contagious. Announce it in different ways for several weeks ahead of time. Be sure your Sunday school teachers are getting their pupils stirred up about it. Don't take anything for granted. Get the choir motivated. Inspire your bus workers. Excite your young people. Find out everything you can about the speaker who is coming. Play up the things about the meeting that will be of special interest. If he has been a great athlete, a noted musician, an entertainer or a notorious sinner of some kind you have a natural thing to build interest on.

Most evangelists are just Spirit-filled men who have a concern for souls and a great burden for revival. But you can get testimonies from them or from others where they have been. Tell the people about him. Put his printed sermons up on the bulletin board if he has messages in print. If he works with young people or has thrilling things of interest to the children be sure they are aware of this and can never forget that such and such a day is when the crusade starts!

(6) *PRAY much* and set your people to praying. Have cottage prayer meetings or other kinds but do not tie the people up so many nights that they are exhausted before the evangelist gets there. Some pastors print prayer reminders so the members have them at home on the table or in their Bibles. Have some men's prayer meetings and some times when the ladies pray. Have your youth man working with the teens—set *them* to praying. A chain of prayer is good.

Prayer meetings before the night services during the campaign will be of real value but I would not set them up too early, perhaps only 15 or 20 minutes before the service each night. And don't lambast your people if they do not come early to pray. Remember that the people who would be most likely to come to pray are also the people who might be most successful at bringing the lost and other visitors. If they can bring prospects by coming at the last minute I would rather they would do that (and I'd tell them so) than to come early to pray and then have no lost or backslidden people there to preach to each night!

By the way, if some interested (and patient) adult will take the junior children under his (or her) wing and pray with them before the service each night you may be helping not only to get some good praying done and some lost parents brought to the Lord, but you'll keep down the noise and confusion before the services begin. Don't sell the kids short. They can pray, too.

(7) *Advertise widely.* The earlier chapter (5) on advertising and publicizing your church will help you in revival preparation, too. If your church is small you may want to take up some expense offerings for advertising and such in the weeks ahead of the campaign. Large, attractive, colorful and inexpensive posters can be obtained by writing Tribune Showprint, Inc., 401 Oak

Street, Box 188, Earl Park, Indiana 47942. These posters are outstanding enough that it is impossible for people not to see them and be impressed with them. Smaller handbills or unattractive paper posters will not do nearly so much good. The posters should be put up about one week to 10 days before the campaign starts and be taken down the day after the meetings conclude. Be as nice to the grocer, bank or department store manager about taking them down afterwards as you were when you wanted him to let you put them up and he will be more agreeable about it next time.

Have an attractive sign printed or a nice banner hung up in front of your church at least a week or ten days ahead of the meeting. Let a professional do the job. Signs scribbled hastily or concocted by the young people will not make a good impression and may do as much harm as good. Some class or women's group will probably raise the money for your sign if you work on it a couple of months ahead of time.

Highway billboards will be good if you can afford them. Sometimes you can get them donated.

Newspaper stories and ads are a must. Plan ahead. Note the difference in chapter 5 between a story (which is free) and a (paid) advertisement. You will probably need more than one ad. Plan them well and seek professional help from an ad man at the newspaper if you do not know how to lay one out. Notice the ads of the churches where crowds go and where things are really happening and you can learn something about good advertising. Even if a lot of people could not actually tell you that they came as a result of the ad it is still a fact that the ad keeps your meeting before the people and reinforces all of the posters and cards and phone calls that have already helped them to make up their minds to come. Also the ads let people know that you are in business and that your church is doing something. People may come later even if they do not get there during the revival. The ad is not a lost cause.

If just one family finds your church and comes to the revival as a result of the advertising, they may (if they join even later) give enough tithes and offerings to the church to pay for many ads in the months to come!

Print up attractive, slick, pocket-size cards announcing your revival. Cards are better than dodgers or handbills. They do not scatter and blow away as easily, they do not so soon become dog-eared and bent out of shape, and, best of all, they fit into a man's shirt pocket or a lady's purse so your members can always have some of the revival cards with them. What man could haul handbills around in his pocket or business suit and what shape would they soon be in if he did? Saturate the whole community, door to door, with the cards, giving a personal invitation. Your ladies can do this, or your teens can, or the whole church can get involved in it as a special Sunday afternoon project the Sunday before the crusade starts.

Radio stations and TV bulletin boards will take your revival announcements if you write them out properly and take them to them well ahead of time. Some of your spirited men will help you with this if you'll appoint an enthusiastic advertising committee for the crusade and help them get started on it well in advance of the meeting. (See again the suggestions in chapter 5).

In your advertising don't just say, "Brother Jones from Jonesville will be here to preach." Give the man's name in large letters and tell where he is from! If he is from half-way across America the town will be impressed with the fact that you have brought a man so far and will figure he must be worth hearing. If he is an author, an editor, an educator—say so! If he is nationally known then I would say so, but don't put down "Internationally Known Evangelist" if he is just 23 years old and fresh out of Bible school. Be honest in your advertising.

IMPORTANT: Be sure and give the full address of your church and a short description or small map as to how to find it if it is off the beaten track. Make sure that you have the *time* of the service stated prominently.

Be sure you print enough cards so that you have a couple of hundred left for the evangelist to use and for others to take and give out during the actual crusade. On many occasions I have arrived only to find there is absolutely nothing for me to hand out to people to tell them about the revival and the church where I am presently engaged. Everybody in town ought to know about your meeting by the time it starts and no one should be able to forget it once it gets under way.

(8) *Sidetrack* all other things just before and during the revival. Don't confuse your people by having several things going on at once. The revival meeting will take all of the time, prayer and effort they can possibly generate. Deacons' meetings, building meetings, school meetings, socials—all of these things should be postponed until after the crusade. "This one thing I do" should be our cry! Let your people think of nothing else but revival, getting right with God and soul winning. In some places it seems that the revival is just a necessary evil that we must work into our busy schedule somehow along with the many other things the pastor already has us doing. No wonder there is no revival!

(9) *Have "special days"* during the meeting if the evangelist does not have such already planned. If your guest speaker does not use a "Pack-the-Pew" or a Host-and-Hostess plan then he will probably welcome your suggestions for such nights as Sunday School Night, Neighbor Night, Twin Night, Family Night, Fellow-Worker Night, etc. If your preacher is coming in on Monday night it would be well to call it "Welcome the Evangelist Night" or "Church Loyalty Night" with an all-out effort to get the entire membership there to encourage the evangelist and get the meeting started right. Some evangelists like to have the first Monday of the compaign to be "Sunday School Night." There is no point in calling it Sunday School Night, though, if you do not have your workers organized to put everything they've got into getting 100% of the classes there—particularly from the older primaries on up through adults. If you can have a couple of hundred extra people there on the first week-night of the meeting by calling it "Sunday School Night" then there is a good chance you can keep a good crowd coming all week if they like the evangelist and if the Lord blesses that first service.

If you are going to have "Family Night" plan it well ahead of time so that your people can line up relatives and family members before they get something else to do. The same can be said of other special nights. Some workers will come from stores, factories, etc., if properly invited and given plenty of advance notice that Fellow-Worker Night will be on a given night, and especially if they like the fellow-worker who invites them.

Dr. Fleming at the Dayton Baptist Temple had several dozen pew-packers lined up before I arrived for the meeting. They were to serve on three different nights. He had secured wooden-covered Jerusalem Bibles, Family Bibles, commentaries and other good books for awards. The people really worked at it. Eighty-two people had volunteered to pack a pew one night. Many were saved that night and I think 141 were saved during the week, most of them brought in by the pew-packers. Be sure your evangelist is in accord with your special night plans.

(10) *Choose personal workers carefully* and be sure you train them well on how to deal quickly and efficiently with those who come forward. In most cases you have but to get them on their knees and ask God to save them at once. To let personal workers get involved in all kinds of questions about the Bible, and denominations, and separation and such matters, will delay the decision and may result in the would-be convert not getting saved at all. Use personal workers who will assume that all who come forward are unsaved unless they positively declare otherwise. Many church members are really not saved these days. Dr. Ron Comfort tells of the lady who was brought by a worker back out of the inquiry room stating that this "Christian Scientist" had just "rededicated" her life! Make sure your workers are trained to get genuine, clear-cut decisions. For help on using your personal workers at the invitation read chapter 9 carefully.

(11) *Explain to your choir* the importance of good evangelistic music and spirited singing each night during the crusade. The choir should be there ahead of time each night but I wouldn't have too many long rehearsals during a campaign lest you wear them out. A wise choir director will have them practiced up well on good revival songs ahead of the actual crusade. Read again the chapter on music and be sure that appropriate music is used. Don't spring outside musical groups on your evangelist without

discussing it with him. It would be good if your philosophy of music and that of the evangelist concur. Don't use weak, doubtful singers who are lacking in confidence or who do not have a good testimony for your revival special music.

Rousing choir numbers, beautifully arranged duets or trios—these will be best for your special music unless you have a truly outstanding soloist who can greatly move people with his (or her) singing.

(12) *Introduce your evangelist properly.* If Sunday is the first day of the crusade I would take him to your young people's departments and other classes and let him say a friendly word of greeting unless you're going to have them all in the main auditorium for Sunday school. If possible, and if he wants to do it, I would have him speak to your Sunday school (at least to the adults) on the first Sunday as it will help to break the ice and prepare the people for that all-important first Sunday service. You may want to also have a big evangelistic rally or a family service with the whole Sunday school present on the closing Sunday of the campaign.

When introducing your evangelist tell the people who he is and where he is from and a little bit about him. The introduction does not have to be long and it should not be flowery or extravagant but it should be proper. People will have a bit more confidence and "take to him" better if they know something about him. Even though you have talked about him to your own people ahead of time there will always be people there who are seeing and hearing him for the first time. If his wife is with him introduce her to the people, too.

It is not necessary to introduce the evangelist every night after that first Sunday (or Monday). If you do, I would simply say, "And now, our evangelist, Brother _____," and turn him loose.

(13) *Be sure your Sunday school superintendent* and teachers realize the importance of their task and of having every pupil present at all services, if at all possible. A teacher can get pupils saved by having a special class night when all of his or her pupils sit together in the meeting. Teachers should be there every night and should be alert to who is coming and who is not. Telephone

committees can be busy from the first Sunday on, working over the church roll and class rolls, phoning prospects and backsliders. Those who phone need to be alert to notice if the people come who have been called that day. Use pleasant ladies who will use intelligence in calling and who will boost the meetings enthusiastically.

(14) *Deacons* can divide up the membership and work on (or call) those who may be discouraged or out of fellowship. Then it would be good for the deacons to spot those people when they come and sit with them or at least let them know that they are glad they came.

(15) *Bus captains* and workers should visit hard, zero in on the parents of their bus riders, pray much and use every conceivable plan for getting their riders to the meetings. In some cases it may not be possible for the buses to run their entire Sunday route on week nights but at least the bus workers should be reaching all of them they can and bringing the older ones (those who will behave) who are mature enough to be saved.

(16) *Keep in touch* with your evangelist before he arrives and be sure you have a clear understanding on just where and when he is coming in. If you can meet him at the plane it will give you an opportunity to discuss the important aspects of the crusade right away.

On the way from the airport to the motel, a North Carolina pastor handed me three cards. On these 3 x 5 index cards, he had written for me:

1. The time of each service;
2. Anticipated schedule for the services;
3. Names of the song leader, pianist and Sunday school superintendent;
4. Plans for meals;
5. Whose car I would be using;
6. How offerings would be taken;
7. A request for my travel and other expenses;
8. Who would be handling the book table;
9. Time of the radio broadcast and all of the special speaking engagements;

10. The plan for packing-the-pews, already assigned.

Needless to say, in that meeting I could give myself to prayer and the ministry of the Word. What a blessing that pastor was to me and the revival!

I often travel by motor home as many others do now. It is always a blessing to me when the pastor has sent me specific directions on how to find his church. If the pastor or custodian lives right by the church then usually someone is available to show me where to hook up the motor home. If not, then it would be well to have someone there to meet the evangelist or tell him someone to call so that he can have the help he needs in getting situated on his arrival. A few churches are providing a pad for parking on now with electrical and water hook-ups (in rare cases even a sewerage hook-up!), and this is a great help. Since even many missionaries are now traveling to their churches in motor homes or campers this is a wise thing for a church to do. Providing these facilities is considerably cheaper than motels, plane fares and restaurant meals!

(17) *Ushers* should realize the importance of their work during the revival. Be sure and read the chapter (10) on Ushers, the Pastor's Special Task Force. Never are they needed more than during special meetings.

(18) *Start your services on time.* This is a help to the evangelist and it will impress people with the efficiency of your church. To start with punctuality and then not keep them too long will surely do much to keep them coming back.

(19) *Maintain a good nursery for the babies* and train your people to use it for the babies and tots. Don't ruin some of your revival services by letting crying little ones disturb. Use your hired nursery workers and then if additional help is needed the good Christian ladies can sign a nursery chart and take turns. Don't make the poor pastor's wife have to do it and it is best not to let teen girls do it, at least not more than once during the revival, and only then if they are good Christian girls. Worldly girls sometimes want to keep the nursery and they are the ones who need to be hearing the preaching.

(20) *Try to appeal to all ages.* I reach children with a brief

dramatized Bible story each evening. The children get enthused and bring others. Teens are invited to stay for a short session each evening on courtship and dating. We also use a simple plan to have adults reach their friends and neighbors.

Where an evangelist does not have special sessions for the youth, the children can possibly be organized into a "Booster Band" by a talented and personable teacher, while the youth director or a young people's worker in the church can band the youth together for prayer groups and visitation effort during the crusade. Over pizza and Pepsi you can accomplish a lot with energetic teens before the campaign ever begins.

(21) *If you have a Christian school* try to schedule your meetings when school activities will not conflict. Use your evangelist to preach to the school children, too. Have a special school night and try to get all of the student body there. Use your school glee club or a giant choir from the school that night and it may help to get many of the parents there, also. When I was with Dr. Bruce Cummons at Massillon, Ohio, he canceled all homework and assignments in the schools there that week so students would have no excuse for not coming to the crusade. What a delight to work with a pastor like that!

(22) *Be sure the grass is cut* and the building and grounds are in good shape before the campaign starts. People are going to be coming to your church as visitors who may decide by what they see and hear whether they will make yours their church home. Put on your best "front" for the revival.

(23) *Use good psychology* when making announcements and addressing the people. Don't fuss at them for not coming sooner. Rejoice that they came at all! Don't say (with a mournful look), "The crowd is down tonight," but rather, "We're glad you are here. Others will be coming in. We are so glad the Lord is blessing. Let's sing and rejoice in all that God is doing for us in these meetings!"

(24) *Invite groups to come* from scouts, clubs, sports teams, other churches. Probably someone in your church will be just the man (or woman) to contact each of these and get them lined up to come one night in a group. Be sure and recognize them when

they come. Fellow pastors should be noticed, also.

(25) *Extra meetings* can often be scheduled (with the consent of the evangelist) in schools, pastors' conferences, radio programs, television interviews, factory meetings, etc. These often will help in swelling the crowds in your campaign.

(26) *Keep the service moving* with no long, drawn-out announcements. Jot down what you have to say or announce and make it brief. Don't let the song service drag. Let one singer or group be coming to the platform as you finish something else. Don't talk on and on after the evangelist has finished his sermon. Let the people go home with the message on their hearts. A preacher should be into his sermon within 35 minutes or so of the opening song. This means the song service will have to move right along and the other preliminaries be brief.

(27) *Send the people away on a high plane.* Rejoice in "what we have heard tonight." If people have been saved tell the congregation about it. Let the saints come down and rejoice with those who have found the Lord. Smile, and be optimistic in your prospects of the service the next night. Sing a rousing chorus just before they go home. Have sparkling music played on the piano as the people leave the building or let the choir be sending them away with a happy song so that all will rejoice in what God is doing at your church!

Chapter Seventeen

What Should an Evangelist Expect of a Pastor and Vice Versa?

A revival campaign in your church should be one of the happiest and most glorious experiences of the entire church year. And it should be eminently successful. At a Christian college I was asked to speak to the "preacher boys" on the subject, "What Should a Pastor Expect of an Evangelist and What Should an Evangelist Expect of a Pastor?" It was a hefty subject! Let's elaborate a bit on this very important theme. First,

WHAT SHOULD A VISITING EVANGELIST EXPECT OF THE PASTOR. . .

. . .who invites him to invest a week or more of his life ministering in that pastor's church?

1. *Is it just an inquiry* about the possibility of a meeting or is it a bona fide and definite invitation? Some pastors have been known to play "roulette" with several evangelists at the same time giving these men (each of them) the impression that the pastor wants them for a meeting. This is unfair, of course, for the *schedule* can sometimes be a nightmare for an evangelist and he may spend much time and many dollars on long-distance calls trying to re-arrange his itinerary to accommodate that pastor only to find out that several men had been contacted and the pastor has already chosen one of the others. That's sort of like proposing to several girls and then selecting the first one who is convenient enough to the wedding date set by the suitor!

Now it is certainly all right to write to several men and inquire about the possibility of getting together in the spring or in the winter of some year on up ahead, as the case may be. A pastor should feel free to ask all the questions he might want to ask about the evangelist, his beliefs, his methods, his travel arrangements, his preferences, etc. I'll assure you that a busy evangelist keeps a constant stream of mail going out and coming in, and his correspondence never ceases. But when a pastor writes an evangelist to say: "We believe God wants you to be our evangelist and we want you to give us a date for a meeting—when can you come?" the evangelist has every right to believe that the pastor means business and that he is correct in trying to arrange a definite date for that campaign.

If a pastor wants to contact several men and find out more about them before making a decision he should do his planning well in advance of the year he anticipates having that campaign. Or, better still, if he wants immediate results in his planning, phone these evangelists and very frankly tell them that he is seeking an evangelist and wants to make some inquiries.

Don't give up on an evangelist if you don't reach him at his home telephone the first time or two you call. Most evangelists are out on the road and it may be a rare time that you'll find him sitting at home by the phone. Find out from the operator if he has an alternate phone number, or in most cases just read his letterhead or his brochure carefully and you will probably find some numbers listed where you can find the whereabouts of the evangelist. If he sends out an itinerary (as many do) you may reach him by phoning the church where he is engaged at the moment.

2. *Have a clear understanding* about the date, the year, the length of the meeting, the size of the church, the potential, etc. When a pastor writes an evangelist it is an act of courtesy to tell that evangelist what you have in mind and what the possibilities for revival are in your church. An evangelist does not want to have to ask, "What is the size of your church, how many come and how many people will your auditorium seat?" but he *does* wonder, and he has a right to be told, when he is seeking the Lord's will about coming for that meeting. It is not that a God-called evangelist will only go to big churches or that he has to have some kind of guarantee. I have never demanded "so much"

or asked for a guarantee, and know of no Spirit-led evangelist who would do such a thing, and some of my best meetings have been in small churches. But an evangelist has only so many weeks that he can be out in meetings. He wants to go where he can do the most good, win the most souls and influence the most people for God. Why should he deliberately go to a church with 100 people if he could be preaching to 2,000 in a city where he would possibly win ten times more people to the Lord? Of course, he should definitely pray and seek the Lord's will about which church to go to as it may, indeed, be the Lord's will for him to choose the smaller church. But no pastor should try to deceive the evangelist about the church to which he is inviting him. It is always refreshing to get a letter from a pastor in which he tells me about his church—what they stand for and are attempting to do, how long he has been there, the size of his Sunday school and church, the size of his auditorium, and maybe the names of a few evangelists they have had recently at this church.

If the building is small, the offerings are down, and the members have lost interest, the evangelist will probably come on anyway, if he can, but he ought to honestly have an opportunity to evaluate the situation and make his decision on his knees about it.

If the situation is such that there is no motel and the evangelist will have to stay in a private home where there are small children and no private bath, it would be only fair to share this information with the man before booking him definitely for the campaign. Sometime ago I received a letter from a church officer wanting me to come to a church and assuring me that the people wanted me and would be anxious to have me come. The letter sounded encouraging but when I called the pastor about the meeting I found that he worked for a living in another town, did not live near the field, that the church had only 35 members and that he was not too enthusiastic about having a meeting, anyhow! So it is only fair to let a prospective evangelist know what he is *in* for.

3. The evangelist also has a right to know *that the church will go all out* to properly prepare and lay other things aside in order

to give themselves to the matter of having a real revival.

4. The pastor could well assure the evangelist that the church will spend to promote and advertise the crusade and that every effort will be made to get crowds there for the opening days of the campaign. (If the crowds do not *keep coming* the evangelist had better check up on himself!)

5. The sound system should be checked out ahead of time as well as anything else that is essential to the success of the meeting. Don't make an evangelist ruin his throat because of an inadequate sound system or faulty "mikes."

6. A thoughtful pastor will start the services on time, keep announcements at a minimum, and have an understanding with his music man that a limited number of songs will be used without a needless waste of time, in order that the evangelist have plenty of time to bring his message. It is a frustrating thing to realize that twenty minutes of your sermon time have been consumed with long, drawn-out announcements or testimonies and that you're going to have to try to whittle the message down "as you go" in order to get the people out at a decent hour.

7. It is the responsibility of the pastor, not the evangelist, to be sure that a nursery is maintained and that the mothers take their babies there, and that parents or ushers take care of their unruly teenagers. Don't bring in a noted man of God and then expect him to have to compete with crying babies and roaming juniors or giggling teens while he is pouring out his soul.

8. The evangelist should be informed ahead of time if long visiting sessions will be demanded of him or if extra services are being planned in other places outside of the church where he is engaged. The more successful pastors frequently say, "We want you as the evangelist to have the time you need for prayer, study, correspondence and sermon preparation. We do not expect you to come here and do our visiting for us." Of course, any real man of God will be glad to make necessary and strategic calls with the pastor when called upon but he cannot run around promiscuously making visits and contacts if he is to be his best for the work he has been brought there to do. Some evangelists may *want* to visit some with the pastor—others may feel that it drains them too

much and weakens them for the services at night. One great preacher who won multitudes told me that he poured out his heart and worked as hard at winning *one* man as he did in preaching to a crowd. I think I would have been most unwise to have demanded that he thus wear himself out making house calls.

When I was a pastor in the earlier days I used to take my evangelist around to visit the "hard cases," the tough unsaved husbands, the infidels in the area, but I cannot recall that it usually did much good and I learned that the tough cases soon had been educated to have their "guard up" and be ready to exert all of the opposition possible when the pastor brought his evangelist around. Others figure we were coming and managed to be out of town or "off hunting" when the revival was going on so they wouldn't have to encounter the evangelist. Of course, there are exceptions to all this and there are times when a visit from the evangelist may, in some cases, be just what is needed. But give the visiting preacher time for his rest, study and prayer, too.

9. Load the members down with attractive cards and educate them to work as ambassadors for the campaign. They can boost the meeting and talk glowingly about the evangelist and his messages. *He* cannot do so but *they* can! People ought to get so excited about what God is doing that they will arouse the interest of people who otherwise would not come.

10. The pastor and his staff and members ought to work hard during the crusade. I would call myself blue in the face contacting prospects and trying to get promises out of sinners and backsliders during our revivals. With an evangelist doing the preaching this frees the pastor to visit and phone and pray more than ever.

11. Before the evangelist ever arrives it would be well for the pastor to consider preaching some messages on the obstacles to revival. Ask God to help you burden the people about unforgiveness, holding grudges, temper, jealousy, poutiness, impatience, worldliness, pride, dishonesty, a critical spirit, worry, lust, unbelief, neglect of prayer, refusal to witness, bitterness, gossip and slander, covetousness, finding fault, inconsistency,

slavery to television, unconcern and lack of burden for lost souls. These are just a few of the things that Christians need to repent of if a glorious revival and/or a blessed ingathering of souls is to be experienced. And, Pastor, make sure you have personally repented of these things!

12. Pastor, be in all the services yourself. If an evangelist was preaching to my adults in the main auditorium at Sunday school I felt I should be in there, too, not only to boost and encourage my guest speaker but also as a testimony to my people. Not only that, but I need the message for my own soul. Some pastors have been known to "abandon" their evangelist and run around looking in on the Sunday school classes or seeing how the offering count was going on in the church office. On more than one occasion I have had to close out a Sunday school service in another man's pulpit with no one to help at the front if someone came forward and no pastor there to turn the service back over to when I was through.

13. Keep the minds of the people on the revival and not on everything else. During the week of a revival the concentration should be on repentance and reaching souls—not on ballots, socials, school projects, the church budget, anticipated new buildings, etc. I believe it would be wise to leave off training union meetings, Bible classes, missionary meetings, lengthy choir rehearsals and anything else that would take time or strength away from the revival. Instead of your best soul-winning ladies sitting around sipping tea and reading parts how much better for them to be praying for revival and visiting prospects!

Instead of your best people coming to a training session on Sunday evening an hour before the evangelistic revival service, would it not be wiser to give them this hour to go gather up some people they had been praying for and bring them to the revival? I think we often defeat our own purpose.

14. Check out singers and "groups" ahead of time before inviting them to sing in your campaign. If you have not seen or heard them you may be in for a shock. Don't make an evangelist have to blush and bite his lip as he tries to get up and preach

after some boisterous and worldly group has just butchered the song service!

15. When you take your evangelist and his wife into a home for a meal do not just assume that they know all the members of the family where you are dining. Usually they do not, and often they have not even yet met the host or hostess. Introduce them. It will also be helpful if you let the evangelist know a little about that home and family before you arrive. This often prevents some remark being made that might prove embarrassing. For instance, the lady may be a widow or divorced and so it would be best for the evangelist or his wife in making conversation not to ask her about her husband!

16. Have meals in homes planned by a wise and discerning lady or by a carefully chosen hospitality committee instead of merely putting up a notice on the bulletin board and letting people "sign up." When I was a pastor we sometimes found that unsavory situations could thus be avoided. Don't take an evangelist into a place where there is disease or contagious sickness. You would not want to take him to dine in a place that was dirty, foulsmelling and nauseating, so observe the golden rule here. Evangelists have to travel all the time, eat under all kinds of circumstances, change drinking water every week and constantly fight to stay healthy so don't subject him to unnecessary situations where he may encounter difficulty in maintaining his well-being.

This is not to say that an evangelist is unwilling to eat with poor people in a modest home. But the place should be clean and the food appetizing. Your church hostess or hospitality committee should be trained to understand this.

17. The pastor should go, too, when the evangelist goes out for a meal in a home. The people should be trained about this. Most evangelists do not want to go without the pastor and many positively refuse to do so. It is awkward, the evangelist has to try to make conversation with strangers who themselves sometimes are bashful and embarrassed, and then, too, some people want to have the evangelist alone because they don't particularly like the pastor or they may be out of fellowship with him. If this is true

the evangelist has no business being in that home without the pastor. If the pastor has several children then, of course, it is not necessary to invite the whole family but at least the pastor should go and if the evangelist has his wife with him then it is best for the pastor's wife to go, also. The hostess or hospitality chairman can explain this to the ladies if the pastor feels he cannot mention it.

18. Try not to consume too much of the evangelist's time. He'll want some fellowship with you but cannot take time to go great distances for meals, get involved in long, drawn-out counseling sessions or wait through the great tribulation for the pastor to make calls before he is returned to his room after a broadcast or a service. Be considerate.

19. It is a comfort for the evangelist when the pastor stays on the platform during the service and can thus survey the situation and be there to handle anything that needs attention. Usually children behave better, teens are less likely to disrupt and even adults listen better when the pastor is up there observing the congregation while the evangelist is preaching. The pastor, too, can thus see when people are under conviction and is more likely to know for sure whether certain people were there or not. In most cases it is probably best for the pastor to be seated on one side of the platform and his assistant on the other side. This is the greatest business in the world and demands our best.

20. Sometimes pastors spend a good bit of time during special meetings publicizing future events that will be coming later in the month or year. It is best, generally, to save such announcements for the last day of the revival. During the campaign keep it upon the hearts of the people that this revival is the most important thing in the world and demands our all.

21. Be sure your own family sets a good example. A pastor's children should be seated near the front and should be well-behaved. I have been in at least one campaign where the pastor's own teenage children did not stay for the special sessions we had for teens. This hurts what we are trying to do for the young people, of course. Most pastors' children are outstanding, by the

way, and usually they are the best behaved and most spiritual in the church. This speaks well for our pastors!

22. The pastor and church should be responsible for taking care of the travel expenses and other matters such as food and lodging while the evangelist is with them. Then a worthy love offering should be given for the support of the evangelist and his family, as an honorable investment in evangelism. If an evangelist could hold as many as 40 meetings in a year that would still leave him with 12 weeks (3 months) with no income. Most of the time, though, taking into consideration December-until-after-New-Years, summer vacation time, travel times between meetings, cancelations, etc., most evangelists preach only 25 to 35 meetings in a year, the average being about 32. This leaves 20 weeks (almost 5 months of the year) with no income. A pastor should realize this and help his people to see the need for a proper offering. Since this is (to some people) a delicate matter and subject to misunderstanding, and since I have asked my pastor, Milton Ker, to write a portion on the subject of the revival offering, we will reserve this matter for chapter 18. Now. . .

WHAT SHOULD A PASTOR EXPECT
OF AN EVANGELIST?

1. THE EVANGELIST (as well as the pastor) SHOULD BE DILIGENT AND PROMPT in *answering his mail!* I've had pastors mention that some evangelists are not careful about their correspondence, nailing down dates, sending pictures, and such matters. Now, in defense of the evangelist, let me say that many times our mail is slow in catching up with us on the road. Then about the time we're ready to answer it we're moving to the next meeting and things get behind. Also evangelists spend much of their time waiting to hear from Pastor B and Pastor C so they can give a definite reply to Pastor A. So it is an act of courtesy for both evangelists and pastors to answer their letters and to try to decide something as quickly as possible. It is distressing both ways just to be kept "dangling" about dates. Evangelists need to be organized, keep their files carefully and not lose their mail. And they need to be conscientious.

2. SEND DATA, PICTURES, etc., to the pastor at a proper time so that he will be able to adequately prepare. The pastor should have our materials in hand at least two months before the crusade and in some cases three months ahead. Some pastors want the material even sooner, but if sent a great many months or a year early the pastor may have misplaced it before he needs it.

3. LET THE PASTOR KNOW HOW YOU WILL BE TRAVELING, when you will arrive and what you will need when you get there. If coming to the church in a motor home, bus, or travel trailer advise the pastor what you will need in the way of space, hook-ups, and such matters. If you pro-rate your travel expense it is probably best to let this be known to the pastor in your information letters sent out ahead of time. If coming by air be sure the pastor has your flight number and expected time of arrival. Be sure and advise him if there is a last-minute change.

4. THE EVANGELIST CAN AND SHOULD BE PREPARED to make suggestions about promotion and getting crowds unless the pastor assures him that this is already taken care of. Some pastors need help and will appreciate suggestions from the evangelist.

5. LET THE PASTOR KNOW WHAT YOUR PREFER-ENCES ARE ABOUT MEALS, but be flexible. Don't be hard to live with. If you have a health problem or special diet needs, then, of course, the pastor should be advised in advance before a hospitality committee has already set up a meal schedule.

6. SHOW RESPECT FOR THE PASTOR'S PULPIT AND HONOR HIM AS A MAN AND AS THE LEADER OF THE FLOCK. Boost the pastor. Do all you can to help him while you are on his field. Never do anything to embarrass the pastor. I would be very careful about making jokes about the pastor or his co-workers. Even if you and the pastor are good friends there are many people who do not understand and feel that you are not giving proper respect to their pastor. The evangelist can do much to build him up in the eyes of the people.

7. THE EVANGELIST SHOULD NOT BRING OTHERS ALONG UNINVITED. If your wife travels with you let it be

known in advance. If you travel by air or train the church should not be expected to pay her fare unless she is part of the team, nor should they have to pay her motel bill. Some churches will *want* to and it is a blessing if they do, but do not demand it or expect it. Do not bring children or friends along to a crusade unless it is clearly understood that it is perfectly all right to do so. My wife travels with me in the motor home a good bit of the time but since we have our motor home this takes care of both travel and accommodations while on the field so there is no extra expense to the church, and the pastor always knows that she is coming with me.

8. DO NOT MAKE "DEMANDS" OF THE PASTOR. I have been surprised to learn that some pastors are pleased that I do not make demands of them and that I am easy to get along with. Obviously some of them have had some unpleasant experiences with cantankerous evangelists. If there is no spare office I frequently set up my study in a Sunday school room in the basement or back in some quiet area. The chairs are not usually comfortable and the light is not always the best but I get along fine and most pastors do the best they can with such matters. You might make suggestions about addressing the Sunday school or meeting with the workers but I would certainly not demand it. Some evangelists have made it hard on the rest of us.

9. EVANGELISTS SHOULD USE DISCRETION AND KINDNESS IN DEALING WITH PEOPLE. Pastors tell me that some evangelists have come thundering down out of the pulpit to point out (and embarrass people), and shout at them or take them by the arm and try to make them come forward. I would hope such are few and far between. This often makes it hard for the pastor to get those people to come if he ever has another meeting. Evangelists should be thoughtful, compassionate, tactful and kind in their pleadings. Leave the door open for the pastor to continue his work with those souls if they do not yield under your ministry. Be completely honest in your invitations. The people should know you are a man of your word.

10. BE DISCREET AND VERY CAREFUL AROUND THE LADIES. Give no cause for suspicion. Avoid the very appearance of evil.

11. BE MANNERLY. Arrive on time for meals and for services. Be a perfect gentleman in the pastor's home and in the homes of members. Eat what is put before you with gratitude. Always express thanks to the hostess after the meal. If you stay in a home always write a note of thanks soon after your departure. A small gift of appreciation would be nice, too. And *always* write to the pastor to thank him and the church for the love offering and other kindnesses. This should be done within a day or two of the end of the campaign. This should be in addition to the words of thanks you say from the pulpit on the last night of the meeting. If someone loans you a car be sure and thank him, and you should at least *offer* to refill it with gas, unless you know the church is going to do so.

12. BY ALL MEANS BE PRAYED UP AND PREPARED for each service. The people may neglect to pray and the pastor may get busy and forget it, but you as an evangelist can never afford to neglect prayer, much prayer and more prayer. And if we neglect our own Bible study and devotional life it will surely show up in our preaching.

13. BE FRIENDLY. Don't be a recluse or a bore. I know we evangelists are not called upon to be social butterflies and we are prone to become impatient with small talk but we have to be kind, friendly and gracious to people. Be patient with elderly people and with children. Consider it a privilege to sign their Bibles or answer their questions.

14. DON'T PUT PASTORS ON THE SPOT. The Lord can impress their hearts if He wants you in that pastor's church. Pastors resent an evangelist who writes or phones them, wanting a meeting. The exception here, of course, would be in a situation where a pastor has asked an evangelist to let him know when he would be in the area or if he had a cancelation. Then it would be fine to contact him.

15. BE NEAT IF YOU STAY IN A PRIVATE HOME. Most evangelists now stay in a motel or in a prophet's chamber or a motor home, but if you do have to stay in a private home take care of your own room. Make your bed, keep things picked up

and by all means keep the bathroom clean and tidy. Don't be sloppy.

16. DON'T JOKE TOO MUCH and be sure they are always clean jokes if you tell one. Off-color stories will be your "fly in the ointment"—your Waterloo!

17. AVOID TEMPTATIONS to laziness. Keep busy. Study, pray, witness, read, walk, exercise, write, keep up your correspondence. Do not let the Devil make you careless and lazy about such matters. Be careful about the dirty magazines that may be lying around in a hotel. Whatsoever things are pure, think on these things, the apostle has reminded us. Abhor that which is evil. Make no provision to the flesh. Watch out for newsstands and the wrong kind of bookstores. Do not become a slave to the television set. Watch it sparingly or it will stifle your spiritual life and rob you of precious study time.

18. DON'T BE MONEY-MINDED. Do not become bitter if the pastor seems not to work hard at getting you a good love offering. Some pastors do not know how and have never been in your shoes. Sometimes he knows his people and knows they'll be generous even if he puts little emphasis on it. If your offering is small just praise the Lord for it, say, "Thank you, Brother," to the pastor and remember for whom you are working. God will make it up to you some other place, or in some other way. Many pastors do not realize all of the expenses that an evangelist has and they do not stop to remember that the evangelist pays for his own house, his utilities, taxes, insurance and other things that are often taken care of by a church for their pastor. I hope this book will help both pastor and evangelist to better understand the position of the other.

19. DON'T LET A JEALOUS BONE DEVELOP IN YOUR BODY. If the pastor drives a better car and has a nicer home than you do, just thank God for what you *do* have and remember that you don't have many of the headaches and problems the pastor has! If other evangelists seem to get the bigger churches and prosper more than you do don't forget that we are called to suffer with Christ "outside the camp" and that *whatever* blessing we have, it is more than we deserve. Read the tract, *Others*

May, You Cannot, at least several times a year. Maybe you should memorize it! (Source of Light Missions, Box 8, Madison, Georgia 30650, publishes this tract).

20. IF YOU PREACH OLD SERMONS BE SURE THEY ARE STILL "HOT"! Don't just run through them like a parrott. Work them over and pray over them and be sure the unction is still on them—and on you! Some of us need to freshen up our illustrations more often, too.

21. DO NOT GIVE EXAGGERATED REPORTS OF YOUR MEETINGS. Be honest. We are not to think more highly of ourselves than we ought to think.

22. *"Wallow in the Word,"* to quote Dr. Appelman. Stay much in the Book. In this way your faith will stay strong and your sermons fresh.

23. DON'T PREACH TOO LONG. Some preachers preach their people into a decision and then keep on until they have preached them out of it again. Spurgeon said we keep on until we get one blessed thought after another and after awhile the people are getting thoughts that are not blessed!

24. AVOID OBNOXIOUS HABITS. Read *Spurgeon's Lectures to His Students* every now and then and watch out for those mannerisms and habits we get into.

25. DON'T BLAME FAILURE ON THE PEOPLE. I can think back to weak meetings I had in the past and I feel now that perhaps my attitude was wrong or I got off on the wrong foot somehow. People up North need a bit more time to "warm up" to you than Southerners in the Bible Belt. Country people may not take to a "city slicker" until he has been there a few days and they learn he is human. Gain the confidence of the people. When they love you they will respond.

26. DON'T TRY TO MAKE FRIENDS WITH CERTAIN PEOPLE on the pastor's field to write back to or come back and see. Do not get up a mailing list of people to seek contributions from later on. Pastors resent this, and rightly so.

27. DRESS CONSERVATIVELY. Perhaps an evangelist can get away with a jacket that a pastor would not want to wear, but I would not be too flashy and certainly not give the impression

that I was dressing lavishly or extravagantly. At the same time, dress properly—wear clean suits, fresh shirts and shine your shoes! Avoid outlandish hair-dos and garish colors. Be very careful about body odor and never let Job 17:1 be your life verse—especially the first four words!

28. EVANGELISTS TO STEER CLEAR OF! In a college boys' class on evangelism I was asked to suggest the type fellows I would avoid inviting to my church (I was a pastor in those days). I told them I would steer clear of the following men:

(1) Big-time "wheels," the professionals who seem obsessed with themselves.

(2) Those given to crude speech and vulgar terminology.

(3) Any one who told off-color stories or seemed to be a "ladies' man."

(4) An evangelist who whined all the time about money or raised Cain about it.

(5) Preachers who talk about themselves all the time instead of the Lord.

(6) Evangelists who are ill-mannered and who do not show appreciation.

(7) An evangelist who would belittle the pastor or seek to play him down before the people.

(8) One who tried to be funny all the time and who told jokes that were not relevant to the sermon—just to entertain.

(9) Any preacher who was effeminate, prettily precise or too dignified and stiff.

(10) One whose sermons were frothy and had no meat or content to them. One who did not truly "preach the Word."

(11) I'd avoid the ones who ride a hobby horse, the "Johnny-one-note" variety.

(12) An evangelist who was dishonest in his invitations or in his dealings, or the preacher who could never find his terminal facilities.

29. WHICH EVANGELISTS WOULD YOU INVITE AGAIN TO YOUR CHURCH? That question was asked, also. I would invite back to my church the men who are earnest, compassionate

men, and who get results—the fellows who warm the hearts of my people and lead them to love the Lord more and serve Him better. I would invite back the man who uses common sense in his dealings with the people, the man who is easy to be entreated and who does not make a scene if things do not go to please him. I especially enjoyed the men who had a good sense of humor, who were versatile and colorful in their preaching. I invited more than once the men who were intense in soul winning and who had a real burden for people. I liked the men who were uncompromising and who warned my people about sin and worldliness, yet who did so in tenderness and brokenness—these were men who had been to Calvary themselves.

Our people came to hear these kind of men, especially if they were interesting to listen to, and if they did not hold the people too long—especially on Sunday mornings.

As I look back on the men we used in evangelism I'd like to combine the plainness and concern of John Rice with the earnestness and dynamic of Lee Roberson; the Hell-fire preaching of Jesse Hendley with the colorful and interesting messages of Bill Rice; the logic and common sense of Bob Jones with the tears and tenderness of Joe Henry Hankins; the simple brevity of Glen Schunk with the powerful effectiveness of Jack Hyles, and the plain, meaty preaching of Fred Brown with the tangy and sharp thrusts of Walter Hughes. If you could combine all of the above in one man you would possibly have a mixture of Paul, Isaiah, Jeremiah, Stephen and Moses! Thank God there are some good men on the scene today. When the older men lay aside their mantles God will have some of the younger ones ready with polished shield and whetted sword, ready to step into the arena.

Chapter Eighteen

The Revival Offering

How to Get a Good One Without Hurting Your Church

There are actually some preachers who are timid about urging people to give a good revival love offering. There may be as many as three reasons for this hesitancy:

1. Some are afraid that if they say much about money it will make visitors and others say that the "church is just after their money."

2. Some are afraid that a generous love offering for the evangelist may hurt their own church budget for the next week.

3. Some, I believe (hopefully only a few), believe that evangelists earn so much that it would be better not to spoil them by giving them too much money!

All of these fears are groundless.

Intelligent people know that it takes money to live and that a full-time evangelist must have an income to survive and to stay on the road. People who give out of gratitude and blessing, and to invest in the life of a man of God, will do so over and above their regular church gifts, generally, and even if they do not, no church suffers from investing in evangelism any more than they would suffer from investing in missions.

It is hardly possible to give a godly evangelist too big an offering. Expenses are staggering for those who live on the road, maintain a home away from home as well as his permanent residence, too, and have no church or board paying for their insurance, auto expenses, taxes, house payments, etc., as most pastors do. And a generous love offering from your church, even if it be several times bigger than a pastor's weekly income, simply helps make up for the small offerings he gets which are totally inadequate, considering that the evangelist receives probably only about thirty to thirty-three paychecks a year compared to the pastor's fifty-two. So don't worry about giving an evangelist too much money.

The "healers" and charlatans have, of course, given evangelists a bad name about raking in huge offerings, but spiritual people in our good churches know the difference and must be educated to realize that there are real needs in the lives and families of true evangelists and that many of them are sacrificing and having a rough time taking care of their obligations and staying on the road.

My pastor (and my successor) at the Central Baptist Church of Panama City, Florida, is a jewel of a pastor. He is one of the most generous men I've ever known, and he is an experienced expert at taking a good revival offering (or any other kind!). So I have asked Pastor Milton Ker to write an article for us for this book on "what every preacher should know about receiving an offering." Here it is just as he gave it to us:

WHAT EVERY PREACHER SHOULD KNOW ABOUT RECEIVING A REVIVAL OFFERING

The primary principles of stable church finance are well-known. They are summed up in the three R's. . .(1) *Receiving* the offerings graciously, (2) *Recording* the offerings accurately and (3) *Reporting* the offerings faithfully.

It is with the *receiving* aspect we are presently interested. . . and specifically in receiving an offering for an evangelist. How should it be done? The following 14 propositions answer that question.

1. *The pastor should prepare the congregation for an important event.* The evangelistic meeting must be considered a vital matter. Wise people do not support that which is insignificant. The pastor should begin well in advance of the meeting to lay the burden and potential of the meeting on the hearts of the congregation. The members should get the idea that the forthcoming crusade is big business.

2. *The pastor should realize the responsibility of receiving a good offering is squarely on his shoulders.* If the offering is insufficient, it is because the pastor failed to lead the people as he should have. The pastor needs to determine in his mind that the offering can and will be a good one. Giving way to excuse-making at this point is evasion of duty.

3. *The pastor should accentuate the truth: "God gave some evangelists. . . ."* The church should realize that the man who is coming is "sent from God." He has a divine call, a divine unction, a divine insight, a divine ability and he is to be in the midst by divine appointment. He is one of God's best gifts to the church. He should therefore be received warmly and royally.

4. *The pastor should acquaint the people with the special financial needs of an evangelist.* The members should be told about the facts such as: (1) an evangelist goes to churches of all sizes and receives offerings of all sizes; (2) an evangelist cannot possibly conduct 52 meetings per year. Therefore there are some weeks without pay; (3) an evangelist often has two homes—a mobile home and a home back home. Both are expensive to maintain; (4) an evangelist usually has no one to underwrite his expenses; (5) an evangelist depends on God and God's people; and (6) an evangelist wears out and needs more clothes since he is before the public nightly.

5. *The pastor should capitalize on the importance of goals.* "He that aims at nothing, generally hits it." Wise is the pastor who sets a goal concerning the revival offering. It is not necessary for the people to know it, but the pastor should. He should be willing to hock his socks to meet that goal. He should settle for nothing less.

6. *The pastor should enumerate the expenses of the meeting.* The congregation should be given a ball-park figure as to the expenses incurred by the meeting. Informed people are usually happier people. However, if the expenses are exorbitant, that rule of thumb may not hold true.

7. *The pastor should create a church pride about taking care of God's evangelists.* The people should be taught to glory in doing a good job for the Lord's servants. They should know and

practice the idea "inasmuch as ye have done it unto one of the least of these. . .*ye have done it unto me."* The question, "How would we treat Jesus?" should be emphasized. The church should be challenged to do more than the average congregation because it is unto the Lord.

8. *The pastor should train the church membership in Bible truth concerning giving to and supporting God's work and servants.* Passages like Luke 6:38, Matthew 6:33 and Philippians 4:19 should be memorized and understood.

9. *The pastor should enjoy the blessing of "second-mile" courtesies and share the blessing with his people.* The pastor ought to buy fruit baskets or something similar and take to the evangelist. He should be conscious about the little needs that may arise while the evangelist is his guest. Care should be taken to provide the best. Every possible courtesy and kindness should be shown.

10. *The pastor should avoid buffoonery during the offering time.* Some think that the offering period is the time for all the jokes, antics, humor, etc. It is not! It is a time of prayer. It is a time of worship. It is a time of gratitude. It is a time of love. It is a time of investment. It is a time of faith.

11. *The pastor should employ a definite plan of receiving the offering.* "He who fails to plan, plans to fail." The following plan is borrowed from the late Dr. Bill Rice. It works.

(1) The key word is *Invitation.*

    a. Prepare ushers.

    b. Prepare envelopes.

    c. Prepare what you are going to say.

(2) Steps to receive it:

    a. Tell the congregation to receive a love offering envelope and wait for prayer.

    b. Have the ushers to pass them out quickly.

    c. Call attention to the envelope.

    d. Read the envelope and use it for your text.

    e. Stress the *need* of the recipient and the *responsibility* of the giver.

f. Pray briefly and pointedly.

g. Receive the offering.

h. Announce the next opportunity to give.

i. Next time repeat exactly.

12. *The pastor should rejoice with the people when a good job is done.* The service after the meeting he should relate to the people the amount of the offering and thank them for it. They should praise God together for being able to help further the work of one of God's servants.

13. *The pastor should lead the people in giving.* If the pastor is selfish, the people will be. If he is gracious and liberal, it will be contagious.

14. *The pastor should trust God for the needs to be met.* He should make it a matter of earnest prayer. He should plead the promise and believe God for the victory. . . . It will come!

—Pastor Milton Ker

Brother Ker has covered the subject well. But a few added thoughts may help from others, also. This is an important matter. I am alarmed about how many good men with great gifts go into the evangelistic field and then have to give it up in a few months or a year or so because they simply do not receive large enough compensations to keep them on the road and take care of their families at home!

Evangelist Darrell Dunn has reminded us that if an evangelist holds thirty meetings in a year (about average) that this means he has twenty-two weeks a year with no income which is the equivalent of someone taking a five-month vacation every year without pay! No pastor or very few people could afford to do this, but an evangelist has to!

It is important for the pastor, himself, to take the offering. Sometimes a well-meaning pastor may use a layman or a staff member to handle the offering-time just to give him something to do. But an assistant, no matter how talented, will not have the same wisdom, authority and success as a pastor, nor will he usually quite understand the need like a pastor will.

You will get a better offering by using special love-offering envelopes (if used properly) than by merely taking a loose offering in the plate. Since most evangelists are reluctant to bring boxes of offering envelopes along with them (for fear of being misunderstood) it is best for the church to furnish them.

It is poor psychology to tell the people before taking an offering that the offerings are "already good." God may have a man out there who plans to take care of some needs for that evangelist, but who may decide that if the pastor says the money has already come in good, his is not needed, after all.

Make it clear what the offering is for. If the first two nights of the meeting are given over to getting the expenses (travel, motel, advertising, etc.) out of the way, then the people should understand this. Then when the love offering begins it should be crystal clear that all of the money taken from now on is your investment in evangelism and goes to the support of the evangelist and his family, or the revival team—as the case may be.

Some pastors just take the expenses and the love offering all at the same time, but this can be a bit confusing sometimes and will probably result in smaller offerings since people always will give more to an evangelist they love and enjoy than they will simply to the "expenses" of the campaign. When you say "expenses" some people automatically think of the light bill, nursery workers, handbills, the custodian, etc., and they do not think "big."

Expenses are terribly high these days both by air or on the highways, so it is well to tell the people this and let them know approximately what the travel expense will be. Keep in mind that an evangelist does not really get an "offering" until his travel fare is out of the way so you may need more for travel expenses today than you would have raised for a love offering twenty years ago! If the need is made known there may be one man or woman in the congregation who might just decide to write you a check for the travel ticket and get that on out of the way!

IMPORTANT! Take at least three or four nights for the love offering to be received. To wait until the last night or two of the meeting can be disastrous. Heavy rain floods, tornado threats or a blizzard on the last night can just "wipe you out"!

Urge the people at the beginning of the love offering nights to take an envelope, pray over it and ask God what kind of an investment or sacrifice He would have them make. Suggest that they make their check as generous as possible. (Some preachers say "every penny (or every dime) given will go to the evangelist—and some people *do* give pennies and dimes!) When you mention "the *check* you are going to write," it puts it on a generous and businesslike investment basis. Most pastors want their people to give a good offering but do not always use the best psychology in their terminology.

If you take an offering for the evangelist each night it is also good to have one night near the end of the crusade when you stress a large gift and urge the people to make their investment in the life and ministry of the man of God who has been a blessing to them. It is also good to have the offering envelopes available at all services (preferably in the pew racks) so that visitors who come (and may not be back) can have an opportunity to give to the evangelist.

Do not pass out visitors' cards or make announcements while the offering is being taken. People should not be distracted when they are worshiping the Lord with their gifts. Have your announcement time separate from the time you are instructing the people about the offering. People many times do not listen to announcements and instructions very well.

Evangelists tell some sad stories of how they have been treated about the offering in some places. "Let's get this evangelist a little gas money to get him home," may be exaggerated but I do not doubt that it has actually been said. It is embarrassing to an evangelist and his family to have a pastor make it sound like charity: "We've got to help this evangelist out now, so let's take a collection for him," has often been said.

"Borrow a dollar from an usher," is another jewel used by pastors to try to be lighthearted at offering time. At least one man brought in an evangelist who was well-known in the city and then made a big appeal to the people who were personal friends of the evangelist to give to support him. Not much was said to the pastor's *own* members about giving. It was plain that the pastor hoped his own people would thus be "spared," but the responsibility for the support of that evangelist *did not* rest upon friends from other churches!

Some make a big joke out of the offering hoping to make the extractions less painful. All of this cheapens the Gospel and is embarrassing to the man of God. Once the love offerings are being taken the people should not be confused with other projects. Some have been given a sad picture of the church's plight at that time, others have reminded the people that the school or the building fund needs money at the very time they are attempting to take the offering for the evangelist (or for missionaries).

In one church on love-offering night a sad story was told of a little old lady in need and the church was asked to give to help the lady. Now the evangelist may have received a blessing by sharing his love offering that night with the little old lady he didn't know, but the wise and fair thing in such a case would have been to have taken a bit from the missions fund or the church treasury for the charity case and not have confused the woman's needs with the love offering for the support of the evangelist the church had invited there for the week.

It will never hurt but will only bless your people to teach them to give generously. Truly, "it is more blessed to give than to receive."

You watch it, the church that is generous and gives good offerings to evangelists and missionaries will always be the church that God prospers. The income for the church will be good and the church will be growing and making headway. "Give, and it shall be given unto you," the Saviour said. When I was a pastor we always had all of our own church needs met during the week and after the week we had given love offerings to others. It just works that way.

If the church is constantly "bleeding" the people for special offerings for buses, school projects, new buildings, new pews, etc., it would be well to at least let up a little bit a few weeks before special meetings are held. In this way the people will be able to give a worthy offering that will not leave the church feeling a bit embarrassed because they did not do what they should have done. Pastors need not feel they cannot afford a full-time evangelist. It just takes a bit of planning and preparing along with good common sense and the education of the members in generous giving.

If you say, "There are envelopes in the pews," it will be well to have a staff member, secretary or usher check it out each day to be sure that the envelopes have not all been used or mutilated the night before. Sometimes people are advised to "take an envelope" when there is not one to be found in sight at all! (Read again Chapter Six on "How to Get Bigger Offerings.")

Pastor, it is good to let the evangelist know what you are planning to do about his expense needs and his love offering. He does not want to be thinking about money or wondering if his plane ticket will be paid while he is preaching in your church. But he *is* human and he may have some payments or bills that are staggering at the moment. Why not relieve his mind and let him know that the treasurer has a check for him for his travel fare and that his meals and other things are going to be cared for while he is your guest? It is easy to trust the Lord to supply through His people if the people are going to be given ample opportunity to give.

Should an offering be taken *every night* during a crusade? Well, it doesn't hurt anything and it does give people a chance to give who may not be able to get back to the meetings later. If someone gets sick or is called out of town he (or she) may miss the blessing of giving altogether if the offerings are only taken at the end of the week. Sometimes, too, a family may drive a distance from another city to hear the evangelist and would be delighted to put in a good offering for him. If the offering plate is not passed the family, the evangelist and the church will all be the losers.

Be sure you use plenty of ushers in taking the offering. Read the chapters on giving and on ushering for suggestions for improving this.

WHAT IF A MEETING IS CANCELED just a few weeks before it was scheduled to begin? Then surely the church should feel some responsibility to the evangelist in such a case. Dr. Bob

Gray suggests that a check for his travel expense should be sent to him by the canceling church immediately (since he will spend money trying to rearrange his schedule and may even lose a whole week because of it). Then additional monies may well be sent depending on how close to the actual date the cancelation occurred. If a church has to cancel a year ahead of time or even six or eight months ahead the evangelist probably can reschedule. But if the meeting is canceled just a few weeks ahead of time it often means that an evangelist will sit idle that week even though he could have been holding a good campaign somewhere else had the canceling church not had him tied up. In one such case when a meeting was canceled shortly ahead of the scheduled date I flew my wife home from the North, pulled into a campground in my motor home during freezing weather and shivered it out for a week, and then went on to my next meeting. I lost the love offering that week, the cost of an airline ticket and the cost of food and a campground because of the cancellation. The pastor was simply "sorry" that something had come up. I stood on Romans 8:28, but it *is* something for the church and pastor to consider!

Let me say that most pastors have been just "great" to me. Most have been fair and kind and generous. They are some of the most wonderful fellows I've ever known. I have no complaints. But I think there are both pastors and evangelists who will be helped by this chapter and, if so, I will be very grateful. Some small churches have surprised us in their generosity. Some larger churches are overextended and are really in a bind. The thing for an evangelist to do is look to the Lord and remember that *He* is the One who has called us and He will sustain us! Philippians 4:19 still works.

Chapter Nineteen

The "Bull" in the Bulletin
(and Other Office Tid-bits)

What do they really find in your weekly bulletin? Is it worthwhile? Does it really do anything for your people? How could it be improved?

Most church bulletins are a disaster. Is it any wonder that a great number of them remain in the songbook racks and others are found made into paper airplanes on the church parking lot?

First, the bulletin should be well-printed on good paper. It is best to have it done professionally unless you have good printing facilities at your church. The visitors and prospective members who look at your bulletin may decide on your church by what they see here. If you do print it on your mimeograph machine then make sure it is a good machine and is in topnotch condition so you can turn out neat and easily-read bulletins.

Some bulletins say almost nothing and others are so full of chitchat and quotes from "the four winds and the seven seas" that it doesn't really help to sell the people on your church or inspire them to want to come back to the Sunday night service or the mid-week prayer meeting.

Most bulletins list the order of service in elaborate fashion (more or less) for the morning service. Then in small print at the bottom of the page (or on the next one with the calendar of activities) there will be a brief reminder that "the Sunday night service will be at 7:00 o'clock."

But the Sunday *morning* crowd is already *there* when they get that bulletin. The *big* thing is to get them back that night! A brief order of service for Sunday a.m. may be fine (though not entirely necessary in our evangelistic churches) but I would put on the rousement for Sunday night! Perhaps a border around the BIG PRINT announcements about our exciting Sunday night service with many exclamation points after the capitalized topic of the pastor's Sunday night message. Emphasize the good special music for Sunday night ("Surprise" by the choir, quartet or by the ladies' sextet, etc.). *Name* your groups—the quartet might be called "The Harmoniers" or the ladies' quintet "The Sunlight Singers." One young girls' group we called "The Melodettes." People like this sort of thing and it builds interest.

Then if you are having special treatment of an interesting subject in your evening training hour you can stress that in your bulletin. Next a brief run-down on the important things that will happen that week. If you're having a revival or some other big event several weeks away it is good to mention it off and on through the bulletin and weekly mail-out well in advance of the starting date.

If you are having an important series in the mid-week services then I'd be sure and stress that. Give your visitors something they'll want to take home so they'll have access to it during the week. If you are on radio or television be sure and give the time of such programs along with the channel or call letters of the station.

If you can do all of that and still order bulletins that have a beautiful picture on the front they will less likely be thrown away. But you have to watch out for some bulletin companies. See many samples ahead of time. Some of them may be slipping in some propaganda (or some pictures) you'd not care about your members seeing.

The Weekly Mail-Out

We called ours *The Central Challenger* when I was pastor of Central Baptist Church, and *Echoes From the Cove* when I pastored Cove Baptist. You can think of a good title for yours.

I always used the first three paragraphs as a personal pitch from the pastor, capitalizing the first two or three words in each paragraph. If we were having special services then, of course, that was the first paragraph emphasis. Otherwise, I made the first paragraph a bit of bait for my message the next Sunday morning or evening. Thinking up good titles ahead of time helps to build interest. Make it sound as exciting and interesting as possible.

The first three paragraphs at the head of the paper will be the things first seen. Usually I used these three paragraphs to say what I most wanted them to read. Then I would divide the rest of the page and put the attendance, offering report, etc., in the first column along with other causes for rejoicing. In the second column we had other pertinent announcements. On page two was the prayer list (sick folk, hospitalized, etc.), youth column, word about our school, etc. A catch phrase or quote here and there helps to keep the people reading, too.

Update your addressograph plates often enough that the name of the recipient is clear. If the name and address are sharp people are more apt to feel that the message inside the paper may be sharp, too. People like the savor of their own name. Don't let it be dull, shabby or misspelled.

Mail your news letter (or paper) in time for it to be sure and get there. The mail service is becoming more and more of a problem. Don't antagonize your postal clerks. Be fair and try to do your mail-outs to suit them. If you have a friend in the post office get his assistance. Try to find out for sure when the mail will go out to your members. I don't know how many times pastors have told me that their weekly paper announcing the meetings did not arrive in the homes until several days after the campaign started! Mail early. Plan ahead.

Pastor, let this mail-out be *personal*—from *you!* People will feel that it is important if you have special and personal messages to your people in the paper. Keep it fresh and vital. If people get the idea that it is just something the secretary or some assistant drummed up to fill space, that it is canned material and endless chatter from here and there instead of real "news," most people will just "junk it" when it arrives.

Be sure that you stress what is happening now and what is about to take place in your church. Keep the people on the edges of their seats with anticipation about what is coming next in your church.

If you make announcements in your mail-out and others in your bulletin you'll not have to spend so much time with announcements from your pulpit. I think it is good to stress important things in your bulletin and call attention to them from the pulpit but some pastors lull their people to sleep by reading the bulletin to them or spending too much time repeating announcements.

Urge the people to cultivate the habit of keeping the bulletin with them in the front of their Bible and putting it up in a conspicuous place so they'll have the information during the week. (This might save some of those calls to the pastorium asking the time of some meeting that has already been listed in the mail-out *and* in the bulletin!)

I am looking at a mail-out paper from the Grace Baptist Church of Kankakee, Illinois, that was received just before I arrived there for a revival. It is called *Grace Notes*—good for the Grace Baptist Church. The big headline at the top reads: KANKAKEE TO WELCOME DR. HUGH PYLE AND CSEHY MUSICAL MESSENGERS NOVEMBER 10-15. Then my picture was on the front along with the musical team. The time and the pertinent information about the revival was front-page news. Also on the front page was a column which was headed "NEW ATTENDANCE RECORD SET." The whole front page would have inspired and encouraged the readers. Inside there was a brief message from the pastor, a list of the missionaries, pictures from the Christian school, notes about weddings, deaths, etc., in the church family, and then the back page was exciting information for the youth of the church. No one would have thrown away that mail-out without reading it first. Even then I believe they would have kept it around for awhile. Pastor John Marvin was wise in so arranging it.

If you make your paper or mail-out sharp and attractive you can also send it around the town to many prospects and to the unsaved as well as to your own members. Many pastors do this and it is a good evangelistic arm and is helpful in getting crowds for special meetings. If you send it to the unsaved, though, you may be limited in the things you would say to your own people since there will be some "family" matters you would not want to publicize generally.

Find churches where things are really happening and crowds attend and you will probably find a sharp bulletin and some effective mail-out ideas. Look around and ask questions. You can learn good promotional ideas even from churches whose doctrines and methods you would disagree with.

Erma Bombeck had a column on "When the Church Bulletin Is Like Sominex" and suggests some jolting ideas similar to the racy tabloids which most of us could not use in our papers but at least the idea was good. Beef it up and spice it up and you'll have more readers.

I arrived at a good church one week-end for a Family Life Conference and when I looked at the Sunday bulletin there was not one single word in it about the conference that was beginning that day. Other things were mentioned for future Sundays, and various youth activities, but people would certainly not have been led to believe that the present conference was important. The pastor evidently had not made connections with his office staff in preparation for that meeting! Organize, plan, think ahead. Be careful about schedule overlapping. Quite often I find that churches have announced that certain activities will take place during the week of the meetings. Then the pastor has to take time to explain that, since we are engaged in special meetings, those activities will be postponed. It would be better to have educated the people well ahead of time to realize that all else was to be sidetracked for the revival or conference.

On your church letterhead it will be helpful to those with whom you correspond if you put full address and telephone area code. Some churches do not. Read copy on all material that is going out from your office. It is easier to correct errors ahead of time than to try to explain them later!

Keep your office workers happily busy. Be sure they have full worksheets and instructions on their duties. Don't let good workers "beat the air," not knowing exactly what they're supposed to be doing. Have a regular coffee break (or rest period) for them and they may not "goof off" as much otherwise. Be sure files are kept fresh and up to date. Good books on management will help you here.

Have your offices well lighted and ventilated. Don't keep the thermostat too warm for efficiency. Make sure the secretaries have comfortable chairs. Try not to have windows that open out onto too much activity. Keep distractions to a minimum. Good office equipment will pay for itself. Don't skimp on proper repairs and upkeep. Give your workers the proper tools to work with.

There are exceptions, of course, but generally it is best not to try to hire people from your own membership. If you do, keep it on a businesslike basis and have a thorough understanding from the very beginning that they are working for the pastor (and for the Lord) and that personalities, peeves and prejudices cannot be considered when doing our best work for God.

Chapter Twenty

The Books I Would
Not Part With

"Bring. . .the *books*," Paul insisted (II Tim. 4:13). The preacher who would succeed had better be a lover and a reader of good books.

"What *books* have helped you most?" has been an oft-asked question. Well, here are the books I'd hate to part with, along with some other good suggested reading matter.

When I first surrendered my life to the Lord I'm glad that someone put a *Scofield Reference Bible* in my hand and suggested that I buy a Fishers-of-Men New Testament. These were my greatest treasures.

I took THE SWORD OF THE LORD as soon as I saw the first copy with a steaming sermon on Hell in it by Evangelist Jesse Hendley. The sermons and counsel of Dr. John R. Rice helped to steer my course in those difficult early days of Christian service. I purchased *The Soul-Winner's Fire* by Dr. Rice as well as his incomparable book, *Prayer—Asking and Receiving*. Next it was *Blood, Bread and Fire* by Vance Havner and some of the expository books of Dr. H. A. Ironside. I still have all of these books and perhaps every copy of THE SWORD OF THE LORD from 1941 on to this present day!

I still use the old *Scofield Reference Bible* (how many of them have I worn out!) but as far as I can learn, the Fishers-of-Men New Testament is no longer printed. I have also used the *Thompson Chain Bible* as well as others. I sometimes read through other Bibles so I won't limit myself to just the spot on the page that a verse appears in the Scofield. I have never used any other than the King James Version of the Bible except as a commentary or reference. The Scofield is a KJV. I preach only from the King James.

Long before I ever thought I'd be a preacher I began to memorize the verses on the plan of salvation in my New Testament and then I learned a whole raft of verses that would answer the excuses people would give me for not becoming a Christian. The Word of God you will never go wrong on.

In those early days I also accumulated every booklet of messages available by the late Dr. M. R. DeHaan. I devoured them greedily. These along with the weekly issues of THE SWORD OF THE LORD gave me my first ideas for sermons. You will still profit greatly by getting every book Dr. DeHaan ever wrote. Order them from The Radio Bible Class, Box 22, Grand Rapids, Michigan 49555. They are worth their weight in gold. You will possibly not always agree with *every* thing that Dr. DeHaan said, nor always with *everything* you read in THE SWORD nor in the Scofield notes, but you will find great enrichment from these materials. Every preacher ought to have them. Order THE SWORD at Box 1099, Murfreesboro, Tennessee 37133.

For illustrations I would take *The Prairie Overcomer,* Prairie Bible Institute, Three Hills, Alberta, Canada. Though not as evangelistic as THE SWORD this monthly magazine will be worth much in illustrations, outlines and sermonic ideas.

Get the booklets of Dr. McCall Barbour on the deeper life.

Deeper Experiences of Famous Christians by James Gilchrist Lawson is a book every preacher should have.

Pilgrim's Progress should be read again and again.

Crowded to Christ by L. E. Maxwell is a masterpiece.

Young's Analytical Concordance you should have as well as smaller concordances.

Get a good Bible dictionary. Smith's and Peloubet's are good ones.

Always have a good dictionary of words and phrases in the English language at your fingertips. *Roget's Thesaurus* and a good rhyming dictionary also will be indispensable. Some dictionaries of quotations, too, will be helpful.

Ten Sermons on the Second Coming by I. M. Haldeman is a classic in prophetic literature. Get it at any cost.

Spurgeon's Lectures to His Students was one of the first books I bought and devoured after surrendering my life to be a preacher. It is great! I still enjoy reading it.

A Quest for Souls is a great book of heart-warming sermons by Dr. George W. Truett. Read also *The Passion for Souls* by Jowett. Both of these will help you keep the burden for the lost.

Notes on the Pentateuch by CHM you should have for Old Testament studies. These come, I believe, in 5 or 6 volumes.

Billy Sunday—the Man and His Message is another good one that meant a lot to me, and still does.

Newell on Romans is outstanding. He also has a good exposition of the book of Revelation.

Proximities of Calvary was one of the first books I read by Dr. R. G. Lee. It meant much to me and I have perhaps all of his other books. Just don't try to preach them as he did. You'll disintegrate!

Thomas DeWitt Talmage has a set of twenty volumes of messages. It may have been reprinted in ten volumes. Get them! He was a master preacher. I have about a dozen other books by Talmage besides the twenty volumes.

Things I Have Learned by Dr. Bob Jones, Sr., is a book you ought to have. Also the compilation of sermons by Dr. Jones in the book, *"Do Right!"* published by Bob Jones University Press.

Life by the Son and other earlier books by Dr. Donald Grey Barnhouse were a blessing to my ministry. These may now be out of print.

Halley's Bible Handbook, Hyles Church Manual and *Nave's Topical Bible* you will find helpful.

Gleanings in Genesis by A. W. Pink is excellent on the types of Christ and most of Pink's works on books of the Bible are very good. Be careful of his extreme views on the sovereignty of God, however.

The devotional books of F. B. Meyer are among my favorites. You'll find many good thoughts and outlines for messages to

Christians and for prayer-meeting lessons here.

Memoirs of McCheyne is wonderful. Read it for soul-searching inspiration.

Dispensational Truth by Clarence Larkin will help you better understand your Bible. *Jesus Is Coming* by WEB you should surely have. *Some Golden Daybreak* by Dr. Lee Roberson is a good book of messages on the second coming.

A Spiritual Clinic by J. Oswald Sanders has been a favorite of mine. Also his *Spiritual Leadership* you should have.

The Kneeling Christian by An Unknown Christian is a classic. Bounds on prayer you should have also. I profited much, too, by *The Revival We Need* and *The Man God Uses* by Oswald J. Smith.

Matthew Henry's Commentaries will be of real help in sermon preparation especially for their devotional value.

Hudson Taylor's Spiritual Secret is great, along with the biographical books on such men as Judson, Livingstone and Carey.

Saint's Rest by Baxter you should have, along with Finney's *Lectures on Revival* and his autobiography. Moody is always refreshing and inspiring.

Simple Talks on the Tabernacle by Dolman I found very helpful.

Vance Havner's books will provide a spiritual tonic and encouragement.

Great Chapters of the Bible by G. Campbell Morgan I think is one of his best. I also liked *The Miracles and the Parables* by Morgan.

God's Plan With Men by T. T. Martin is excellent if you can find it.

The Bible of the Expositor and the Illuminator, a set by W. B. Riley, will be of great help.

The Harmony of Science and Scripture and other books of apologetics by Harry Rimmer I greatly enjoyed.

Always a favorite is the *Treasury of R. A. Torrey*. And for sermon ideas you'll want *Handfuls on Purpose*. *Fully Furnished* by F. E. Marsh is a gold mine! The books of Herbert Lockyer are good for getting material together for sermons.

Old timers who wrote good sermons were W. L. Watkinson, Louis Albert Banks, J. Stuart Holden and A. C. Dixon. Any of their books you'll be glad you bought.

The New Topical Text Book is great for outlining sermons.

C. E. Macartney is great on character sermons. He makes the men and women in the Bible come alive.

I enjoyed the works of W. L. Pettingill, Ironside and Sam Jones.

Spurgeon's sermons are immortal and you should read some often. You can get good ideas from sermons from Spurgeon but don't be disappointed with yourself if you can't preach them as he did!

Dr. John R. Rice has not only good books of exposition and timely booklets on problems but also some strong revival sermons in print.

If you can get some of the older books of Keswick and Moody Founder's Day messages you'll find some good material.

I've only scratched the surface but the above constitutes some of my book favorites—books I found most helpful. Some pastor friends responded to my request by listing some books that have helped them most. They include:

Spurgeon's *Treasury of the Bible.*
Ironside's commentaries.
Things to Come by Pentecost.
Walvoord on Daniel and Revelation.
Warren Wiersbe's commentaries on various books.
G. Campbell Morgan on the Parables of Jesus.
Walvoord on the Holy Spirit.
Ryle's Expository Thoughts on the Gospels.
Systematic Theology by L. S. Chafer.
He That Is Spiritual by Chafer.
Life Is Tremendous by Charles Jones.
Preaching Without Notes by Charles W. Koller.
Proverbs by Ironside.
Spiritual Depression by Tim LaHaye.
Keys to the Word by A. T. Pierson.

Balancing the Christian Life by C. C. Ryrie.
The Epistle to the Romans by James Stiffler.
Bible Expositions, I and II, by I. M. Haldeman.

Every preacher should read some self-help and motivational books. One of the very best is *See You at the Top* by Zig Ziglar. Get it!

An All-Round Ministry by C. H. Spurgeon will help preachers. Other books for pastors and preachers include: *Ideas for a Successful Pastorate* by Huss, *Pastoral Problems* by W. B. Riley, *The Pastor, His Life and Work* by Charles Wagner, *The Preacher and His Preaching* by W. B. Riley, and *Big Ideas for a Better Sunday School* by Clarence Sexton (assistant to Dr. Lee Roberson).

Dr. Robert L. Sumner's books will also be very helpful. He is an outstanding writer.

Liberalism, a Rope of Sand by Don Boys (published by the Sword of the Lord) gives information preachers should have.

Get *The Preacher and His Preaching* by Alfred P. Gibbs for additional help.

My brother, Howard Pyle, a fervent preacher in Georgia, suggests earnestly that every young preacher read carefully *Blue Denim and Lace* and *Strength and Beauty* by Dr. Jack Hyles. I concur.

Every pastor and evangelist needs often to look into the fires of Hell to keep his burden for souls and to remember what we seek to save men from. Booklets like *Hell, What the Bible Says About It* by Dr. John R. Rice; *The Gates of Hades* by M. R. DeHaan; and *The Truth About Hell, Sheol and Hades* by Pettingill are excellent. The most powerful book on Hell that I have is by William Elbert Munsey and is called *Eternal Retribution* (published by the Sword of the Lord). Get it, whatever the cost.

Christ Incomparable by J. Oswald Sanders was a book that blessed my heart. It is excellent preaching material, too.

Fresh-Minted Gold by Hy Pickering, and other Bible study outlines by this author will be used and enjoyed.

Confident Pastoral Leadership is one of the newer books for preachers by Howard Sugden and Warren Wiersbe, and has helpful material and counsel.

Dress for Success by John Molloy is a book a pastor might want to have on hand. It may need to be updated from time to time, and I do not think preachers should be vain about their clothing but we *should* look sharp and dress properly and this book has some good suggestions for buying clothing.

Managing Your Time by Engstrom and Mackenzie, and *Manual on Management for Christian Workers* by George Ford you will find helpful.

Literature Evangelism, a manual by George Verwer, I think was once a Moody Colportage book and at last report was available from Walterick Publishers, Box 2216, Kansas City, Kansas 66110. It has a unique plan for evangelizing a city or town with literature distribution. Pastors have used this successfully, especially in areas that are greatly unchurched or that are Roman Catholic.

How to Increase Your Sunday School Attendance by J. Vernon Jacobs is good.

Get the *Church Usher's Manual* by B. F. Sylvester (Zondervan) for further help in training ushers.

Other helpful material in smaller booklet form would include *What a Supervisor Should Know About How to Delegate Effectively* by Raymond Dreyfack, from the Dartnell Corporation, if you can find it; *Winning Souls and Getting Them Down the Aisle* by Dr. Curtis Hutson (Sword); *Let's Go Soul Winning* by Dr. Jack Hyles; and a leaflet, *Why the Christian School,* by Row Lowrie, from Christian Schools Today, Newton Square, Pennsylvania. Any soul-winning material by Tom Malone would be fine.

From Dr. Dino Pedrone, The Open Door Church, 600 Miller Street, Chambersburg, Pennsylvania 17201, you may order his paperback *Conference Manual* on church growth and building "Pennsylvania's Largest Sunday School."

So many pastors hop around and have a hard time getting situated. I believe the book, *The Restless Pastor,* by G. W. Gillaspie (Moody Press), might help the man who feels he ought to keep moving—on to another charge, or is wondering if he ought to leave or not.

Keep in mind that I do not recommend all of the books mentioned for their doctrinal content, but many of them for their practical value. Most of them have helped me and I think they can help others. I *know* most of them will!

Where can you get these books? I wish I could tell you in every case. So many of them I have found in secondhand bookstores, way back on dusty shelves in the back of out-of-the-way places. Some are now out of print, I am sure. Keep looking in the used book places, the book warehouses, even Salvation Army family stores. Keep your eye open for book sales. Some can be obtained from book sheets from the discount book places. Your reputable book dealer in a good (noncharismatic) bookstore may help you secure good books. But be careful in buying books. So many preachers waste money buying worthless books. So many of the bookstores that are called "Christian" today are anything but that; many of them are operated by charismatics or New Evangelicals, and they will not have many of the best books that men of God could use. Sadly, many book publishers that were fundamental and true to the faith twenty years ago have now sold out to popularity and are in the business to make money. Some of their books will be good—others will be shallow and almost worthless for a real man of God. So be careful!

Read a good news magazine like *U.S. News and World Report.* It is the more conservative of the big three, though on some special events you may also want to refer to *Newsweek* or *Time.* *Reader's Digest* will also help keep you abreast of things. If you try to read too many magazines or wade through all of the papers and materials that come to you from religious sources you'll waste precious hours and your study of the Bible may suffer, too.

For good music and good books about music write to Dr. Frank Garlock, P. O. Box 6524, Greenville, South Carolina 29606.

It is said that the trail-blazing preachers, like Wesley, "rose every morning at four and preached most mornings at five. They commonly divided each day into three parts—eight hours for sleeping and eating, eight for study and meditation, and eight for preaching, visitation and social labours" (Bready). Wesley urged upon all his preachers the necessity of spending at least five hours in twenty-four in reading the most useful books! Make friends of your books.

Chapter Twenty-One
In the Thick of the Battle
(A Potpourri on Church Building, Finance, Weddings, Funerals, Youth Programs, Standards, Etc.)

Others far more adept have written volumes on these matters so rather than devote an entire chapter to each I will let others help me speak and then add a few personal and practical suggestions.

Many pastors get in over their heads when starting a church building program. Others encounter difficulty and end up in a split while the church building is under construction. Still others, to their chagrin, find that they have not built adequately or that they have hurried into the matter without thinking through what they were really going to need in a building.

How many are lamenting that they did not provide ample space for parking, or that the rest rooms are in the wrong place, or that they should have hired an expert for their sound system instead of letting Brother Sound-off do it "for the discount." Far too many church vestibules are too small and inadequate.

CHURCH BUILDINGS

Pray, think and plan with your good men about the proposed building. Decide about what you want and then start out to look at many church buildings. Don't jump at the first idea for an auditorium that you see. Get a good nucleus of earnest men for a building committee. Take some of them with you to inspect and observe a number of church buildings that appeal to you.

Order books of church plans and study them carefully. Sound out many sources of financing. Raise as much money as you can before you start. Try to get your whole congregation involved. Preach enthusiastic sermons on the great "building" themes of Scripture. Get good advice from successful pastors who have built strong, evangelistic churches. Some of them, too, can put you in touch with good builders and good architects. You may even be able to use the plans of another church under some circumstances. But be sure you get what you need for your own situation.

If you think you might some day start a school then it would be good to build your educational plant with that in mind. Rooms have to be so big and hallways and rest rooms must be adequate for a certain number of pupils. You may save yourself money and headaches later. Here are some practical things to remember:

Have enough space between pews. Many evangelistic preachers have lamented the fact that their pews are too close together. People are jammed in so that it is very difficult for a person to get out of the row during the invitation. If a stout person happens to be on the end of the row it may be an impossibility! Don't sacrifice your soul-winning success at the invitation just to get one more row of pews in the building.

Leave room at the front. You need room to deal with people and for folks to come by and welcome the new converts. Allow space for a prayer altar for Christians as well as sinners.

Have your platform high enough or be sure you have a slope to the front in your auditorium floor so that people can see the preacher. In many churches it is almost impossible for some worshipers to look at the man of God as he preaches. Many platforms are too low.

Make your vestibule large. People need a gathering place for fellowship. Ushers need room to navigate. We don't want the kids to talk in church but we rarely give them room to before and after if they stay in the building. There is rarely room for a book table in the good churches who invite authors and other Bible teachers whose books would be a real blessing to our people. A large, well-lighted lobby or vestibule will go far in creating a good taste in the mouths of visitors when they come to your church. The Open Door Church at Chambersburg, Pennsylvania and the

Dayton (Ohio) Baptist Temple are churches with large, ample vestibules. The Northside Baptist Church at Charlotte, North Carolina, is a good example of a rounded vestibule that follows the shape of the circular auditorium.

Plan on ample parking. In many cities now it is demanded by law and it is always good to have off-street parking, preferably with entrances that are not in a stream of heavy traffic. Try not to have your entrances and exits on hills and curves. Think of the safety of your parishioners.

Plan your sound system before the last minute and don't skimp on it. It often takes time to get the equipment and to get it functioning properly.

Place some rest rooms off the lobby so that if people *do* have to go out they'll not have to traipse through the auditorium and past the preacher to get back to some isolated rest room. Of course you will also want some additional rest rooms in your educational buildings, one on each floor. Think carefully, also, of where your water fountains should be placed. At least one should be off or in the lobby, probably near the rest-room doors.

Plan for enough speakers so that sound is evenly distributed, and enough air-conditioning and heating vents so that some will not bake while others freeze.

Be sure you have some outside faucets and electrical outlets. Most churches do not have them or do not have enough of them. You'll need them for lawn work and power equipment on your grounds and parking lots. Also a great number of evangelists and missionaries are traveling now in trailer homes or motor homes and will need outside hookups. While installing plumbing also put at least one outside sewer hole (sanitary dump station) for your traveling guests to use. Wise pastors now are making a parking pad for motor homes and trailers with full hookups at hand. Be sure your outside electrical outlets are on a separate circuit and can carry at least 20 to 25 amps.

Place thermostats out of reach of children—in fact, it would be good to put them out of the reach of most of the parishioners. Have your sound controls easily accessible, especially to those on the platform. Plan your lighting well—far too many churches are gloomy and/or the pulpit area is not bright and cheerful.

An overhanging shelter over a prominent doorway will make you more popular with parishioners on rainy days. Have enough exits to your parking area so that people can get on out and away when the weather is bad.

Place your telephones so they do not ring near enough to the auditorium to disturb the messages. A blinker light or soft "buzz" can alert the ushers without ringing so that people become distracted or edgy. Many people automatically wonder if that "emergency call" might be for them if they hear a phone ringing.

Think carefully about color schemes. Soft, subdued colors are best. Blue or pale green are restful and cheerful colors. Gold is not bad for a carpet but may show dirt more than the darker colors. It is believed that a red carpet is "exciting" and may cause tempers to rise readily—especially in business meetings! Look at many colors for walls and carpets before deciding.

FINANCING THE BUILDING

I have asked Dr. Gary Coleman, successful pastor of the Lavon Drive Baptist Church, Garland, Texas, to write us a brief on finances and since much of what he has to say is relative to financing a building program, here it is, with appreciation:

Here are some quick thoughts in regard to church finances:

1. Integrity

One of the keys to a successful ministry is building a testimony of handling finances in an upright manner. The people and the community should be convinced that we are honest and dependable when it comes to handling the monies that come through our church. The integrity of the church is in a sense the integrity of the pastor. This means that the pastor and the church must meet financial obligations. Integrity would also mean not using our position to be pushy in getting a discount or bargain deals. Business people resent such a wrong attitude and prefer to work with a church as they would any other business.

2. Accountability

Accountability involves having full disclosure of income and expenditures. I think it is advisable to have a regular deacons' meeting where a financial report can be discussed by a pastor to his deacons. Then, a report could be given to the people at a regular monthly business meeting of the church. Disclosure eliminates questions and controversy. A pastor's ministry can be severely handicapped by refusing to be open about the church's finances. Problems can also arise when funds are not used for the purpose for which they were given. For example, in regard to a bond program, if bonds are issued to build a building, then bonds must be used for that purpose, etc. One person should approve all purchases. Purchase orders should be used. The handling and depositing of the money should be done under a certain procedure. A good bookkeeping system should be used.

3. Planning

A realistic budget should be prepared, presented to the people, and approved annually. The approval of the budget gives the pastor the authority to spend the funds that are allocated in the budget. This helps the pastor in that he does not have to come back to the people for the approval of every expenditure. A control factor can be put on the spending of budgeted funds.

An annual stewardship emphasis will help the people to grow in the grace of giving and will raise the money to meet the budget. The stewardship emphasis allows the pastor to discuss finances, the church needs, and the matter of giving in a context that is not offensive. Information on how to conduct a successful stewardship program can be secured from a sister church or some other organization that publishes such materials.

Expansion and building programs should be entered into with great caution. A thorough study should be made in regard to the need for the building, the cost of the building, and the church's ability to take care of the additional obligation. While taking into consideration anticipated growth, no building program should be entered into on just the basis of projected growth, particularly, if paying for the building is based on the income from projected growth. The following things need to be considered in regard to the building project:

1. Do not enter into cost-plus contracts. All work must be done on a contract basis. The exception would be if there is volunteer work done by your own men.

2. Plan the building well where there will have to be very few changes in the building. Changes after the building project has started causes the cost to rise considerably.

3. Be careful not to be intimidated by businessmen in your church who feel they should have the business just because they are a church member. They should submit competitive bids just like the other contractors.

4. Principle of Giving

Without a doubt, one of the main factors in making the church successful financially is the ability of the pastor to understand and practice the principles of giving. Generosity breeds generosity. The pastor's willingness to give liberally and generously to the Lord's work and to others will have an impact on the whole church to help them to be involved in giving to the Lord. The pastor needs to demonstrate his giving without being boastful or having a "poor-man" complex that would hinder his influence upon his people. The pastor needs to lead the church in not only tithing and regular offerings, but in giving to other ministries and people. The principle of giving and receiving is related to the principle of sowing and reaping. A giving attitude can be developed in a church by bringing before the people needs of others and a willingness to take up offerings to meet those needs.

—Gary Coleman.

SUCCESSFUL STEWARDSHIP IN THE CHURCH

Dr. E. J. Brinson, pastor of the Bethel Baptist Church and President of Bethel Baptist School of Arlington, Texas has a church with over 2,500 members, has added 40 new missionaries to those supported by the church in the past three years (bringing the total to 85), employs seven full-time male staff members as well as five secretaries, and the church budget has grown from an average of $3,400 per week a short time ago to over $12,000 per week in 1979. The annual mission budget is over $100,000. I have asked Dr. Brinson, who speaks frequently on evangelism, stewardship and Sunday school work across America, to write us his philosophy of stewardship. Here it is, along with some other vital suggestions for pastors.

THINGS YOU SHOULD KNOW ABOUT STEWARDSHIP

Introduction:

1. *STEWARDSHIP DEFINED:* "An organized effort to teach biblical concepts of Stewardship accompanied by an invitation and opportunity to obedience."

2. *STEWARDSHIP'S GOAL:* "For God to control all that the Christian is and has in order to provide him with complete freedom from the world's system of life and finances."

3. *STEWARDSHIP'S BASIC PRINCIPLE:* "God owns everything including the believer. God wants His children to be custodians of all His possessions for His glory."

EVERY CHRISTIAN SHOULD KNOW:

I. *STEWARDSHIP IS BIBLICAL*

1. *Stewardship is* a declaration of God's ownership of all things—Ps. 24:1; Haggai 2:8; Exod. 19:5; I Chron. 29:14; Deut. 32:6; Ps. 50:10-12.

2. *Stewardship is* the believer's responsibility to manage, supervise, and administer all things for God's glory—Luke 19:13; Matt. 25:14; Gal. 6:5; Prov. 9:12.

3. *Stewardship is* an accounting system to which every Christian must one day be audited—Luke 16:2; Rom. 14:12; Matt. 18:23; 21:33-41; 25:19.

II. *STEWARDSHIP MUST BE TAUGHT*

1. *Teaching*—we must *declare* the whole counsel of God.

2. *Testimony*—we must *demonstrate* the practice of God's principles.

3. *Testing*—we must *depend* on God to provide and bless.

III. *STEWARDSHIP IS GOD'S ONLY PLAN OF PROVISION OF RESOURCES FOR HIS WORK*

1. God has *committed* Himself and all He has to us—Rom. 8:32; I Cor. 16:1,2.

2. God has *commissioned* the church to world evangelization—Matt. 28:19,20.

3. God has *challenged* us to claim His resources through the principles of faith giving—Phil. 4:19; Luke 6:38; II Cor. 9:6-13.

CONCLUSION:

1. *If God* gave His Son for the sins of all men. . .and He did;

2. *If God* gave the message of that Redemption to His church. . . and He did;

3. *If God* desires that the Gospel be preached to all nations. . . and He does;

4. *If God* has provided a plan to finance His work. . .and He has;

5. *Why then* do we not have all we need in order to get the job done? The simple answer is we have failed to understand, teach and implement God's biblical plan of finances into His work.

SOME SUGGESTIONS FOR PASTORS

1. Plan to attend *at any cost*, one of the Stewardship Seminars sponsored by Stewardship Promotion Associates, Dallas, Texas. Information may be obtained by contacting Dr. John Williams, 3106 Palmdale Cr., Dallas, Texas 75234.

2. Read Dr. Truman Dollar's book, *How to Carry Out God's Stewardship Program*, Thomas Nelson, Inc., Nashville, Tennessee. An extensive bibliography of many excellent books on Stewardship is contained in Dr. Dollar's book.

3. Acquire one of the fully developed Stewardship Programs from Stewardship Promotions Association, 3106 Palmdale Cr., Dallas, Texas 75234.

"Stewardship Is Lordship"—Published 1976
"Growing Thru Giving"—Published 1977
"The Grace of Giving"—Published 1978
"Learning to Give—Discipline"—Published 1979

We have used each of these programs, as have hundreds of other churches, in establishing strong stewardship programs.

—E. J. Brinson

Now read again chapter six in this book on "How to Get Bigger Offerings."

ON NAMING YOUR CHURCH

Names can help to make or break a church. Think of the churches you know that are big and flourishing and then study their names. The First Baptist Church is a good name if you happen to start a church in a town or village that does not already have a Baptist church. Central Baptist is a good name if you are centrally located. Calvary Baptist has become well-known enough, and since prominent churches in many cities have this name it is a good one to use. Because of the prominence of several churches in Ohio and other Northern states that have used the word "Temple" (such as Akron Baptist Temple, Canton or Dayton Temple, Landmark Temple of Cincinatti and the Massillon Baptist Temple) this may be a good name for pastors to consider if they're starting a work in those areas, that is in towns or villages near these cities. After the Jim Jones catastrophe, of course, it would be suicide to name it "The People's Temple"!

Northside Baptist Church of Charlotte is *on* the north side and therefore is properly named, especially since it is located on the interstate and can be readily seen by thousands on the north side of Charlotte, North Carolina.

Highland Park Baptist Church of Chattanooga designates a well-known area of that city and a large population center, so it is a good name.

The Baptist Tabernacle may be a good name, in some states, for an evangelistic ministry. Grace Baptist Church (like Calvary) seems to be a name in good repute. That is strange since the *grace* of God is so despised by the world.

Thomas Road Baptist Church in Lynchburg, Virginia, is a church that has a "localized" name and also is not situated on a main thoroughfare, so there are exceptions to every rule, but a nationwide television ministry plus a dynamic soul-winning crusade has beaten a well-worn path to the door of this big church.

Names like Forrest Hills Baptist, Rochester Hills, Sylvania Heights, South Sheridan, Temple Heights—these are good names if they identify a growing church in a large, well-known area and if the name helps visitors to find the church.

The Open Door Church of Chambersburg seems to have picked a good name for a growing, evangelistic church in that Pennsylvania city. Bible Baptist may be a good name (and should be) but remember that most churches in the Baptist Bible Fellowship call themselves by that name so you may sometimes be identified with a group to which you may not belong.

The New Testament Baptist Church is a name to be considered. Trinity Baptist and Emmanuel Baptist seem to be names that have weathered the storms and stood the test of time.

Keep in mind that if you give your church a name from some town or church in the Bible that most people are not familiar with you will make it necessary for people to constantly inquire about the meaning of such a name. Before you pick a name stop and think if you have known other churches with that name that have flourished and grown. Don't limit the outreach of your church by giving it too much of a localized name, or by giving it a name that sounds "peculiar."

To sum up, I would choose a name which identifies your city or area and has a good "ring" to it. I would stick to a name that has a "citywide" quality to it and will make people feel that this is *"the"* church for such a day as this. And I would pick a name that is easy to spell and easy to pronounce. Truly, "a good name is rather to be chosen that great riches."

DON'T BE A MARRYING SAM

Weddings are a "must" since we believe that people should get married and establish homes and families. But weddings can take up an awful lot of a pastor's time. Like many other preachers, I've lost two full evenings many a time because of a wedding. There are some of your people who will insist, of course, that the pastor, and he alone, can perform the ceremony.

How can you keep weddings from consuming too much of your study and soul-winning time? For one thing, don't marry just anybody who comes along. Some pastors make it a practice never to marry anyone who has been divorced, under any circumstance. If this is your conviction then, of course, you can eliminate an awful lot of weddings pronto. Also if there are doubts in your mind about whether a couple is telling you the truth about their marital status or their salvation experience you can just say that you only perform ceremonies for couples who are both saved and have no living mates.

There are some pastors, I am told, who never perform a wedding except for their own members, and this would narrow the field down, considerably.

In some cases you may be able to turn a wedding over to an assistant or associate pastor, if you want to, and they are willing.

Another way to save time on weddings is to talk thoroughly with the young couple when they come to you for counseling about it. In addition to talking to them about spiritual and home matters let them know what you want and expect at the wedding. Tell them if the rehearsal is scheduled to begin at 7:00 p.m. that you expect the wedding party to be there at that time since you have other duties and obligations. It is unfair for a family to expect a pastor to sit around for an hour or more waiting for some tardy participant to finally put in an appearance. Insist that they know for sure what time the organist, the singer and other members of the party can be at the church. If they cannot all be there at 7:00 then it will be best to move the rehearsal up to 8:00. Don't let them run over you. It is your church.

Still another way to save time—I used to wait for the bride to make up her mind about just what should happen first and who should come out first, and usually a bride can waste a good hour trying to decide just how she wants the procession to flow. I soon learned that brides didn't do this very often and that I could best decide it *for* her, in many cases. You don't have to perform very many weddings before you learn how they are pulled off, and you could conduct one in your sleep. So, where possible, I would lead the faltering bride to see "just how easy it is to do it in this fashion," and usually they are glad to have the suggestions of the pastor.

Many brides spend money on some "director" (usually from a florist shop) to come in and "direct" her wedding. Here, again, you frequently run into a lot of wasted time. I soon learned to suggest to the bride that she could save both money and time by letting me direct her wedding. And then I would keep it as simple and uncomplicated as possible.

If the bride wants songs or musical productions that are not proper for a spiritual church I would just tell her that we use only hymns or traditional wedding music in our church. If you have other convictions as to dress, candles, arrangements, and such matters just be sure the bride understands this before you get into finalizing of the plans. If you suspect that something may be amiss or embarrassing I would surely spell it out for her long before time for a rehearsal.

Be sure that the bride understands that a fee should be given to the custodian who opens and closes the building for her rehearsal and wedding. Also if she does not have someone to clean up after her wedding this should be taken into consideration, too. An additional fee may be necessary for the sound technician if one has to be there to handle the P.A. system or any recordings of the wedding. Most brides realize that they should have a gift for the organist and/or singers but some of them are totally unaware of this so it does not hurt to remind them of these things. Have a check list handy to go over with the bride when she comes to you to plan her wedding.

Usually you can take a wedding form from a pastor's manual and then "doctor" it up to suit yourself. Don't hesitate to pray and read Scripture and bring whatever spiritual remarks you deem appropriate and important. Do not hesitate to make it a *Christian* wedding. If they don't want that kind of wedding they can always get it done somewhere else. At the same time you should not be too informal and certainly never be light or flippant about the wedding. Make it sacred and sweet with the proper amount of dignity and finesse.

If they invite you to the rehearsal dinner (which they should), and if they do not include your wife, then I would just *ask* them if the invitation includes her. Many times the bride is nervous and forgets such matters.

I understand that some busy pastors of large churches have an assistant to "stand in" for them at the rehearsal, thus making it possible for the pastor to have one more night free. If you do this you would have to always use the same "format" or there would be awkwardness and perhaps mistakes at the wedding. You'd have to have a trusted and true (and smart) assistant to do this. And you'd have to share some of the honorarium with him!

You can calm the nervousness of both bride and groom if you have a brief prayer with them in their respective "waiting" rooms before the ceremony begins. Assuring them that all is well and everyone is on hand will settle their anxieties. And if you use notes (even though you have the ceremony memorized) it may keep you from making a mistake and leaving something out by accident.

After the ceremony you should announce the reception if the bride and groom want everyone present at the wedding to attend the reception. While pictures are being taken will be a good time for you to get witnesses and to sign the certificate and the license. Then don't forget to give the certificate to the bride and/or groom before they depart that night. And of course don't forget to mail in the license so it will all be legal. And speaking of legal, you should check with your courthouse before performing your first wedding in a new area to be sure that proper and legal steps are taken in such a ceremony, for this is both a spiritual and civil transaction.

One thing more, unless you know both bride and groom to be dedicated and spiritual Christians it will be wise to remind them that no booze of any kind is to be served at the reception. Relatives of some of these couples may surprise you by "spiking the punch" otherwise.

DEATHS AND FUNERALS

When someone dies who belongs to your congregation you should go at once to the home (or the hospital, as the case may be) and have prayer with them. Be gentle and extremely considerate at this time. You do not have to talk a lot or wax eloquent. Sympathetic silence is often appreciated, but they do expect their preacher to pray with them. Usually a few choice verses from the Word will be in order, also. If people are milling around the room or the house, as often they are, you should just take charge (briefly) and suggest that you'd like to have prayer with them. You probably will also have to return to the home again as funeral plans are being made, or to confirm these plans.

If people want the funeral at a time when it would be impossible for you to be available then do not hesitate to say so, gently, of course. Also if they want to have it in some unusual place or if they make strange requests about it, you can usually steer them into the proper decision if you handle the matter carefully and kindly, yet with authority. People are upset at a time like this and generally will welcome suggestions from a poised and spiritual man of God.

You can usually save time by having the funeral in the funeral home chapel instead of in your church. One thing more, some people feel sad when they come to church after attending a funeral of their loved one there. This is another good reason for having it in the funeral home chapel. However, if they insist on having it in the church then I would proceed as requested and make the service as inspiring and cheerful as possible.

Make friends with your funeral directors. They will generally be cooperative and helpful if you are easy to get along with. You can be sure they will appreciate you (even if they are not saved) if you conduct yourself properly and if you are not long-winded.

The funeral is not the time for long discourses or for a lengthy musical presentation. Usually I would steer the family into having one or at the most two vocal numbers if they wanted singing. If they want some outlandish song you can usually get around it by saying that your singers do not know (or use) that number but that they can pick something just as good that would be very comforting.

Normally, in such cases, I would move into my place behind the pulpit at the time set for the funeral and begin with an opening prayer. Then after the first song some appropriate Scripture can be read, and then the other song. Following that I brought my message, usually 10 to 12 minutes long—never more than 15 minutes. People afterward would tell me how much the messages meant to them and often would comment on the fact that so much was said in such a short time. Some of my brief and effective messages have been published by the Sword of the Lord in my book, *Beyond the Sunset.* This book would not only give you some good funeral sermon ideas but it would be (and has been) extremely helpful placed in the hands of the sorrowing after a funeral is over. The book also is used as a comfort and help to people who have lost loved ones in other places or who may just want to "bone-up" on Heaven and the life beyond. The messages are cheerful and scriptural and have brought peace to many troubled hearts.

Should you give an invitation at the funeral? Where there were a number of unsaved people present and where there was definite conviction I have sometimes done so, but usually just asking them to raise their hands if they would then and there trust Christ, and then, after leading them in a brief prayer (while all heads were bowed) ask how many had prayed that prayer of surrender. Many have done so. On other occasions I have waited until after the funeral and have won some souls personally at the cemetery. Still at other times I found it best to wait until the family had returned home from the cemetery and have been able to win some of them at the house. The Holy Spirit will lead you about it if you are careful and sensitive to His leading.

What if other ministers are involved? If you are asked to assist another man then you have to adjust and just pray or read Scripture as you are asked to do. But I have read or prayed the plan of salvation to a family many a time in such cases. Often a liberal or a lazy preacher who has been asked to conduct the service is glad for you to bring the main message since most of them don't have anything much to say, anyway. But be considerate and be fair, of course. And be brief. The funeral is no time to try to expose the errors of the liberal preacher. But you can preach the truth with such clarity and power that the contrast will be obvious.

Suppose the funeral is in your town but the actual burial in some distant city? Well, there may be some times when you'll have to make the trip or when you feel you should go. But usually it is possible to carefully steer the family into letting you have the main funeral service before they leave town and then let the local pastor (usually a friend of the family there) handle the brief graveside service at the other end of the line. In such cases it is best for you to drop back by their home after the family returns from the distant town, usually the next day.

Make notes on the names of lost relatives and neighbors and other prospects who may hear you at the funeral and may be impressed with the gospel message. Hearts are tendered at a time like this and often the seed is sown for later reaping. And don't forget the bereaved family in the weeks that follow.

Should you take an honorarium for holding a funeral? This is a question often asked. Certainly you should charge *no fee* for your service. But usually the family has been so blest by your help and thoughtfulness that they really do want to do something to show their appreciation. If they offer you an envelope (or a check) I would accept it with thanks and say that you were certainly glad to be of some help. You can assure them in your note of thanks for the gift that while they did not "owe" you anything that the check is most appreciated and that you will accept it as unto the

Lord and use it for His glory. If you have to make a trip to a distant city and they want to pay your travel cost then I'd surely let them do so. It is only right that they should.

Times of sorrow help to endear your church to the people if you are considerate and consistent. Your secretary or some dependable person should be absolutely sure that flowers are sent to the family if someone dies who is a member of your flock. Also if your ladies will help out with dishes of food and other thoughtful gestures at that time they will probably always be grateful.

I would discourage long vigils at the funeral home. Don't feel that you have to stay with the family by the hour. You have your other responsibilities and most families want to be with their own loved ones at that time, anyway.

Don't give a flowery eulogy. A lot of those people knew the deceased better than you did. The safest thing to do is stay with the Scripture and the simple plan of salvation. And if you are burying an unsaved man try not to torture the bereaved by reminding them that he is in Hell, but at the same time don't lie and pretend (or assume) that he is in Heaven. Your message is for the living.

Learn how to pronounce any names ahead of time that you will have to read or refer to at the service. Be ahead of time for the funeral. Save some wasted time by having a small booklet to read (or else read your Bible) while waiting for the funeral to start. No use to sit there staring into space. I have outlined a good message in the back of my Bible at such times instead of "killing" time.

Generally it is best not to make too many references to the family (or the deceased) at this time. Lift up Jesus!

THE YOUTH PROGRAM OF THE CHURCH

There are some good ones—Awana, Brigade, Word of Life and Pro-Teens are all to be considered. If you have a real sharp youth director he may be able to take the better facets of these programs and make up his own.

Make friends with your young people. Be considerate of them. Make a practice of remembering their names and their hobbies and accomplishments. Applaud them when they do something good.

Don't make a practice of railing on them or low-rating them. Sometimes you may *have* to call them down from the pulpit but you will probably accomplish more if you can win their confidence and talk to them as a youth group or even individually.

Go on some of their youth activities with them. How much you do this may depend upon your age and your physical condition. Teens can wear you down! But be a friend to them and let them know that you are genuinely interested in them.

Make sure your youth pastor or youth director is not building up his own little "church" for the young people and alienating you from them. Keep in touch with him (and with them) enough that you know what he is doing and he knows what you expect. Make sure he keeps the standards high.

Be frank and honest with the young people. I'm sure the long hair on boys did not need to ever get started in our fundamental churches. But so many pastors were afraid they would offend the young people and appear too straight-laced if they took a firm stand about it. Love the young people, pray much for them and then be perfectly honest with them and you can get them to do (and be) almost anything they ought to do and be.

I have just come from a church where they have a great host of consecrated young people. The pastor's own son is a spiritual boy, a senior in high school. The pastor's daughter, about 14, is a fine and faithful girl. The preacher *does* preach hard against sin. He does not compromise. About thirty teens sit closer than half way down in the church auditorium. They listen to the messages. There seems to be little or no cutting up or horse play in the services. Some of these teens help with personal work at the altar with younger folk who come forward. Others are busy in other things like the bus ministry, music, etc. What a church! And the boys look like boys. The girls are modest and proper.

On the other hand I've been in churches where the young people hug the back rows of the church (and some of them hug *on* the back rows!). They grin, they whisper, they write notes, they misbehave. What makes the difference? I believe that what Dr.

Roberson has said holds true here, too: "Everything rises or falls on leadership!" It is up to the preacher to train his parents and his young people. It takes time. It involves blood, sweat and tears. But it is worth it!

Be patient with young people. They are facing battles. Keep your sense of humor with them. But don't try to be a clown or a comic. Command their respect by setting a good example as a man of God. They expect you to be a spiritual giant. Don't disappoint them.

See that your own children sit near enough to the front that it is a good guideline for the others. Level with your own kids. Let them know that you desperately need their help. Let them see how important their testimony is to Christ and to the work God has called their daddy to do. Let them share in the triumphs of your ministry and they'll help in the hard places, too. See that your own boy looks like a man and that your own daughter dresses modestly and is feminine. It will go a long way toward growing a good crop of young people in the church.

Give attention to the young people's department. Take note of them when they are involved in a project. Reward them for victories won.

Don't try to just "entertain" them all the time. Far better to get them involved in visitation and soul winning. Then when you do have parties and funtimes they will appreciate them all the more.

Have plenty of the right kind of books available for them. Show the good Christian films. Bring in other youth groups that are spiritual and sound. Encourage the right kind of athletic program as long as you keep it from eating into the church activities or controling too much of their time—or yours!

Have a good youth revival now and then. Take them to Christian colleges and let them see that thousands of other youth are going on for God. Take them to retreats and to Christian camps. If they are poor get adults interested in "sponsoring" a child. Let some of them get into a (well-supervised) program for raising their own money for such things. Bring in Nicky Chavers and his Academy of Arts sometime for a production that the young people themselves can participate in. (Write Dr. Chavers at Academy of Arts, 134 Bradley Blvd., Greenville, South Carolina 29609.)

To keep them out of bad music have Dr. Frank Garlock come for a seminar on music. Teach them the right way and you won't have to spend as much time knocking the bad way. Train them to cultivate a taste for good music.

See that your music director uses young people wherever possible. Let them help with your radio program or telecast if you have that kind of talent.

If you can get some of them serving on a bus route they may well be a bus captain or a driver themselves in the years to come.

See my book, *The Good Ship Courtship*, for ideas for young people and for suggestions about what they can do together or on dates.

Don't be afraid of standards. They'll respect you more than they will if you have no standards.

Have a few outstanding "big days" for young people during the year. Especially at the time when worldlings are having their annual prom you ought to have a tremendous big time for your own high schoolers. If the meals at local restaurants are nothing to brag about try having your ladies fix their favorite gourmet dishes for this affair and have a smorgasbord they'll talk about all year!

When children are smaller let the parents entertain their own kids. I know you will have to have a few things each year even for the smaller ones since many come on the buses and have no parents who care about them, but for the most part I'd save the fancy and important big times for kids after they get into their teens. Even then keep the activities simple in the young teens and gradually make it better and fancier and longer. So many children today are doing things that only teens did a few years back that by the time they get into their teens they want to do "adult" things! Train your parents in the church to understand this.

Start a Scripture memorizing plan for your young people and stay with it. The Bible Memory Association has a good one. So does Rev. J. O. Grooms at Thomas Road Baptist Church, Box 1111, Lynchburg, Virginia 24505.

"LIFT UP A STANDARD FOR THE PEOPLE"
(Isa. 62:10)

Your regulations for deacons, staff members, etc., you can incorporate in your church bylaws. Then you can have a list of standards for your teachers, workers, ushers, committee members and others who are chosen by the church to serve.

When I was a pastor our standards for Sunday school teachers, training workers, youth workers, superintendents were well known. We had copies of these standards typed out. Every prospective worker was given a copy. This covered such things as salvation experience, proper baptism, doctrinal beliefs and putting Christ first in one's life. In addition to this our standards stated:

* God's Word insists on separation from worldly practices. This would cover such matters as theater-going, dancing, card playing, etc. (I John 2:15-17; Rom. 12:1,2; II Cor. 6:14-17.)

* Second Corinthians 7:1 and I Corinthians 6:19 demand that a Christian's body be considered the temple of the Holy Spirit. Strong drink and tobacco should in no wise be used.

* Such a worker should be faithful to all services, Sunday morning, Sunday night, Wednesday nights, revivals, etc.

* The Christian should believe in and practice tithing.

* The Bible demands modest apparel (I Tim. 2:9). For this reason we do not believe Christians should appear in public immodestly clad—such as shorts or other scant or suggestive attire. We believe women should dress like women and men like men.

* A Christian should not participate in gossip, slander or critical speech.

* He or she should be concerned about souls and should engage in the church visitation program—and should inspire others to do so.

* All teachers and workers are expected to attend the weekly teachers' and officers' meetings. They should also enter into the promotional efforts of the church with enthusiasm.

These are some of the main things that we wrote into our Bible Standards. You can enlarge on these and add others. We gave a copy to every one who became a prospect for an office or who accepted a job in the church. When your leaders have high standards then the other members of the church will soon learn proper Biblical standards, too.

Be true to your own conscience and to God and the Bible. Be kind, but be firm!

THE WIFE OF A PREACHER

Young men are concerned (and should be) about getting the right kind of a wife if they are going to be preachers. This should be a matter for much prayer!

Go to a Christian college where convictions are like yours. You are more apt to find a consecrated girl who is interested in Christian service there than most any other place on earth.

At such schools as Tennessee Temple University, Pensacola Christian College, Massillon Baptist College, Maranatha Baptist Bible College, Hyles-Anderson College, Bob Jones University, and such like, you will find hundreds (if not thousands) of young people who believe as you do. Most of the pastors I have been with have found their wives on the campuses of such schools.

Look for a wife who is concerned about souls and who has high ideals. You may even find a girl who really longs to be a preacher's wife.

Lean upon the Lord and wait patiently for Him. Don't get in too big a hurry. He will lead you to the right one at the right time. Don't let the flesh dictate. Walk in the Spirit.

When you think you have fallen for a girl who may be the one for you be sure you go together long enough to find out all you need to know about the girl, her parents and background, her aims, dreams and ambitions. This is the most important step you'll ever take after you become a Christian. Many a pastor has been ruined because he married wrong.

Pray for her and pray with her, too. Make sure you are compatible and that you both desire the will of God more than anything else on earth.

What should you expect of your wife in the church? Some demand too much. Let her first be a wife and mother. If she has a talent then she should be used in the church but you'll save yourself heartache if you do not try to project her too much into the forefront of things. If she is "in charge" of the music or the ladies' activities or something like this, you'll be more likely to find jealousy and resentment building among the other women and trouble may be brewing before you know it. Some women are a great asset to a pastor by being a teacher, a singer, a children's worker. Perhaps in some cases this is as God intended it.

But a pastor's wife can be a great help to a pastor by just being a devoted mother, a loving wife, a faithful Christian, and a lovely example of a modest, unselfish and consecrated lady.

Don't demand the impossible. Do not insist upon her doing things that she is not fitted for or that would make her a nervous wreck to attempt. If she goes to visitation faithfully (and she should), if she teaches a class, if she fills her place in the pew, if she welcomes people and helps the pastor keep up with names, and remembers important matters for him, if she goes to the weddings and the funerals, if she answers the phone for him, and helps him raise godly children, if she is a devoted and affectionate wife, if she is a good cook and homemaker, you may be sure she will have her hands full—and *then* some!

Read again chapter fourteen about the pastor's home and personal life. Make your wife queen in the home. Be considerate of her, be courteous, be thoughtful, show appreciation. Never play her down. Encourage her. Her lot will not be an easy one. Be her friend and lover as well as her husband. She's going to need you!

Help her to see the importance of knowing what your children are doing at all times. The behavior of your kids will greatly determine the success of your pastorate. Don't let your children be brats. Train them with all the prayer, time and effort you can muster. They need the attention of both a mother and a father.

Be careful what you discuss with your wife in front of your children. Don't let your wife (or you, either!) get too thick with people in the church. You can't have close friends among the people without arousing the jealousy or ill feeling of others. This is one of the heartaches of the pastorate—you have to be friendly to all and close friends of none. There will be some people you and your wife will like (even love) more than others but don't let it *show* if you can help it. Love the Saviour first and foremost and the friendship of others will be all the sweeter even if you cannot always show it as you would like to.

MAINTAIN A SPIRITUAL, SOUL-WINNING PROGRAM

In a Southern Baptist state paper the following paragraph appeared about a prominent church in the convention:

The Baptist _____ (bulletin) from the First Baptist Church of _____ says, "Nearly every phase of our work is progressing splendidly. The auxiliaries show marked improvement in attendance. Two scout troops are doing better work. Music groups are progressing nicely. Art, dramatic and hobby groups are being organized. Our church is more and more fulfilling its mission for Christ in the community and around the world"!

There was not one word about soul winning, preaching or Bible study. Not any indication that the prayer meeting was important or even attended. Yet the church felt it was "fulfilling its mission." The leaders of that church need to read again the Great Commission.

Of John Wesley it was said, "He left a good library, a well-worn clergyman's gown, a much-abused reputation, and the Methodist Church." The advice Wesley gave to preachers: "Your business is to save as many souls as you can!"

Again it was Wesley of whom it was said, "He was out of breath, pursuing souls."

Vance Havner writes, "To know Christ, and to make Him known—anything less is useless, anything more is superfluous."

Chapter Twenty-Two

Questions and Answers
(The Preacher and His Perplexities)

"Being told things for our own good seldom does us any" *(Reader's Digest).* But preachers do face difficult decisions and the answer can be found either in the Bible, in common sense or in the experience of another. So here goes with some of the questions preachers often ask and some practical, common-sense answers.

The pastor could well learn, with David, that God "in whom I trust" is the one "who subdueth my people under me" (Ps. 144:2). When *we* try to "subdue them" ourselves, we run into trouble. My help is in the Lord. We preachers are spiritual advisers and instruments of God but, "we have not dominion over your faith" (II Cor. 1:24), "but are helpers of your joy."

The following questions are not particularly in any order or sequence nor am I mentioning them according to their importance, but they are some that have been asked me by young preachers (and others) or they are some I have heard of others having problems with.

(1) ABOUT MOVING AND
CHANGING PULPITS:

(1) Q: HOW LONG SHOULD I STAY IN A CHURCH, HOW DO YOU KNOW WHEN TO MOVE, AND HOW MUCH NOTICE SHOULD BE GIVEN?

A: One of the most important articles to be printed in recent months was by Dr. Truman Dollar on "Musical Pulpits." He deplores the fact that so many preachers today are simply using one pastorate as a waiting station and a stepping stone to a bigger and "better" field. (The message was in *The Baptist Tribune* for August 10, 1979, and if you can get it it will be invaluable.)

"Son, find a city, put down your roots, and stay a lifetime," Dr. Dollar quotes this as standard advice given young men in the early years of the Baptist Bible Fellowship. Then he names the large, flourishing churches that have really made history and reminds us that their pastors have stayed there from twenty to forty-seven years, respectively. He refers to the "staying mentality" of successful preachers. The author lists a number of important reasons why it is good for a pastor to "stay put" and build a work through the years. This was an exceptional quote: "Strong pastoral leadership is often destroyed because of rotating pastors. . . .Leadership must be established before structural problems can be resolved. Credibility with a congregation does not come overnight. It is a long process of working, praying and suffering together." Other reasons Dr. Dollar lists for staying in one pastorate is: "personal growth of the pastor, learning that people are basically the same everywhere, making your congregation a part of your family, taking the long look in solving problems, and viewing the ministry as God does."

Sometimes, of course, God *will* lead you to make a move; especially may this be true in the early days of your ministry. But I would go to the church expecting to make it a life's work unless the Lord definitely leads otherwise. Just the fact that you have difficulties or problems does not mean that the Lord is leading you to change pastorates. What is your own attitude in resigning? Are you going off in a huff because your ideas were not accepted? Do you grab the first invitation that comes along, letting your wife pack while you "pray about it"? Are you considering leaving because of an "ornery deacon"? You can be sure there will be more of the same over at the next place.

Of course, in some situations, you do come to the point where you have done about all you can do. If the outward evidence is that you should move, and the inward conviction is the same, and then a real challenge to a much greater and more opportune ministry comes along, you should probably consider it. In most cases, though, you would have to stay in one place from three to five years to be sure you had given it your best.

If you are itching to move on, then it is not fair to lead the people into a building program or some other expensive project that you are not willing to stay and face with them.

And, when you know you are going to move you should give them at least thirty days' notice, a little less or a little more if they request it. Usually they are not going to make a move until you are gone, and your heart is not going to be in the work there once you have made up your mind you are going.

(2) Q: BEFORE ACCEPTING A CHURCH WHAT SHOULD I LOOK FOR OR INQUIRE ABOUT TO DETERMINE IF THIS CHURCH IS FOR ME?

A: Well, I hope they check *you* out more thoroughly than most churches do before calling a pastor. But, by the same token, you should check *them* out. Find out why the former pastor left. Determine what kind of preaching they like and/or will tolerate. Discover what kind of music they like and whether or not they are willing to change if you think they should. Find out if they are willing for you to be the pastor or do they just want a "yes" man. Will they let you bring in evangelists and other speakers as you feel led or do you have to check with the deacons or the church to see if it is OK?

Will they be willing to expand and branch out in the work? For instance, if you are enthusiastic about a bus ministry find out if they will follow you in starting one. If you feel you should build a camp, will they help you do it if the Lord leads in that direction? If they are on the radio once a week and you feel it is a field where you should be on every day, you probably should sound them out about it.

If they desperately need buildings, will they follow you in a building program if you plan to stay there and see the matter through? If your wife is an accomplished organist what kind of problem will this make about the lady who is now the organist? Is the choir in that church the "war" department?

Do members of the church like and promote the charismatic movement? Will they put up with your exposing error and warning them about false doctrine?

Is the church independent or is it tied in to some denomination or conference? Do they support their own missionaries? What do they think about the Christian school movement? Will they follow you in a soul-winning and visitation program?

How do they elect their officers, deacons, etc.? How strong are they about the King James Bible being used exclusively? Will some of the key workers be promoting other "versions"? Would they be expecting you to cooperate with the local ministerial association or with civic affairs?

What about the role of the women in the church? Are they willing for a preacher to preach hard to their young people about modesty, clean living, separation, etc.?

Do they like the same schools you do and how will they feel about your promoting your choice of colleges for the youth?

Are they willing to have high standards for their workers in the church? Will they allow you to hire and fire your own staff workers?

These are just a few of the things you'd better look out for. It is easy to see that if you have strong convictions you may come out better to start your own work "from scratch"!

(3) Q: DO NOT MANY PREACHERS HAVE TROUBLE IN CHURCHES BECAUSE OF POOR PSYCHOLOGY?

A: Well, common sense is not a required subject in any school I know of. Good psychology is mostly just using common sense. "Horse sense" *really is* largely "stable" thinking! You'll find that many of the answers in this book are just common-sense suggestions. It is true that many preachers use poor psychology.

For instance, a pastor said to a mother whose child was cutting up and giving her a rough time, "That kid needs a good paddling!" Well, it was true, of course, but the mother was offended because he used such poor psychology. He could perhaps better have said, "Children are sweet and we love them, but they sure have to have a lot of patient training and discipline. Could I leave you a good booklet on the subject of child rearing? I believe you'd really enjoy it." And then I'd give her my *Taming of the Toddler* or some such book.

To a long-tongued woman a pastor bristled, and said, "That's not showing me the proper respect!" Again, she was *not* showing him the proper respect, but a woman like that obviously did not *have* any respect for the man of God. His feelings were probably entering into it, somewhat. He could have turned her off with a sweet reply or a kind and gracious word about her that would possibly have completely disarmed her, as he "heaped coals of fire on her head."

One church leader told another to "go take a long walk on a short dock," which was hardly the way to bring the man around to his point of view!

Use your head, study people, pray for them, ask God to give you a love for them and then as you mature spiritually the "good psychology" should come with experience and years. And study the book of Proverbs. It is the *best* psychology!

(4) Q: PEOPLE SAY I AM *TOO ROUGH* ON THEM. YET ALL I AM DOING IS TRYING TO GET THEM TO LIVE SEPARATED LIVES. WHAT SHOULD I DO?

A: We are living in a day when churches have become so worldly and the world has become so "churchy" that preaching on separation is not popular. You might try preaching simple salvation messages in the morning and hitting your own members more at night when the "cream" crowd is there. All members are not going to agree with you about separated living. You have to take time to gradually lead them into a spiritual life. And get them busy winning souls and learning the Bible and the separation preaching will come easier.

You can lambast them every Sunday morning and evening about women who wear "pants" to church. Your good members will abstain whether they agree with you fully or not. But the people you drive away may be the people who most needed to be saved or to learn spiritual truth about things more important than mode of dress. I found that I could teach my own people most anything on Sunday night and Wednesday night. I also let them know that we needed to be patient with people who came to church on Sunday in ungodly or outlandish garb, or boys or men who came with girlish hair. After we got them saved most women looked around and realized that our ladies wore *dresses* to church. And most boys when they became Christians went out and got a haircut. If they didn't they often would drift on to another church, but at least we had a chance to evangelize them first. And in the process our own people were strengthened about their own convictions regarding proper dress and separated living.

In my revival meetings I do not spend a lot of time preaching about long hair on boys and improper clothing on ladies. But they get the message because we stress the "new creature in Christ" truth, and we also use illustrations about the perverts and others with long hair, such as the rock stars, in such a way that people begin to see the difference. Then, as my book, *Skimpy Skirts and Hippie Hair,* begins to circulate among the people you can see the difference. Also as my booklet, *How to Quit Smoking,* gets around we learn of people who are quitting. When they learn that there is wonderful deliverance from such habits for them they are more likely to quit than if you just rail on them for smoking all the time.

In my stories to children I warn them about never getting started on bad habits like that. In the process I am preaching to their parents but they "take it" because they do not want their *kids* to start.

I hate to see women parading around in slacks and other male-looking attire. But I'd rather preach to them in slacks than to have them go to Hell in slacks. One good way for a pastor to help his women to dress properly is to make easily available to them such booklets as *Pants-Suits and Christian Women* by Dr. Horace F. Dean, P. O. Box 676, Havertown, Pennsylvania 19083, and *God Drew the Line* by Dr. S. Franklin Logsdon, printed by Tabernacle Baptist Church, P. O. Box 3100, Lubbock, Texas 79452. I would have a quantity of these in every church vestibule or Sunday school book rack in America. They'd get the message!

Concerning the dance, the theater, rock music and such matters I would use such blood-curdling illustrations in my judgment preaching that to participate in such matters would scare the daylights out of them.

But don't preach on "judgment" and sin *all* of the time! Vary your preaching, as the Bible does, on many and various themes.

And give your people time to learn and grow.

(5) Q: HOW DO YOU BEST STUDY THE BIBLE, HOW DO YOU OUTLINE A CHAPTER, AND HOW DO YOU KEEP FROM RUNNING "DRY" AS A PREACHER?

A: That is a big order! The best way to learn the Bible is to "read the Bible"! Just keep on reading, marking, digging, praying over it, memorizing choice portions and using what you learn. Take good sermon papers like THE SWORD OF THE LORD and read books often by preachers who were experts at outlining and preaching. Vary your study habits. I read some in the Old Testament and some in the New Testament each day. I use a *Scofield Reference Bible.* I keep a concordance and Bible dictionary handy, as well as a good English dictionary. I make notes.

Along the way I observe which chapter portions would lend themselves to alliteration and outline. Sometimes the outline is right there in the text. In other chapters it seems difficult so I do not try to *force* an alliterative outline if it doesn't come easily. There are some good Bible study books which a reliable Bible bookstore can suggest to you. But I've dug most of mine out for myself. See chapter twenty for some good book suggestions.

I learned 1,500 verses of Scripture in two-and-a-half years after I surrendered my life to Christ. This has been a great asset to my preaching. And some of those verses I memorized have fallen right into a fine outline for preaching. Nothing has helped me more than learning the Word.

To keep from "running dry" take in as well as give out. Read much. Meditate in the Word. Take walks alone with God and have fellowship with Him. Pray for God to keep you constantly filled. Announce series of sermons that will keep you on your toes studying for those messages. Then read the great messages of good men along those subjects, keeping notes and gathering illustrations. And keep your own heart hot in personal soul winning!

(6) Q: WHAT ABOUT PEOPLE CALLING ME (THEIR PASTOR) BY MY FIRST NAME?

A: I would not encourage that. And I think it is not best to get on a first-name familiarity with most of your members, either. Of course, you will have some folks who will just be insulted if you do not call them by their first name, and they have the respect they should have for you too, so in some cases you can call them "Joe" or "Bill" without their calling you by your given name. They do not need to call you "Reverend" or "Doctor," of course, but it is good for them to call you "Brother ___" or "Pastor___" as the case may be. They should have respect for your position and your authority. It isn't that you are proud or "high and mighty," but you *are* the man of God and the shepherd of the flock, and they need to have you in proper esteem. Walk with God and they will not consider that you are just "one of the boys." And I do not think it sounds good for young pastors to call older members of their church by their first names unless they just insist upon it.

(7) Q: WHAT ABOUT THESES CRUSADING PREACHERS? SHOULD I JUST NOT "PREACH THE WORD" AND LEAVE WORLD EVENTS AND MORAL IS-SUES ALONE?

A: Well, of course, soul winning and Bible preaching should hold priority. But in reading the Bible it is easy to see that God is concerned about morality. History, both biblical and secular, reveals that nations that live like America lives today have been destroyed. And if things continue to go as they are going now we may not have any freedom left to open our churches and our Christian schools each week. So we *do* HAVE to take a stand for our very survival. Also you'll find that (particularly in the Old Testament) God's prophets and God's appointed kings *did* do something about idolatry, homosexuality, corruption in leadership and the slaughter of the innocents. So for a preacher to hide his head in the sand and say he is not obligated to fight sodomy, abortion, pornography and national drunkenness is, I believe, a cop-out.

Read Don Boy's book, *Liberalism—a Rope of Sand* (published by the Sword of the Lord) and you'll get your blood to boiling. Also from that book you'll get plenty of ammunition for messages on moral issues of the day.

Of course, some preachers go overboard on "crusading" and neglect their own ministry to their people. This is wrong. Ask God to help you keep a proper balance, by all means. But you have to fight sin! Evil forces are determined to destroy our churches and schools today.

The preachers of this country could have prevented the so-called "Gay Rights" movement if we had stood up and exposed this thing in churches all over America. We could have led our ladies to so protest pornography in stores and public places that at least the smut would have been driven back underground. Our professing Christian people in this country could have driven the profanity and much of the vulgarity from the airwaves had preachers led the crusade before excessive sin got such a foothold. Millions of our church members should have stormed our congressmen long ago to demand legislation about abortion, gay rights, pornography and booze in grocery and drug stores all over our once-Christian nation. If we had stirred up our church members about sin like we should have we could have demanded that certain members of the liberal (and sometimes insane?) Supreme Court be impeached. We could have prevented much of the total ruin of our public school systems. But we sit back and let the perverts march and the abortionists butcher babies while our people never hear crusading messages about these things. My book, Let's Start an Avalanche (about such matters), is the most ignored book on our book tables! When the "Avalanche" message appeared in THE SWORD OF THE LORD thousands of preachers could have used it to start a reform and revival movement that would have sent shock-waves throughout the land, but only a few tried it, from all reports.

Thank God, it is not too late. If we hurry, the preachers of this land may yet save the day. Yes, moral issues should concern us and our people should be kept informed!

(8) Q: OUR CHURCH IS INDEPENDENT, FUNDAMEN-TAL, PREMILLENNIAL. IS IT BEST TO ADVERTISE THIS OR JUST LET PEOPLE FIND OUT WHEN THEY ATTEND?

A: It might depend on where you are in the country. In a hotbed of liberal churches it might not be a bad idea. Still, I wonder how many casual readers of church advertising would even know what you meant by such terms. I think I might put "Independent" in my church ad in the yellow pages since some good fundamental people could be looking there for an independent church. On the other hand, in Southern Baptist territory in the deep South I think I'd just put (as we did) the name, CENTRAL BAPTIST CHURCH, on my sign out in front of the church, along with the pastor's name, of course. My contention was that all Baptist churches *should* be fundamental and independent and that it was the *other* crowd that had gone astray while we Bible-believing fundamentalists were the *real* Baptist churches. By just putting the simple name of the church we attracted many Baptist people, some of whom were hungry for Bible preaching. In so doing we were able to lead some convention Baptists (who were sick of liberalism) into a sound, biblical ministry.

(9) Q: SHOULD PREACHERS BE POLITICAL AND "PREACH POLITICS"?

A: Not "preach" politics, of course, but a preacher should certainly pray for his nation and president (both privately and publicly), and he should keep the people abreast of matters that concern morals and freedom. At election time he should lead the people in prayer about such matters, and he should do all he can do (in a nonpolitical way) to help people realize who the conservative and decent candidates are when he knows of such candidates.

(10) Q: SHOULD A PREACHER PREACH ON CERTAIN SINS AND WORLDLINESS OR JUST GENERALIZE, AS SO MANY DO?

A: Yes, indeed, he should lift up his voice like a trumpet and show "my people their transgression" and "their sins" (Isa. 58:1). If you do not specify about the theater, dancing, rock music, perversion, drugs, booze, smoking and such matters the people will never take it very seriously. Hit sin hard but don't ride a hobby. Don't see how obnoxious you can be about it. Use your head. Love the people and let them realize that you preach against sin because you do not want them to be ruined. When they learn that you love them and want the best for them they will take it, and someday (if not now) they will appreciate you for your honesty and courage.

(11) Q: IS IT ALL RIGHT TO USE PERSONAL ILLUSTRATIONS—THINGS THAT HAVE ACTUALLY HAPPENED IN MY LIFE?

A: It is all right and sometimes it is proper to do so. But I would not make a career of it! Too many references to yourself and too many personal anecdotes may give the impression that you think too much of yourself. I would try to leave "I" out of it as much as possible.

(12) Q: AM I OBLIGATED TO VISIT MY PEOPLE ALL THE TIME? IT IS HARD TO TAKE PERSONAL INTEREST IN SO MANY MEMBERS.

A: You ought to visit all of your people at least once, I feel. And you should keep up with your shut-ins, the troubled, the spiritually weak and the backslidden. If you do this and then visit the unsaved you'll have your hands full! Read Jeremiah 23:1,2 and see how God feels about pastors who do not visit the people, thus allowing them to become scattered. You should keep up with your people and know what's happening to the sheep. But you can't do it all by yourself. (See Chapter Eleven on "How to Visit.") And train your deacons and people on how to help you do it. People will love you and appreciate you more if you are concerned for them in their sicknesses. The relatives and friends of these sick people appreciate the pastor who reminds the people to pray for their ailing loved ones and who announces their recovery, etc. But I would not give long sick lists and "organ recitals" of the afflicted from the pulpit.

(13) Q: I GET SO LITTLE DONE ON VISITATION. TIME GETS AWAY AND THERE ARE STILL SO MANY TO VISIT.

A: In a world of lost and troubled people we'll never catch up! But I think probably many pastors stay too long at one place. Be brief, state the purpose of your visit, pray and be gone! There is a temptation to stay too long and get bogged down in casual small talk.

(14) Q: IS IT WISE OR UNWISE TO READ FROM VERSIONS OTHER THAN THE KING JAMES AUTHORIZED VERSION?

A: I think it very wise to stick with the KJV. I remember in my late teens a pastor who read from (and quoted) some other version. I was perplexed and did not fully understand him. He didn't have much power in his preaching. He was soon gone. Stay with the beautiful King James Bible for its reliability and accuracy. Thus you'll encourage newcomers and even the unsaved to bring their Bibles with them to church and junk their *Living Bibles, RSV, Good News for Modern Man,* etc. I have used other "versions" only for private comparisons and personal reference and study.

(15) Q: HOW DID YOU GET SUCH BIG MEN AND FAMOUS PREACHERS TO COME TO THE CHURCHES YOU PASTORED?

A: Well, for one thing I took them when I could *get* them, summer, winter, whenever they were available. Another thing, I would honestly write those men, telling them about my work, how much I had admired them, how big (or small) my church was, and how I felt they could really do something for our people. I would assure them that their plane fare would be covered and that we would do our best for them otherwise. And I assured them that I would advertise widely and do my best to get good crowds. God sent us some of the greatest preachers of this century. There's a right and wrong way to go about such matters.

(16) Q: SHOULD A FUNDAMENTAL PASTOR BELONG TO OUTSIDE CLUBS AND CIVIC ORGANIZATIONS?

A: I really don't see how he has time to do so. I certainly would not belong to any organization that might put you in an embarrassing or compromising position. Avoid the very appearance of evil. And don't get into something that is time-consuming if you hope to succeed in your ministry. We are called to be preachers and spiritual leaders—not "hail-fellows-well-met."

(17) Q: WHY IS IT THAT THE PULPIT COMMITTEE

THAT CALLS YOU SEEMS OFTEN TO BE THE FIRST
ONES TO TURN AGAINST YOU?

A: Perhaps if they do it may be that they are the most discerning and most critical members of the church because often that is what qualified them for the pulpit committee! And they feel personally responsible for your being there, so may feel it is their solemn duty to "police" your ministry. Perhaps they now feel they can do better and would like to try again.

(18) Q: WHY DO THE MIDDLE-AGED AND OLDER FOLK SEEM OFTEN TO RESENT THE YOUNGER AND NEWER MEN WHO WANT TO BECOME ACTIVE IN THE CHURCH.

A: They shouldn't, of course, but sometimes they do. Older folks who worked hard to get the church where it is feel threatened by newer and younger workers. They see their jobs being taken over. Sometimes middle-aged people (both men and women) are going through a change-of-life experience and are unusually nervous and touchy right about then, anyway. If they were as spiritual as they ought to be they should be able to overcome this feeling. But some of them get backslidden in heart and are not praying and reading the Word as they should be. Pray much for them, be patient and try to understand them. And try to keep them busy doing something that they can do even when younger and more aggressive men come along. Try to stay out of situations that would lead to this. Try to avoid family blowups by foreseeing what too many of the same tribe may do to your staff of workers. In your school it is best not to have the wives of board members working as teachers, etc. Don't let one man get in as superintendent and stay forever until he is so old and "settled" that he is difficult to move.

(19) Q: WHAT DO YOU DO ABOUT CONSTANT INTERRUPTIONS?

A: Sometimes they are divine instructions. In most cases you just have to learn to "roll with the punches." But a good secretary and a wise wife can "screen" many of the calls (and callers) and help you avoid some of the worst. And you have to learn to cut some of them short if they do get in to see you and have nothing really important to talk about. (See Chapters 2 and 13.)

(20) Q: I STAY SLUGGISH AND HAVE A HARD TIME GETTING THE ENERGY TO DO ALL THAT I NEED TO DO AS A PASTOR.

A: Get a good (complete) checkup from your doctor at least once a year. Don't overeat. Eat wisely. Get plenty of protein in your diet and eat salads that have a variety of fresh, raw vegetables in them. I'd eat a good salad at least once a day—either vegetables or fruit. Drink plenty of citrus juice. Don't load up too heavily on sweets. And it is believed that too much white bread as well as white sugar is bad for you. You don't have to become a food faddist to use common sense in your diet. You may need vitamins. Don't use coffee or certain stimulating foods as a crutch or as a substitute for a good and proper diet. Avoid fatty and greasy foods.

And get plenty of exercise, at least 4 or 5 days a week—such as walking fast in the fresh air, jogging, riding a bicycle, etc., as well as calisthenics and sitting-up exercises. A good exercise plan will keep you toned up and you'll feel like fighting your Goliaths most of the time. None of this should take too much time except the long walks. Walk briskly and even they can be done in a hurry. Tennis is a good game that need not be too time-consuming and is good exercise. Get enough sleep without overdoing it. "Prosper and be in health" (III John 2).

(21) Q: I FIND MYSELF REPEATING MYSELF AND AM TOLD THAT THEY "HAD HEARD THAT STORY BEFORE." HOW DO YOU AVOID THIS?

A: Keep good records of what you have preached and where. As for illustrations I used to put a little circle in the upper corner of a clipping with the date I used that in a sermon at my church. As an evangelist I keep certain illustrations for certain sermons, as a rule, and then if I know when I preached the sermon at a place I usually know that I probably used that illustration, too.

(22) Q: WHAT DO YOU DO ABOUT A FORMER PASTOR'S COMING AROUND?

A: Well, they should not make a career of it. But if the man was a godly man and well respected, and if he did a good work there, it won't hurt you a bit to speak well of him, welcome him when he returns, call on him for prayer, and even have him preach for you sometime. The people who liked him will like you better for this. When *you* become the "former pastor," however, it will be wise for you to stay out of the way of your successor and do not try to give him either trouble or advice. I would not go back on the field very often. The pastor who is there now should have the affection of his people. You had your turn. If you left because of trouble or difficulty it will probably be best for you not to return to the field at all. And never take weddings or any other appointments or honors that should go to your successor!

(23) Q: WHAT ARE THE THINGS MOST PASTORS NEGLECT, TO THEIR OWN DEFEAT?

A: I do not know, but I imagine prayer would be number one. It is so easy to get so busy that one's own personal prayer life goes begging. Then consistent visitation and soul winning would probably be the next most oft neglected.

(24) Q: WHAT IS THE WORSE TRAIT IN A FUNDAMEN- TAL PASTOR?

A: Laziness, perhaps! Just this week I've heard a godly woman remark about how shocked she was when she moved to an area and realized how lightly the pastors seemed to take their work. So many of them talk constantly about hunting or they are off fishing or golfing several times a week. No wonder their churches do not grow! I sometimes felt like a criminal if I took one day a week for rest.

(25) Q: HOW DOES A PREACHER BUILD SELF- CONFIDENCE?

A: Nothing succeeds like success. Keep working at those sermons and at that visitation until you see some results. Every victory won should spur you on. Then read Zig Ziglar and other motivators. Listen to their tapes. Read Jack Hyles. Read Proverbs. And by all means, read the successful men of the Bible—Paul, John, Moses, David, Samuel, Abraham. It is not as much *self*-confidence as it is *God*-confidence!

(26) Q: HOW DO YOU GO ABOUT ESTABLISHING AND ORGANIZING A CHURCH?

A: Some home mission boards among our fundamental groups probably know of towns that need a church and could give you valuable advice. Or you could possibly run an ad in some Christian papers stating your desire to establish a work. New England and the far West have many, many towns with no fundamental, Bible-preaching work. Get a nucleus of even a few—three or four interested Christians and start visiting. From then on it is hard work and plenty of it! Many a church has started in a home, a basement, a storefront, a school, even a tent. As people see you grow and learn that you mean business and are there to stay they will have confidence in you and some will gravitate to your work. When you start a permanent building others will decide to join with you to do a job for God. Win souls. When you get twenty or twenty-five good people it will be possible to go ahead and get a charter and draw up a constitution and bylaws. You can make up your own, but you might want to look at the charter and bylaws of some other good fundamental church for some ideas as to the construction.

(27) Q: I'VE HEARD THAT PREACHERS ARE THE WORST RISK BEHIND THE WHEEL OF A CAR. IS THIS TRUE?

A: It may be, and sadly so. Preachers ought to have a good reputation for driving sensibly and safely. Some preachers boast of their speeding. This is a poor testimony and it is bad business. Do not imitate the fast driving of Jehu (II Kings 9:20). Insurance men have also told me that preachers are a poor risk, healthwise. Read the answer to Question #20 again. Keep your health and you will be more likely to keep your sanity! What is even worse—some preachers are a poor credit risk. No wonder the world looks on and wonders!

(28) Q: COULD YOU LIST THE SEVEN MOST IMPORTANT KINDS OF PREPARATION FOR YOUNG PREACHERS?

A: My guess would be: 1. HEART preparation—make sure of your own salvation and your fellowship with God. "Blessed are the pure in heart." 2. HEAD preparation—study, read, dig, train—go to a good fundamental, spiritual, soul-winning Christian college or Bible school. 3. SOUL—prayer, meditation, keep up your spiritual life, including Bible study. 4. FOOT—beat the bushes, visit, witness, win souls. 5. MOUTH—preach on street corners, in jails, factories, shops—anywhere you can get in. Preaching success comes from much preaching. 6. HAND—the word consecration means "hands filled," serve the Lord, do the menial task, don't be afraid of hard work. 7. DISPOSITION— develop your personality. Learn to laugh at yourself and with others. Don't be sour. Take the view of faith and optimism. Enter into the work joyfully. Learn to smile when the going is rough. Keep looking up!

(29) Q: WHAT ABOUT DIVORCED PEOPLE IN THE CHURCH. HOW MUCH SHOULD WE USE THEM?

A: I was in a church recently that had a split because some teacher in the flock had decided to teach that no divorced person should even be permitted to be a member! If we are not going to use people who were once divorced then what about people who once stole, or cussed or lied, or looked at a woman lustfully? Shall we turn out all the members who ever smoked or took a drink? We'd soon have an empty church and be out of business.

We allowed people who had been divorced to serve if they were now consecrated and separated Christians. Some sang in the choir perhaps or served in the nursery, for instance. One of our very best school board members had married a divorced woman back before he was saved. Sometimes a fine young Christian was carrying the burden of loneliness because his mate had left him to run off into sin with another. I could not see that it would be scriptural to penalize this innocent Christian further by never letting him serve in the church. We did not, however, ever make a deacon out of a divorced man even if he was the innocent party, because of the testimony, as we wanted to be careful not to put a stumblingblock before others. I realize there are numerous interpretations of I Timothy 3:12, but we just wanted to stay on the safe side about the ordination of deacons or preachers.

(30) Q: MY CHURCH NEVER WANTS ME TO GO OFF IN REVIVALS OR ANYWHERE ELSE, FOR THAT MATTER. HOW DO YOU OVERCOME THIS?

A: I would begin by winning some of the deacons or other spiritual men to your way of thinking. Let them know that it would strengthen and help you to get away sometimes, and that you'd come back to them a better preacher because of it. Don't abuse the privilege but it should not hurt your ministry to take a meeting away two or three times a year if you have good help and back-up men to hold the fort at home for you. The church will also share in the blessing of the souls you win in other places. Help them to see that they can help other churches by sharing you with them for a day or two in conferences, etc. Hard-working pastors put in from 50 to 70 hours a week and need a break sometimes by getting away to a Bible conference or a preachers' meeting somewhere. You can gradually train your men to see this. Remind them that a faithful and busy pastor rarely gets a whole day off any week, even if he tries to. As you win some key men to your way of thinking they can pretty well take care of the others. In the same way you can educate people to see the need of paying your hospitalization insurance or making the payments on a home for the pastor, and such matters.

(31) Q: OUR MUSIC PROGRAM LEAVES MUCH TO BE DESIRED. PEOPLE CRITICIZE US NO MATTER HOW MUCH WE TRY. AND WHAT DO YOU DO WHEN MRS. "SCREECH-OWL" VOLUNTEERS FOR A SOLO?

A: Carefully read Chapter Seven on "God's Music." Vary your selection of hymns. Use songs with real meaning—songs that can be understood. Don't let your song leader get in a rut. When an instrumental number is to be played at least announce the title of it—and maybe you should even read a few of the words if it is not a familiar song. People need to know that this is a spiritual song and if it is not familiar they can be told what it is. In some churches the choice of special numbers is poor—all people are not hillbillies, but you'd think some pastors and song leaders must believe they are.

Pastor Al Bradshaw of Tampa says, "When the music goes

down the church soon goes down, too." Dr. Victor Sears has recently written a much-needed article, "Modernism Takes a New Form." He states that the new modernism has crept into our churches in the production of carnal music known either as contemporary or as "soft rock," and is often backed with the sound of "canned music" that could be produced by the average dance or disco band at the corner honky-tonk. "With its sensual tones, jungle beat and nightclub presentation it appeals to the flesh rather than to the spirit. . .this off-beat style of music was connived in Hell, hatched among the charismatic crowd, and printed in their publishing houses. Good fundamental Baptists and others that refuse the teachings of this crowd concerning tongues, signs, etc., are now singing their music in our churches. Many say it carries the same beat they used to dance to in the world before they were saved. There is sort of a hippie-oriented "pop" flavor that is disgusting to any consecrated Christian and must be repulsive to Almighty God. Train your people. Help them cultivate a taste for good music.

If you have a music director he ought to be able to so arrange the music program that Mrs. "Screech-Owl" would be taken care of. Sometimes you might *have* to use someone in a Training Hour or Prayer Meeting service that you'd not want to put on the platform on the Lord's day. She *might* fit into the choir without ruining it. But if it is *too* bad you may just have to hurt her feelings by telling her that your music is already taken care of. Or the music director perhaps can give an "audition" for special singers, and thus eliminate Mrs. Owl.

One other possibility: You might think about giving her a job in Children's Church or letting her direct the nursery to get her off the platform of the church.

(32) Q: WHAT DO YOU DO WHEN SOME OF THE PEOPLE ARE AGAINST YOU?

A: Be glad they're not *all* against you! If you really do business for God you're going to *have* opposition. Dr. Bob Jones, Sr., said, "The door to success swings open on the hinges of opposition." Jesus said, "Beware when all men speak well of you." But I would try to learn from my opposition, too. Sometimes they are justified in opposing you. Make sure of what you are doing, and be sure it is what God is leading you to do. As for criticism, Lincoln said, "If I tried to answer all the criticisms of me and all the attacks leveled at me, this office would be closed to all other business. My job is not pleasing men, but doing the best I can. If in the end I am found to be wrong, ten legions of angels swearing I was right will not help me; but if the end proves me to have been right, then all that is said about me now will amount to nothing."

(33) Q: I HAVE A TIME WITH MY TEMPER. IT IS HARD NOT TO COMPLAIN AND TO LASH OUT AT THE PEOPLE. THEN THEY REBEL AND SOME OF THEM LEAVE.

A: Remember who you are working for, and there will "be no complaining" (Ps. 144:14). Be cheerful. If you stay joyful as a Christian and walk with God they'll take what you say better. Your temper should not be "distemper." Die to yourself. Many times that "temper" is in the flesh—not the Spirit. Let the Word you preach do the "lashing." Don't be sour. Spurgeon said, "There are more flies caught with honey than with vinegar."

(34) Q: HOW DO YOU STAY ON TOP OF THE SITUATION? I AM PRONE TO DISCOURAGEMENT.

A: Discipline yourself to be master of the situation. Schedule your time—your workday. Plan on some recreation, too. Get up and get at it. Don't lay around and groan about your tasks. Spurgeon said, "Woe unto the minister who dares to waste an hour." Eat right and exercise properly—keep yourself trim and healthy.

Answer your mail! Make yourself do this and other tasks that may be hard for you to want to do. Good schoolmasters insist that their students take at least some subjects they do not like. Master these things—don't let them master you. If you hate hospital visitation then sing and rejoice as you go to the hospital. And thank God as you walk out—the patients you visited would like to be walking out, too.

Pray as you go. Practice the presence of God. It is *His* battle, not yours. If you suffer some loss, remember that your property was really His, anyway. He can replace it. Don't be gloomy. Let others do some of the work. Don't try to do everything yourself. Read the story of Moses and Jethro. Moody said, "It is better to get ten men to work than to do the work of ten men."

Be hard on yourself. Look out for such things as laziness, jealousy, pride, lust, covetousness, sidetracks, vanity, gluttony. "Let him that thinketh he standeth take heed lest he fall" (I Cor. 10:12).

(35) Q: MISSIONARIES TELL OF NEGLECT BY PASTORS AND CHURCHES; WHAT CAN WE DO?

A: It is true. Sometimes missionaries come to their home church and are virtually ignored. Again, the victory depends on leadership. Pastors should train their people to love their missionaries, to pray for them, to write to them. When missionaries are coming the pastor should make a big thing of it with his people and get them excited about it. Let them give their testimony and show their slides.

Be sure someone opens their home to the missionary. Think of their needs while they are with you. Maybe they need rest most. Perhaps they need a car to drive while they are in your town. They may need medical or dental care.

Don't leave a missionary standing around looking lonely at the end of a service. You might be amazed at how many do. Stay at the front sometimes after church (or let your missions chairman do it) and see how few people come down to welcome or greet your missionary. It is sad! And if the pastor does not see to it that someone takes the missionary home for dinner he may end up eating at the local hamburger stand by himself. Your people will benefit greatly by having their missionary in the home. Keep a good, up-to-date missions display board where it can be seen.

Many times a pastor can help the missionary by calling ahead to other churches, by mapping out an itinerary or by allowing him to use the church phone.

I don't know how many times missionaries told me that they appreciated the letters they received from me, their pastor. They seemed so pleased that a pastor would write them and indicated that very few pastors did so. Missionaries have enough burdens and trials without our adding to them by neglect.

(36) Q: SOME CHURCHES ARE CUTTING BACK ON THEIR MINISTRIES BECAUSE OF THE ECONOMIC CRUNCH. ANY SUGGESTIONS?

A: Police your bus routes to make sure gasoline is not being wasted. To drive a 44-passenger bus six extra miles to pick up one little girl may be heroic but there may be a member coming by there who could save that bus trip. Make your bus workers economy-wise.

Some churches run their heating system or air conditioners all day long when the service is not until night. Especially is this true in churches that have a Christian school. The building is heated up for early morning chapel. Someone is not made to turn off the lights and heat so they all burn and run all day. Many dollars are wasted. Churches are famous for this! Some churches are kept so cold from the air conditioning that people have to bring extra coats to stand it. To cut the thermostat down some would be to save money and make people happier, too.

Many church rest-room faucets leak. Almost all of the outside hoses do. Some toilets run by the hour. Many lights are left burning in rooms that are not in use. It will pay you to map out a job sheet for your custodian on such matters or to plan a workday and let the deacons or trustees fix these things. Train your school workers to turn off lights and heaters when they leave the auditorium and the students to pick up after themselves. Some equipment is left on all night long at some churches.

For other ways to handle finance matters better read Chapter Six and Chapter Twenty-one of this book.

(37) Q: WHAT DO YOU DO WHEN YOU REALIZE YOU HAVE BLUNDERED AND MADE SOME BAD DECISIONS?

A: All of us make some bad ones. It doesn't hurt a bit just to say so. Especially in a young preacher this will be appreciated by the people. Sometimes we need to humble ourselves.

I faced a crisis as a very young pastor and said some unnecessary things to my congregation, and said it rather poorly at that. In principle I was right but in practice I could have done differently. An older, mature man reminded me that I was in a jam because of my position. He taught me that it is "lonely at the top" and that any leader, pastor, president, manager has to make decisions that will often be unpopular. He told me that if I couldn't "take it" when the going got rough and I encountered difficulty and criticism that I would never succeed as a pastor. He was right! So if you know you are right go ahead and graciously lead the way, even if you make some people unhappy. But when you realize you have blundered it is best to swallow your pride, ask forgiveness and back up and start over another way. Read II Chronicles 10:7-13. You can learn from those old men sometimes.

(38) Q: THE FUNDAMENTALISTS ALL AROUND ME ARE ALWAYS FIGHTING ABOUT SOMETHING: CUTTING ONE ANOTHER DOWN. HOW DOES A YOUNG PREACHER KNOW WHICH SIDE TO BE ON?

A: Well, you'd better just be on *God's* side. I'm looking at a picture in the paper of tens of thousands of charismatics standing in the rain outside the Capitol at Washington, D.C. in a "Washington for Jesus" rally. They are waving their hands in the air and "speaking in tongues," the story said. This picture is on the front page of the paper. They expect many thousands more at the rally. When reporters asked them what they are protesting they reply that they are "not protesting anything! We are just going down there for Jesus." With our nation steeped in sin, drunkenness, debauchery and welfare-ism; in a once-Christian land where now the Bible is scoffed at, in a nation saturated in pornography, abortion, perversion and profanity these people have nothing to protest! Yet they get together by the thousands to holler, hold hands and "speak in tongues." My heart ached to think that this is what a lost world looks on and thinks is "Christianity"! At the same time fundamental, Bible-believing Christians cannot get together on anything because of our constant bickering, name-calling and criticism of every other Christian who does not do everything just as we would do it.

Through the years I have learned that much gossip and slander of preachers and other Christian workers was not true, when the facts were known, when the evidence was all in. With maturity you learn to grow more cautious before jumping on every wrecking crew that comes along. Don't let someone else do your thinking for you or determine who your friends will be.

Of course we have to take a stand against modernism, heresy and the cults. That is a different matter. But there are many saved people with whom we may disagree and yet we can stand with them against communism, booze, pornography, abortion, homosexuality, etc. There are good Christians who love the Lord who do things in a different manner than I would do them. And they may not yet have learned some things that God has taught me. But I do not need to hate them and vilify them. They probably know some things I don't know, and God has used them to reach some people I could never reach. No one ever built a monument to a critic.

Spurgeon said, "To be burning at the lip and freezing at the soul is a mark of reprobation. God deliver us from being superfine and superficial. . . .I know a class of religious people who, I have no doubt, were born of a woman, but they appear to have been suckled by a wolf. . . .We are not to go about the world searching out heresies, like terrier dogs sniffing for rats; nor are we to be so confident of our own infallibility as to erect ecclesiastical stakes at which to roast all who differ from us with . . .coals of juniper which consist of strong prejudice and cruel suspicion" *(Spurgeon's Lectures).*

Dr. Jack Hyles in a great message on "Sweet Revenge" teaches us that there is *no such thing* as sweet revenge, that when you "get him back" or "give him what he deserves" you know the emptiness of revenge. He reminds us how Joseph, Abraham and David acted in grace, compassion and mercy in their encounters with those who would do them in. Dr. Hyles states, "You may preach some great sermons, but you will never rise to the spiritual peak to which you will rise when you quit fighting back with your enemy." He reminds us that we will never be any more fundamental than when we imitate Jesus with His, "Father, forgive them, for they know not what they do"!

In full-page ads Dr. Hyles states that "absolutely no criticism of other fundamental preachers, churches or schools is allowed by the administration, faculty or student body" at Hyles-

Anderson College. Could this be one reason why the blessing of God has rested upon that school?

Charles Finney said, "To tell the truth with design to injure is slander"!

Somewhere I read and copied this down, "I hate the guys who criticize and minimize the other guys whose enterprise has made them rise above the guys who criticize and minimize."

Bible-believing, fundamental Christians had better hang together in a world that is fast becoming communistic, atheistic and pagan or we may "hang separately" with no freedom left to even open our church doors. Already I have to fight sin, the world, the flesh and the Devil. After that I have very little strength left to start in on my own team! "We are labourers together with God."

About censure, an old divine was quoted as saying, "Before censuring anyone, obtain from God a real love for him. Be sure that you know and that you allow all allowances that can be made. Otherwise, how ineffective, how unintelligible or perhaps provocative your best-meant censure may be."

* * * *

To conclude this book I leave with you a statement I solicited from my brother, Howard M. Pyle, a veteran pastor in suburban Atlanta, Georgia. He directs a Christian school and pastors the Faith Baptist Church of Ellenwood, Georgia.

His comments on "What every young preacher should know" make a fitting climax to all that has gone before:

> I would say that any young preacher ought to be careful not to attempt to mimic nor duplicate the styles and ways of a seasoned preacher. Every man must be his own man. To some is given 1, some 5, some 10 talents. God will require faithfulness to what we have; not to our ability to keep up with another.
>
> Every church doesn't need a Christian school (it may be a blessing to one and a blight and blemish and burden to another), just as every church does not necessarily need a big bus ministry nor a radio or TV ministry, nor a camp program. To be led of God is far better than to be dictated to by tradition, custom or convenience.
>
> I would tell a young preacher to pray for a wagonload of love

for his people, but never to sacrifice principle, conviction and character for love. To do what is right—even if to lose friends and/or members—will always come out RIGHT in the end. "Do not sacrifice the permanent on the altar of the immediate." "Do right if the stars fall."

We do well to glean from the experience and wisdom of older men who have fought the battles. Every Timothy needs a Paul; every recruit can profit by listening to a 5-star General; and every man can be my teacher—IF I will be teachable.

In addition:

NEVER UNDERESTIMATE

The Power of God—Eph. 3:20

The Influence of Satan—I Pet. 5:8; I Thess. 2:18

The Potential of Prayer—John 14:13,14

The Fickleness of Man—Ps. 118:8,9

The Weakness of Flesh—Rom. 13:14

The Worth of a Soul—Luke 15:7

The Reward of Giving—Luke 6:38

Having said all of that, may God crown your efforts with success as you go out to be the preacher He wants you to be!

For a complete list of books available from the Sword of the Lord, write to Sword of the Lord Publishers, P. O. Box 1099, Murfreesboro, Tennessee 37133.